SWEAT, TEARS, AND JAZZ HANDS

SWEAT, TEARS, AND JAZZ HANDS

The Official History of Show Choir from Vaudeville to *Glee*

MIKE WEAVER AND COLLEEN HART

Hal Leonard Books

An Imprint of Hal Leonard Corporation

Published in 2011 by Hal Leonard Books
An Imprint of Hal Leonard Corporation
7777 West Bluemound Road
Milwaukee, WI 53213

Trade Book Division Editorial Offices
33 Plymouth St., Montclair, NJ 07042

Printed in the United States of America

Book design by Damien Castaneda

Library of Congress Cataloging-in-Publication Data is available upon request.

ISBN 978-1-55783-772-1

www.halleonardbooks.com

Dedicated to all those who have sparkled in and behind the spotlight

CONTENTS

PREFACE
FROM THE TOP: WHAT IS A SHOW CHOIR?

Colleen (top, middle left) with a group of her senior friends at their last show choir performance.

What is a show choir? Since graduating from my sequined dresses nearly ten years ago, I've pretty much perfected that answer.

In short, a show choir is a mash-up between a standard choir, a dance team, and a drama club, which competes with similar groups throughout the country. And it's cool. I swear.

After I stepped down from the stage and went off to college, I realized that show choir was like a secret cultlike society, hidden in select pockets of the Midwest, which I just happened to stumble upon and dedicate eight years of my teenage life to. We lived in a world that didn't understand the intricacies of our craft without first—or at least secondhand—experience. And a short description never seemed to give it the justice it deserved.

Until the show *Glee* popularized the genre and raised awareness about this culture of high-energy harmonizers, show choir alumni like myself mostly chalked up their experience to something vastly unrelatable to their friends. We reserved the stories that began with, "This one time in show choir . . ." for friends and family who shared those memories.

My support group consisted of a handful of friends I met through my almost-decade run with E.T.C. The All Americans in Akron, Ohio. The group, which was founded by Bob Heidi and, at that time, was directed by Cheryl Boigegrain, stood for Energy, Talent, and Commitment. E.T.C. was, and still is, unique from other competitive show choirs, as it drew students from different middle schools, junior highs, and high schools in the area. Some groups saw that as an unfair advantage. We just saw it as awesome.

Looking back, those years are somewhat blurred due to my overindulgence in aerosol hairspray, but what I do remember was always feeling like a better version of myself when I was around those thirty-plus other gleeks. Sure, there were rehearsals that involved screaming, when there were more tears than sweat, when certain group members

"WHAT WOULD I DO WITHOUT MY MUSIC?"

Sometimes I stumble home at night discouraged.
Dragging my battered behind.
Wondering if the battle's worth the fighting.
And why so many people's eyes are blind.

But as I disappear into my music,
Dreams start rebuilding strong and high.
And I know though I may not be winning,
I'm a long, long way from losing if I try.

And I think, what would I do without my music,
What would I do without my song?
What I do without my music . . .
To make it right when everything seems wrong.

discovered creative differences, and when frustration beat out achievement. But, for the most part, whether it was performing a Ricky Martin song in silver pants or having head-to-head facial expression battles during a powerful ballad, we had fun.

Every year when sending off the senior class, it was, and still is, a tradition for the choir to sing (sans any twirling or stomping) "What Would I Do Without My Music?" arranged by Ed Lojeski. Ten years later, I continue to remember those lyrics better than most of my computer passwords.

We would hold hands as tears ran down our faces, singing those lyrics as if we had written them ourselves, wondering what life would be like without rehearsal every Saturday and competition season every spring.

After the initial post–show choir shock, I realized that show choir, for me, wasn't about becoming a professional performer or about having a training ground for a future in music. I walked off the stage in May 2001 with an awareness of and appreciation for passion. And because to this day I'm drawn to passionate people, high-energy environments, and creativity, in a way, I never truly left the stage.

It amazed me to be a part of a process that started with a binder full of sheet music and resulted in a thirty-minute production filled with elaborate sets, multiple costume changes, and emotion. Every great show was developed from an idea—from a brainstorm—and had the ability to affect not only performers but also the audiences.

It was eight years of inspiration. The uncertainty of where I would draw that energy and passion scared me. Life without a spotlight seemed boring, mundane, and ordinary.

I went to college. I discovered cheap beer, boys, and sororities, and somewhere during my four years in Athens, Ohio, I found a passion for writing. Words inspired me. I found I could take ordinary writing assignments and breathe life into them with creativity; that I had a talent for tickling the keyboard.

During this discovery phase I remembered a piece of advice that our choreographer, Mike Weaver, gave us upon graduation. He told us, "To truly be happy in what you do, figure out what you're most passionate in, and then find a way to make money doing it. Do that, and you'll never work a day in your life."

My love for writing led me into the world of public relations—and then five years later into discussions with Mr. Weaver himself about pursuing this project. I'm honored and humbled for the opportunity to put show choirs on the bookshelf with the choreographer who led me, like many other performers, in the direction of my dreams.

This book highlights the influential milestones throughout pop culture and pop music history that helped develop the show choirs today. We hope that, upon turning the final page, readers will gain insight into this, until now, unrecorded world (that isn't so small after all) and realize that, while outside factors are affecting the world of show choirs, show choirs themselves are, more importantly, shaping many individual worlds.

Colleen Hart

Mike Weaver (middle) with the E.T.C. All Americans 2001 senior class, including Colleen (left of Mike).

I love good luggage. It's true you get what you pay for, but designer brand or not, most suitcases arrive at the airport baggage claim with fresh bruises and marks. To me, each of those marks help paint a reminder of the miles I've traveled, the people I've met, and the job that I love.

Working as a director/choreographer, I travel 250 out of 365 days a year. I spend more time at Hampton Inn than I do at home. I've brainstormed performance ideas at countless Starbucks, dozens of hotel lobbies, and several different rental cars and cabs.

Throughout the past twenty years, my luggage and I have visited hundreds of show choirs. In that time my interest in theater; show styles, and their history only grew, which led me to this project.

Sweat, Tears and Jazz Hands is intended to answer common questions about the past, present, and future of show choirs. It's not supposed to be an encyclopedia of music, of choral history, or even of show choirs.

Mike and fellow campers posing for a show choir camp publicity photo at Indiana State University, headed each summer by Ron Hellems and Ann Conrad, in Terre Haute, Indiana (1978).

Through a chronological approach, we've created an edutainment-style book, highlighting historical periods and figures, long-forgotten facts, and anecdotal stories that have contributed to shape the show choirs of today.

While we have attempted to present a spectrum of opinions, we tried to avoid taking a particular side or stance. If there is an underlying theme here— it's that the struggle to "figure it out" is the essence of show choir history. It's the sharing, borrowing, and copycat styles of those who succeeded and those who wanted to succeed—whether that meant trying to master vocal directing, staging, costuming, arranging, fund-raising, set building, etc.—that built this entertainment genre.

A second theme realized is the impact of personalities in the show choir story. At many turning points, it was the commanding presence of an individual—Fred Waring, Don Neuen, Hal Malcolm, Milton C. Anderson, F. Ritchie Walton, Ron Hellems, Judith Meeks, or Dwight Jordan —who advanced the industry, rather than the force of an idea or movement.

I came to this project thinking I knew something about show choir. Boy, was I wrong. Beyond show choir, I have learned a lot about show business in general. Each of the eras had a hat in conforming show choirs styles: from the traveling, family-friendly entertainment acts of vaudeville to the big-band orchestras and television shows of the '50s to the MTV generation inspired by the performance idols like the Jacksons and Madonna. It was both eye opening and encouraging, discovering the roots of my livelihood spread so far.

It's those men and women who have created this world, in which I spend so much of my life, who deserve the most acknowledgments. This story isn't about who can sell the best moves or who can outsing who. This story is about an ongoing group of people striving to do what they love and making the world a more interesting and livable place through music; more livable, if not for everyone else, at least for themselves.

Mike Weaver

THE FIRST ACT: VAUDEVILLE

1

There's no business like show business.

—IRVING BERLIN

The first act. The beginning. Step one.

There's a lot of anticipation involved in witnessing a story unfold from the beginning. Opening an unbroken book cover. Receiving a crisp, unbent concert ticket. The future is, in a way, symbolized through those objects, creating excitement for the audience, the reader.

Many times, success rides on the opening performance. After the curtain opens, energy should fill the stage and performers should demand attention by delivering well-rehearsed perfection. Because in a culture of short attention spans and limitless entertainment options, audiences want to be pulled in. They want unforgettable.

The beginning matters.

There's comfort in understanding the origins of a person, place, or art form and in being able to trace back to the starting line. Looking to the beginning allows one to place blame for shortcomings and, better yet, to assign credit where deserved. It provides an identity to a person. It gives context to a place. And it builds connections to an art.

Not everything, however, begins with a clear timeline or with a page one. Not all events have a memorable witness or scribe. Friendships can begin when least expected or can grow overtime, leaving one to wonder, "When did this happen? How did this start?"

When someone or something didn't intentionally press go, history sometimes turns out to be more of an evolution than a timeline; it becomes influenced by many different individuals and events—making for a more interesting and speculative story.

The tale of show choirs doesn't begin with a simple, "Once upon a time." There is no specific birth date, no designated parents or grandparents. Until now, show choir has essentially been an orphan of performing arts history.

Despite their place in the industry throughout the past few decades, these ensembles have quietly infiltrated American towns. One by one, they have marked their territory with jazz hands, sometimes excessive smiling, and a trail of glitter leading back toward their practice hall. So how did these pop music–loving choral ensemble groups come to be?

The answer lies in lifting the curtain to an era of gypsies, tramps, and thieves; when shows were stealing more than just hearts and imaginations; when sequins were practically the mark of the devil and performers doubled as prostitutes. It was the mid-1800s, when show business looked a lot like the red-light district.

PRE-VAUDEVILLE

Before there were family-friendly performances, Disney, and G-rated movies, show business marched to the beat of a different drummer. Those involved in the show-biz clique were often associated with prostitution, thievery, and con games. The business was unorganized and the profession lacked respect from the general public. But as bad as the working conditions were, there were still creative, passionate, and smart performers who saw promise on the stage.

A MAN BEFORE HIS TIME: P. T. BARNUM

One of those upstanding, but unabashedly sketchy, performers was P. T. Barnum. Known in the industry for his tall-tale stories and dishonest marketing techniques, Barnum also helped clean up the entertainment industry by introducing a new performance genre.

Melding education with entertainment, Barnum presented a well-dressed package of musical performers and one-act plays in a family-friendly exhibition setting known now as "edutainment." His original acts took place at his American Museum, in New York City, which looked much like a modern-day circus. Wall to wall were live freak acts, dramatic theatricals, beauty contests, and inexplicable human oddities. The acts and the atmosphere were intriguing, captivating, and alcohol free. The idea seemed to stick.

"Edutainment" museums quickly popped up in practically every metropolitan city, copying Barnum's formula of clean entertainment mixed with outlandish acts. In 1868, the American Museum burned to the ground (for the second time), but not before refreshing

Barnum's Cast Highlights:

- General Tom Thumb, the 26-inch-tall man
- Chang and Eng, Siamese twins
- Anna Swan, the tallest girl in the world at 7 feet 11 inches
- Annie Jones, the bearded woman

RAZZLE-DAZZLE THEM

P. T. Barnum has often been credited for the bamboozler's predatory creed, "There's a sucker born every minute."

and rejuvenating the American entertainment industry. In 1881, Barnum joined forced with James Anthony Bailey. Barnum and Bailey years later sold their production to Ringling Bros. who formed the Ringling Bros. and Barnum & Bailey Circus, an act that would play on long past Barnum's day.

SHOW BUSINESS ARRIVES IN VAUDEVILLE

P. T. Barnum and his circus of freaks laid down a solid foundation for change in the entertainment industry. Before 1870, aside from "edutainment" productions, theater wasn't meant for everyone. Variety shows, or performances that involved several different styles or acts, were found mostly in saloons, called music halls or honky-tonks, and the environment was loud and often raucous and rowdy. It was corner dive bar material for the drunks, the poor, and the curious.

Right before and during Prohibition, from roughly 1880 to 1930, changes occurred in theater. Polite society rejected the slutty stage productions of the past and began embracing the more sober, Puritan-approved purveyors of fun.

ANTONIO "TONY" PASTOR

In 1881, Tony Pastor, a young theater owner, quickly gained a reputation for offering this clean style of entertainment. As a comic singer who had appeared at P. T. Barnum's American Museum at the early age of six, Pastor had an engrained appreciation for polite and tasteful theater. He worked to expand his audience base by appealing to both men and women, alternating between operettas and family-focused programming.

The news of Pastor's success quickly spread to theater managers throughout the country. It became apparent that a cleaner environment resulted in more profitable ticket sales.

BENJAMIN FRANKLIN KEITH AND EDWARD F. ALBEE

Benjamin Franklin Keith and business partner Edward F. Albee, Boston theater owners, played a large part in transforming New York City's vulgar theater/vice district into a respectable middle-class entertainment zone. Following the lead of Tony Pastor, they focused on acts and performers that could deliver family-friendly entertainment. They prohibited off-color jokes or controversial material of any kind and

COMING TO A CITY NEAR YOU!
Barnum's FUNundrum, the latest show was put together to create a two-hundredth birthday salute to Phineas Taylor Barnum (P. T. Barnum). The show, which traveled across the United States in a mile-long train, contained about 130 performers from six continents.

VAUDE-WHAT?

The term *vaudeville*, adopted in the United States from the Parisian boulevard theater (nicknamed "crime theater"), is speculated to be an American version of one of the two French phrases: *voix de ville*, meaning "voice of the city," or "Vau de Vire," a valley in Normandy famous for its satirical theatrical performances.

Show choir competitions have unknowingly adopted the vaudeville method of presenting self-contained traveling acts back to back in a family-friendly format.

How to Enter Vaudeville: A Complete Illustrated Course of Instruction, *published by Frederic LaDelle Company (1913). This book covers the numerous styles, genres, and topics concerning vaudeville entertainment from acrobatics and juggling, to singing and dancing, to makeup, costuming, booking your act, and advertising.*

Simply called the Theatrical Shop, this costume and theatrical supply shop in West Des Moines, Iowa, operates out of the old Lyric Hotel and Theatre, a vaudeville house that served as a performance space for acts performing in the Orpheum Circuit, one of the major vaudeville circuits.

worked to avoid accidentally-on-purpose wardrobe malfunctions.

Keith called this theatrical movement *vaudeville*, and it didn't take long to catch on. The term helped distinguish the new performance acts from the adult debauchery of variety theater, and the "Frenchness" of the title helped rebrand the industry and create a more sophisticated image.

No longer did the industry seek to entertain only men. Productions also focused on appealing to wives, daughters, and grandmothers. Theater was now a family affair. Producers had officially traded the foul language, booze, and scantily clad chorus girls for handsome venues, proper attire, and plentiful profits. It seemed to be working out for everyone.

Although historians might not have an exact date and time when vaudevillians first hit the stage, the easy answer is that vaudeville began when variety cleaned up its act. Like variety bills, vaudeville could feature any random combination or menagerie of acts, including jugglers, magicians, animal trainers, singers, and knife throwers. The difference, however, was that now that randomness had a purpose. A format had been put into place, with an "ah-ha" moment for the audience when they discovered the performers and the acts were presented in a predictable and climactic way.

Vaudeville brought a new air of appreciation and respect for performers and their stage. Most vaudeville talent still got paid ridiculously meager wages and unions had yet to be established to protect their rights, but performers no longer needed to hide in the shadows of booze halls to hone their craft. Bonus.

Vaudeville brought class. It shed a new spotlight on show business. And the theater world suddenly realized that it would never be the same.

VAUDEVILLE COMPANIES

The early vaudeville traveling acts combined the grueling schedule of a campaigning politician with the scrappiness of an eighteenth-century minstrel. Eventually, however, through the hustle and bustle of profit-minded theater owners, the whole business of putting on a show would become organized through grouping their theaters into circuits. This new way of thinking would become the business foundation for the entertainment industry.

BURLESQUE

Not every performance at the turn of the century was Sunday school clean. With the majority of variety theaters heading down the straitlaced vaudeville road, those few shows that continued to cater to the all-male audiences, dubbed *burlesque*, experienced a surge in popularity. Generally found in major metropolitan cities such as New York City, Philadelphia, and Chicago, these were adult-style musical variety shows that proved entertaining and whisper-worthy with their usually naughty, gaudy, and bawdy acts.

Unlike vaudeville's individual performers who traveled week after week, burlesque shows toured as a complete troupe for forty weeks of the year. During the 1930s through '50s, this made burlesque a steady and coveted paycheck for performers willing to strut and strip.

Derived from minstrel shows, burlesque followed a set and expected format, rarely veering from the norm. The all-girl ensemble numbers incorporated singing, dancing, kick lines, and can-cans interlaced with crass jokes from comedians. Although this genre started with somewhat innocent intentions, somewhere along the way burlesque went bad. By 1930, it was well along to having the reputation of a modern-day strip club.

TIN PAN ALLEY

While vaudeville was cranking out performances and bringing in crowds, music publishers came onto the scene to feed the public's growing hunger for music that they could play and perform themselves. Referred to as Tin Pan Alley, the music publishing industry set up shop and thrived in New York City. This was the place to be to sell a song. Tin Pan Alley revolutionized the music publishing industry and marked the beginning of how American popular music, or simply "pop," was produced for public consumption.

Tin Pan Alley introduced music to America in a new way: Publishing companies sent their music salesman on the road. These salesmen, nicknamed "music pluggers," would scour cities and towns, asking performers to buy and play their music. They worked long hours. They got paid crappy wages. It was not a job for the softies. Prior to the advent of music pluggers, sheet music was hard to find beyond professional circles. In 1892, all that work paid off for salesmen of the Oliver Ditson publishing company, when "After the Ball" by Charles Harris became the first sheet music to sell over 2 million copies.

THE WHAT'S WHAT OF VAUDEVILLE THEATER COMPANIES: A CHEAT SHEET

ORPHEUM CIRCUIT:
One of the two big-time theater circuits of the vaudeville era found primarily in Midwestern and Western cities. Created by Martin Beck, the circuit booked some of the biggest European-American (white) acts of the time, including Al Jolson, Sophie Tucker, Will Rogers, and Eddie Cantor.

KEITH-ALBEE CIRCUIT:
Owned by Benjamin Franklin Keith and Edward Albee, this circuit established control over most of the East Coast vaudeville theaters. It later became RKO Motion Picture Company, when combined with the Orpheum Circuit.

THEATRE OWNERS BOOKING ASSOCIATION:
Also nicknamed the "Chitlin Circuit," this band of theaters focused on African American performers, often highlighting jazz and blues singers, bands, and dancers. Famous theaters that hung with this crowd included the Cotton Club and the Apollo Theatre.

CHOP SUEY CIRCUIT:
Popular during vaudeville's decline in the 1930s and '40s, this circuit was made up of a series of Chinese restaurants and nightclubs featuring all-Asian variety shows. Shows incorporated acts involving tap and fan dancers, acrobats, magicians, and jugglers.

Christina Aguilera plays a small-town girl who travels to L.A. to make it big in a neo-burlesque nightclub owned by a former dancer, played by Cher in the 2010 film *Burlesque*, directed by Steven Antin.

Tin Pan Alley was the center of the music publishing industry at the turn of the century, located on 28th Street between Fifth and Sixth avenues in New York City. The name comes from the noise created by dozens of cheap, thin, and tinny-sounding upright pianos furiously pounding out tunes from the dense group publisher's offices. It sounded like tin pans beating together. Great neighborhood. Cheap rent.

"Irving Berlin has no place in American music. Irving Berlin is American music." — Jerome Kern, American composer of musical theater and popular music

Irving Berlin's sheet music, especially, "Alexander's Ragtime Band," became classic show choir staples for decades.

Another American composer, George Gershwin, embraced jazz harmonies and rhythms with the same passion as Berlin. His early pop hits, such as "Strike Up the Band," "Fascinating Rhythm," and "I Got Rhythm," would later become show choir anthems.

"After the Ball" is a 3/4-time melodramatic tale of a man explaining to his niece why he never married. After a dance, because he saw his ladylove kiss another man, he called off the engagement and refused to hear an explanation. Only years later, after she died, did he learn that the man she kissed was her brother.

FAMOUS FORMER SPEAKEASIES IN THE UNITED STATES

- 21 CLUB, NEW YORK CITY
- COTTON CLUB, NEW YORK CITY
- JULIUS', NEW YORK CITY
- BUTCH MCGUIRES, CHICAGO
- CLUB LUCKY, CHICAGO
- CORK & KERRY, CHICAGO
- DURKINS, CHICAGO
- GREEN MILL, CHICAGO
- MAYFLOWER CLUB, WASHINGTON, D.C.

Suddenly there was a demand for sheet music, and Tin Pan Alley was ready to deliver. Now anyone, not just professional performers, could find and purchase their favorite pop music composition for ten cents a sheet. Plus, it was a sign of class to own a piano—and a lot of families wanted to be classy.

IRVING BERLIN

One of the most successful composers and lyricists who jumped on the Tin Pan Alley bandwagon at its height was Irving Berlin. As a member of this exclusive Tin Pan Alley crew, he was determined to write a song inspired by ragtime, a popular musical genre of the era. Ragtime was well known and well liked by many, but it was also slightly scandalous. Its history was rooted in slave songs and in the red-light districts of New Orleans and Saint Louis. At a time when alcohol was about to be outlawed, ragtime was also getting the cold shoulder.

. . . Until 1911. It was then that Berlin struck the right chord with "Alexander's Ragtime Band." Its style captured, commercialized, and exploited a genre originally made famous by Scott Joplin. The hit skyrocketed Berlin's popularity. Suddenly, America opened its heart and wallet to Berlin and pop music.

And Berlin continued to entertain year after year and hit after hit.

ALL THAT JAZZ

Berlin and Tin Pan Alley weren't the only ones scoring musical slam-dunks during the vaudeville era. The Roaring Twenties arrived, bringing brass bands and bobbed hair cuts to the stage and a public fascination with a new kind of music called *jazz*.

Between 1920 and 1933, much of the country was going through one of the most famous dry spells of all time, Prohibition. Mandated by the Eighteenth Amendment to the Constitution, it was illegal to sell or distribute liquor in all forty-eight U.S. states. While this law was successful in decreasing consumption and cutting back arrests for public intoxication, it led to an abundance of bootlegging, organized crime, gangsters, and underground bars, called *speakeasies*. Bottoms up!

Luckily, there was nothing dry about music during the '20s. Speakeasies, found in urban settings, were often filled with popular jazz musicians and flappers. With a booming economy and the passing of the Nine-

Much like rave parties in the late 1980s, speakeasies could pop up, shut down, or shift locations at whim. Sometimes all you had to do was look down.

teenth Amendment—women's right to vote— jazz was a fresh, new, and exciting soundtrack that set the period apart from anything that had come before.

Not everyone was hanging out at speakeasies or selling illegal alcohol. As gangsters were causing mayhem on the streets of Chicago and New York City, a man named Fred Waring was forming a jazz band called the Pennsylvanians. This band's clean-cut, all-American image aligned with the nation's moral compass as well as their fascination with all things jazz.

REVERBERATIONS FROM VAUDEVILLE

In 1927, while Tin Pan Alley was still thriving and Waring and his Pennsylvanians were booking shows and building a fan base, the motion picture industry, which had been quiet until now, suddenly had something to say. Warner Bros. produced the first talking motion picture with new Vitaphone technology: *The Jazz Singer*. Starring Broadway veteran Al Jolson, this movie single-handedly killed the silent cinema genre.

All those vaudevillians perked up because, sudden-

Vaudevillian Mae Questel moved from stage to screen when she provided voices for the animated characters Betty Boop and Popeye's noodle-ish girlfriend, Olive Oyl.

SO LONG, VAUDEVILLE. HELLO, HOLLYWOOD!

Famous vaudeville entertainers who found stardom in motion pictures include: Charlie Chaplin, Buster Keaton, Ed Wynn, Bert Lahr, Milton Berle, Mae West, Fanny Brice, Sophie Tucker, Josephine Baker, Betty Grable, and Bettie Page.

ly, Hollywood was calling. Performers who had transferable skills—actors, singers, and dancers—got screen tests. The dog acts and jugglers had a tougher time.

Although the future of vaudeville was in the air, one thing was for certain: Motion pictures began to dominate the interest of both theatergoers and performers. By the mid '30s, not much was left of variety entertainment other than burlesque.

The era seemed to leave as quickly as it came, but the vaudeville show left behind foundational pieces that can still be seen in theater today. It brought regulations and structure to the entertainment industry and continued to inspire other genres of music and performers well beyond its years of popularity.

BOB FOSSE

As some focused on regulations, others worked to keep the traditions of vaudeville alive onstage. Robert Louis "Bob" Fosse, a Chicagoan born in 1937 at the tail end of the vaudeville period, was to become a monumental force in show business, responsible for honoring and maintaining the foundational elements of vaudeville traditions.

Fosse began his study of dance and theater at the Chicago Academy of Theatre Arts under the instruction of Frederick Weaver, who had been trained to teach and perform with the vaudeville theater state of mind.

The academy didn't host lessons in classical ballet or other performance techniques that could take a lifetime to perfect. Instead the theater school offered training in tap, toe, and acrobatic dancing; musical instruments; radio announcing; and drama. Weaver wanted to create child performers who would be manageable and marketable as "moppet acts."

Under Weaver's tutelage and management it was common to see child stars graduate with honors from the performance school. And Fosse was no exception. In 1939, Weaver paired Bob Fosse with another young dancer at the school, Charles Grass, as a tap-dancing duo called the Weaver Brothers. Eventually the name shifted to reflect their tap skills and the boys, who looked like actual brothers, became known as the Riff Brothers (Dancers Extraordinary).

Although vaudeville was quickly on its way out, Chicago offered plenty of opportunities for the boys to show off their skills. They performed at American Legion, Mason, and Eagle lodges; at amateur shows; and at numerous Chicago theaters.

During these formative years, Frederick Weaver would continuously school the boys about the core values of a vaudeville act. Weaver's philosophy was, "Once you get it right, you can do it for the rest of your life. You perfect an act year after year, but you don't change it."

One of Weaver's favorite vaudeville stars, who also served as a performance icon for Fosse, was Joe Frisco. His stage trademarks included a well-fitted suit, white socks, a derby, and a cigar, and he became famous for doing a snaky dance called the "hootchy-kootch."

Fosse studied, emulated, and incorporated Frisco styles into his own work whenever he could. For example, in both the 1956 stage and 1957 film versions of *Pajama Game*, viewers can see clear Frisco-isms in Fosse's choreography for "Steam Heat."

Throughout his career, Fosse adapted numerous vaudeville-inspired techniques, traditions, and tricks into his work. White gloves, derbies, quirky shuffles, vintage steps, and gimmicks—he did it all. And he did it all very well.

The curtain may have fallen on vaudeville but Fosse provided an encore. Although he died of a heart attack in 1987, he will forever be remembered for his contributions to American musical theater, film, and television.

SETTING UP FOR SUCCESS

As the saying goes, "When one door closes, another one opens."

While the vaudeville door was sealed shut, another had cracked open that would soon reveal a whole new genre of performing—one that could borrow from and incorporate all the pop culture-isms of the day: the exaggeration of P. T. Barnum's freaks; the traveling, family-friendly format of vaudeville troupes; the (innocent) dancing and sequins of the burlesque shows; the energy and excitement of jazz; the styles of Fosse; and the shows that entertained, as well as educated.

The mid- to late twentieth century brought new types of entertainment industries, from live performance to film and television. And now a new type of performance style was warming up. A melting pot of music was in store for America, and the world was about to be introduced to the yet-to-be-named genre, what we now call *show choir*.

Someone had pressed *go*. The red light had turned green. The show was about to begin.

Famous "moppet acts" in history include Shirley Temple, as well as Baby June [June Havoc] and her News Boys (recreated in *Gypsy*).

In Vaudeville terms: A *flash act* refers to the big ending or finale moment when the entertainer goes for shameless applause—relying on props, sets, costuming, or energetic execution to overwhelm the audience with effect rather than actual talent.

A *riff* is a tap term used to describe the making of multiple sounds with a combination of brush scuffs forward with one foot. A basic riff is two sounds (a-one), but skilled tap dancers can create three (a-one-e), four (a-one-e-and) and five (a-one-e-and-a) sound riffs.

TRYOUTS: THE INFANCY OF SHOW CHOIRS

2

Know what you are good at and what you can't do, and find people that you have faith in to make it happen.

—ERIC VAN CLEAVE, FORMER DIRECTOR, LAFAYETTE JEFFERSON HIGH SCHOOL'S FIRST EDITION

Auditions, tryouts, interviews. They are all meant to bring out the best in their participants. All are instructed to portray the best versions of themselves.

Observing an audition, one will surely notice the anxiety, but should also recognize the excitement and optimism of the performers as they step up to prove the worth of their hard work and passion.

A number of groups, individuals, and companies, without knowing, took a lead role in shaping show choirs. First in line was Fred

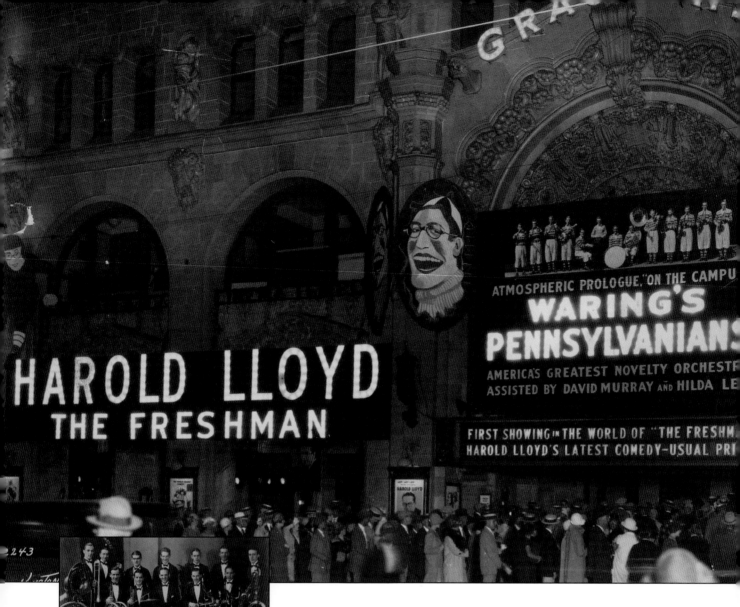

HAROLD LLOYD
THE FRESHMAN

ATMOSPHERIC PROLOGUE "ON THE CAMPU
WARING'S
PENNSYLVANIANS
AMERICA'S GREATEST NOVELTY ORCHESTR
ASSISTED BY DAVID MURRAY AND HILDA LE

FIRST SHOWING IN THE WORLD OF "THE FRESHM
HAROLD LLOYD'S LATEST COMEDY—USUAL PRI

Waring, a popular musician, bandleader, and radio-television personality.

During his teenage years, Fred, his brother, Tom, and their friend, Poley McClintock, founded the Waring-McClintock Snap Orchestra. Throughout the years, the band went through a couple of name changes—Waring's Banjo Orchestra, Banjazzatra—before settling on Waring's Pennsylvanians in 1917.

From the start, this all-male ensemble, led by Fred Waring, alternated between playing instruments and singing, a novel idea for that era. Featuring fresh-faced, all-American, and energetic twenty-something men, the show was an instant hit. The band emanated cool in every way. The boys sang cheerleader style through megaphones. Reviewers called them a "jazz band riot." Everyone wanted to book Waring's Pennsylvanians for events from fraternity parties to weddings to fund raisers.

The group eventually became so successful that

Waring decided to abandon his education to tour with the band. At this time, theater was beginning to combine the technology of radio and phonographic records, which opened many possibilities for entertainers. Within a short time, he learned how to entertain (and market his music) using both types of media. From 1923 until late 1932, Waring's Pennsylvanians were Victor Records' most popular recording artists.

The group's popularity grew beyond Waring's forward-thinking marketing approach. It was one of the first musical ensembles in American history to embrace and entertain with the trendy and entertaining tunes of the day. Folk music, love songs, patriotic hymns, and Broadway showstoppers—this group sang it all.

Before long, Waring's Pennsylvanians loosened their bow ties, added women and a full singing chorus to the group, and adopted yet another name that seemed to better fit their smooth, modern sound. The group became known as Fred Waring and the Pennsylvanians.

Waring's adaptation of chorus with the smart rhythms of the day gave the group's lyrics a fresh face. Odd sounds, the raspy voice of Poley McClintock, the sweet hummingbird-like voices of the three "Waring girls," and talented instrumentalists gave the Pennsylvanians' performances a unique quality.

The troupe sold millions of records throughout the years, filling American radio sets with such classics hits as "Someone to Watch Over Me," "Hello, Dolly," "White Christmas," and "I Only Have Eyes For You."

When asked for the reason behind the band's success, considering the current Depression, Waring said, "The answer's simple when you think about it. We put on a big, fast, breezy show that made people forget their troubles. It was like medicine for beat-up spirits."

The group continued producing records until copyright problems started popping up in smaller-market radio stations, due to the clash of radio and recorded music. Just as many artists became lobbyists to take down Napster in 2000, Waring was personally and professionally invested in reforming the copyright issue. His livelihood depended on it. He lobbied hard for broadcasting reforms so that the authors of recorded music would receive fair compensation for their work. In late 1932, Fred Waring abruptly quit recording. He felt that the recording industry was, in a way, competing against his own radio show.

Syncopation (1929), Fred Waring and his Pennsylvanians providing musical accompaniment for an RKO film.

A *glee club* is a musical group, historically comprised of male voices but could also be female or mixed voices, which traditionally specializes in the singing of short songs—glees—by trios or quartets. The most famous, simply named Glee Club, was at Harrow School in London, England, from 1783 to 1857. *Glee* in this context does not refer to the mood of the music or of its singers, but to a specific form of English song that is homophonic (based on chords rather than on interwoven melodies).

The Shure Model 5B was the state-of-the-art radio microphone used during the 1930s. It featured a patented (and necessary) spring suspension system that allowed the microphone to float in a steel circular frame, which prevented unwanted noise from the floor and the mic stand.

BLENDING MORE THAN VOICES

Waring was also a promoter and financial backer of the first modern electric blender on the market. In 1937, he unveiled the Miracle Mixer (later renamed the Waring Blendor, with an o) at the National Restaurant Show in Chicago, at a price point of $29.75. He was quoted in the *St. Louis Dispatch*, saying, "This mixer is going to revolutionize American drinks." And his prediction came true. Smoothie, anyone?

DEFINING WARING-ISMS

Prior to the uncharted success of the band, Waring made it a point to carve out a style of music all his own. One of his choral arrangers, Luigi Zaninelli, once commented on Waring's approach, "He only conducted words." Meaning, the bandleader had developed a reputation for manipulating musical rhythms to align with the normal intonation of American speech patterns. He was obsessed with how the words were said, not just how they were sung over a melody.

One of Waring's smartest moves during his radio days was employing the talents of young choral director Robert Shaw. According to J. Kevin Butler, a notable choral clinician and historian, it was Shaw who developed the well-known choral method referred to as "Waring's Tone-Syllables." The technique was used primarily as a way to counter the thin tone ranges of 1930s radio microphones. It suggested that singers elongate vowels, round out the tones, and crisply clip the consonants so that listeners could better understand the lyrics.

While frustrating to some (mainly his choral arrangers and performers), Waring's Tone-Syllables became his interpretive stamp and ultimately led to the term known as the "Waring Sound." His style was not merely about choral blend and harmony; it was also about reproducing and singing American songs in a way that listeners could understand (through the airwaves) and find meaningful. In essence, he conducted more than just the words and music. He conducted emotions and expression while dealing with the limits of technology, a lesson future show choirs would strive to achieve.

Interestingly enough, Waring, who was nicknamed the "Man Who Taught America How to Sing," had no formal vocal or musical training. He was quite the Billy Elliot of choral music. Not only did he lack the background, he also lacked the financial support from his family and moral support from his peers. In fact, while studying at Pennsylvania State University, he was rejected from even participating in the glee club, let alone leading it. Whereas some young musicians would see these events as roadblocks, Waring perceived them merely as speed bumps: they may have warned him to slow down, but instead he took a risk and hit the gas, leaving his critics in the dust.

RADIO, TELEVISION, AND BEYOND

Although Waring may not have been recognized at the collegiate level, he was a respected professional. After proving his own and the troupe's talents over the radio waves, some of America's largest companies (with the thickest checkbooks) started to notice this rising star, specifically the mega-electric company General Electric (GE). And so with commercial sponsorship, the molding of the modern-day show choirs continued.

In 1948, GE agreed to sponsor *The Fred Waring Show*, a weekly live Sunday night television program. Fred Waring and the Pennsylvanians were now entertaining families through the newly introduced black-and-white Kinescope television screens. Suddenly the medium of broadcast entertainment was more than just radio scripts and songs transmitted by shaky microphones. Viewers expected to see the musicians playing and the singers singing. Waring, the consummate

Robert Shaw and Fred Waring.

BLACK, WHITE, AND BOOM!

By 1949, there were more than two million television sets in America. New Yorkers alone owned 720,000, which was a 600 percent increase from the previous year. That same year, laws appeared prohibiting the installation of televisions in automobiles.

The Fred Waring Show (1949), on the front cover of *TV Forecast*, before it became *TV Guide*.

TUNING INTO TELEVISION

In the 1950s, Randy Van Horne and his Swinging Chorus, a swing group, were the voices behind the famous Hanna-Barbera theme songs in *The Jetsons*, *The Flintstones*, and *Huckleberry Hound*.

The word *swing* in *swing* choirs came from the 1940s big band era, the popular style of music and dance at the time.

showman, delivered just that.

Just as the industry evolved, so did Waring and his talented troupe of performers. Emotion leading the charge, music memorization was one of the first changes put into place to prepare for their television debut. This allowed the group to create a larger emotional connection and rapport with the viewing audience. Additionally, visual elements and staging were revved up to include themed theatrical sets, costumes, and featured dancers.

The television program demonstrated all the showmanship that made Waring famous: high-quality arrangements, talented singers, tight pacing, forward-thinking, and, of course, "the Waring Sound."

Making it look easy was hard, and Waring found television a constant challenge as the early technology matured. Each week, the new medium required significantly more weekly material from him than any of his previous shows. What it amounted to was producing an hour-long mix of Broadway or Hollywood musical revues, with about four days of preparation. There never seemed to be enough rehearsal time.

In their first ten weeks on television, the Pennsylvanians burned through more than 150 special arrangements of songs, old and new. Like the writers of today's most popular live-studio shows (e.g., *Saturday Night Live*), Waring's show writers and arrangers often found themselves burning the midnight oil to deliver new material each week. In addition, the Waring troupe continued its weekly engagements, which made for an even crazier schedule. During the live-televised run of *The Fred Waring Show*, the Pennsylvanians were at the height of their popularity and typically played in about 150 cities each year, traveling nearly every night by buses to the next city. The cast averaged a total of forty members, including the orchestra and glee.

By 1949, less than a year into the television broadcast of *The Fred Waring Show*, Waring-wannabes were starting to appear in rural community high schools in the form of pop choral ensembles.

Two of these first groups, dubbed *swing choirs*, were (the) Swing Choir in Lacrosse, Wisconsin, and the Swingsters in Manhattan, Kansas. Both simultaneously started filling their high school auditoriums with songs and smiles during the first season of *The Fred Waring Show*. Whether the choral directors were trying to directly mimic Waring or not, it was clear that the bandleader's influence was moving beyond just media and music and into education.

Despite the coincidental timing, Larry Boye, director of the Kansas show choir, didn't necessarily credit Waring for his decision to put together the Swingsters. When asked how he got the idea to create a singing and dancing group, he replied, "Not from Fred Waring. I had heard of Fred Waring. We didn't have television . . . I just did it."

That's the funny thing about influential people in history—especially in the entertainment industry. Individuals start making decisions, start dressing a certain way, start using certain slang, all the while not realizing the inspiration behind the trend.

Consider Justin Bieber, the musical phenom discovered on YouTube. Although he started off as just another teen heartthrob and pop artist, his influence grew larger than his pop chart singles. Average tweens

Say It With Music

Serving as a training ground for future choir members, **Girls' Chorus** holds regular rehearsals every Monday, Wednesday, and Friday during the fourth period. Directed by Mr. Mikelson, each of the forty ambitious singers strives toward transfer into the larger group.

Singing Waring's arrangement of the "Song of Christmas", the newly formed **Swing Choir** made its first appearance during our Christmas assembly. Accompanied by Norma Spangler, this group of twenty selected from the choir has sung throughout the city.

Top Row: B. DeClute, Don Barrett, T. Wheeler, K. Gillmeister, J. Garralin, K. Fawcett, **Second Row:** J. Low, R. Martin, D. Larson, R. Vaaler, L. Hunter, D. Tanke. **Front Row:** L. Melby, G. Rigsberg, M. Standiford, D. Glasbrenner, T. Renner, P. Standiford, A. Schultz, C. Clark, M. Dalzell, S. Sayner.

LARRY BOYE: WARING WORSHIPER?

Maybe not. Boye admitted to taking his students to a Waring Summer Choral Workshop in the early 1950s but was unimpressed with the staging and movement ideas that were being offered. Boye said, "I wanted to see more action, more visual excitement . . . the kids and audiences wanted to have more going on than just moving from picture to picture."

THE MUSICAL MIDWEST

Surprisingly, two of the earliest high school pop ensembles did not appear in metropolitan areas where professional swing and pop music groups were performing. Instead, rural Midwest students were the first to tap to the tunes of Waring. Less distracted than the city teenagers? Perhaps. The saying goes, "The smaller the town, the bigger the show choir."

Fred Waring to his ensemble, "Be on your toes tonight—or I'll be on yours tomorrow."

might not think overtly of him when they sit down to get a haircut or pick out their outfit for the day, but suddenly classrooms around the United States started to have a similar, fashionable look to them. Fifteen-year-old boys began sporting long, shaggy-but-styled haircuts and wearing tight jeans and bomber-style jackets. American teens and tweens, and a few admitted adults, caught a serious case of Bieber Fiever. It happened.

Many could argue that Waring is to show choirs what Bieber is to the long, flippable hairstyles. Although Boye was self-assured in his statement, his few short sentences helped prove that Waring had hit a milestone. Waring's net of influence had been cast so wide, people didn't even realize when they were "doin' a Waring." That credentialed authority became larger than even the bandleader ever expected and continued to grow even when he was no longer on stage or television

In 1955, *The Fred Waring Show* came to a close after seven successful seasons. In the end, Waring and the production crew decided to draw the final curtain on the show not because of ratings, but because Waring was simply burnt out. Each year, the show required him to produce more than 3,100 minutes of music (60 minutes per week for 52 weeks) at the perfectionist standards that he demanded of himself. Although television brought him more fame and fortune, he was spent.

After waving the white flag of surrender to television, Waring lived out every overworked performer's dream—he hit the road and explored the world with his Pennsylvanians in tow.

The across-the-globe production and tour involved strategically planned lighting effects, choreographed transitions, decorated dancers, scripted theatrics, and unforgettable music.

Toward the end of Fred Waring's touring years, he remained active as a music educator and entrepreneur. Every summer, nearly one thousand teachers, in quest of new ideas for their classes as well as college credits, attended the Fred Waring Music Workshop at Delaware Water Gap, Pennsylvania, where they spent eight hours per day learning Waring's choral techniques and elements of showmanship, including program planning, staging, and lighting.

Waring was an avid teacher and devoted himself to

helping young musicians reach their highest potential.
In 1965, he said in an interview:

> So many young singers fail to understand
> a most important concept which I so earnestly
> feel must be taught and taught by every re-
> sponsible teacher. It is this: a song is com-
> posed of both words and music. These two
> ingredients are blended to create a song. The
> singer must look upon them as being equal
> in value. He cannot consider them separately
> except, of course, for purposes of analysis and
> study. Integrated performance will have pow-
> er of communication and conviction . . . and if
> that is not desired, why sing at all?

Waring developed a reputation within the industry
for holding demanding, tough, and meticulous company rehearsals. Tear shedding was not surprising or
uncalled for during a Waring work session.

Dr. Fritz Mountford, an ex-Pennsylvanian and
Waring historian, describes Waring as "patient and sym-
pathetic, while at the same time, a strict and disciplined
conductor." Through all the chastising and grueling rehearsals, those who worked for Waring came to respect
and admire him for the humility and passion he brought
to creating beautiful music. From this unwavering disci-
pline, along with Waring's sincere desire to help talented
young people achieve their best, came the perfection of
sound and performance that rendered the Pennsylvanians an institution. It is a fact in show business that
anyone who worked for Waring got top priority as a potential performer for other quality producers.

By the time Fred Waring and the Pennsylvanians
hung up their traveling shoes, swing choirs were bopping and swaying across the country. By the early
1960s, a small number of colleges had embraced the
pop choral/band concept and launched their own War-
ing-style ensembles. Indiana, the land of corn, cows,
and pigs, was soon to become a major player in the
development of swing choir. And swing choirs seemed
to be cropping up in several places at once.

Whether one credits Waring, television, radio, or
even Mr. Larry Boye for taking the lead in molding a
new form of entertainment, it was official: The curtain
had been lifted on show choirs.

Sit back and enjoy the show.

Your Hit Parade
(CBS) radio, 1949:
from left: John Lau-
renz, Monica Lewis,
and Russ Case.

ACCEPTANCE: SWINGING INTO TELEVISION

There are strengths and weaknesses everywhere—we mostly build on the strengths.

—MILTON C. ANDERSON, DIRECTOR, YOUNG AMERICANS

There is something unforgettable about the first time an acceptance letter arrives in the mail or the first job offer that is laid out on the table. Suddenly, there's merit in the struggles and validation behind one's hard work. Sometimes it takes a piece of paper to make it real. Sometimes it just takes one person or one monumental moment for people to believe in themselves.

In the 1950s, when swing choirs were nearing acceptance from the music industry, watch-worthy programming was often defined by a square box that radiated both sound and light—the television. Just introduced to America, this new technology was becoming as popular as poodle skirts and SPAM.

Beyond allowing parents to entertain their children safely in the comfort of a family room, this new household must-have brought a unique offering to the performing arts world. It provided a new outlet for variety shows and allowed musical performers the opportunity to create a more intense visual connection with their audience—something radio never was able to achieve. It presented a performance language similar to live theater but with the advantages of such cinematic actions as close-ups, dolly shots, panning, and lip-synching. The novelty of watching shows in

The television set was introduced in America in the 1950s, and by 1959, 85 million sets had been sold. Television became the ideal medium for introducing pop music and fashion.

Throughout the decade, television surpassed radio as an income-producing medium and quickly became a significant focus, with families watching a staggering average of six hours of programming a day.

Surgeon General Approved: Interestingly enough, almost every prime-time show—from *The Fred Waring Show* in the late '40s to *I Dream of Jeannie* in the '60s—had a tobacco sponsor. In addition to the ads, family programs often had a reputable celebrity endorsing their product, such as John Wayne for Camel cigarettes. And if tobacco didn't appear in the shows' ads, their characters were smoking. Even Fred and Wilma Flintstone would light up from time to time.

one's own home made television entertainment even more dynamic and intimate than live performances.

The powerful combo of television and variety shows jolted the general public's appreciation and passion for music and musical performances. But to be successful, performers now had to be animated through not only their voice but their facial expressions. The show itself needed to be visually appealing to a large, family-focused audience. Dancing and (G-rated, family-friendly) body movement became basic elements of what was considered a worthwhile program.

AN AVALANCHE OF VARIETY SHOWS

By the mid-'50s, celebrities, producers, advertisers, and record companies all recognized the commercial value of television variety shows and were competing to attract the biggest audiences. As a result, there was a flood of new sparkle and glitter-fied television shows, leaving families with a sizable pool of music-focused features from which to choose. Whether people considered themselves part of the Waring fan club or Elvis groupies, there was something for everyone.

Every Hollywood celebrity wanted his or her own show. The bigger the name, the better the production. The more creative and unusual, the more viewers tuned in. Unfortunately, however, much like the dot-com companies of the '90s, just a handful of the '50s shows achieved long-term success.

To prevent a flop, it was essential to receive corporate financial support. The most popular and entertaining shows were more reactive than proactive, receiving solicitations from large corporate sponsors such as General Electric, Ford, and Philip Morris for paid advertising space. These businesses saw this pop culture wave as a means to increase their own profits through branding.

A handful of the most popular, advertising-worthy musical variety programs included:

YOUR HIT PARADE (1950–1959)

This weekly program, sponsored by Lucky Strike cigarettes, featured a house band and resident singers who performed Top 40 hits. Although the show was fairly popular, it was never as successful as its radio predecessor that began in 1935.

AMERICAN BANDSTAND (1956–1989)

Unlike *Your Hit Parade, American Bandstand* was one of the longest-running music variety shows, perfectly illustrating the American transition from radio to television. Hosted by Dick Clark (decades before he celebrated consecutive New Years Eves with Ryan Seacrest) for the majority of its run, the show featured dozens of teenagers dancing to the tunes of a selected pop artist performer. The show's regular guests included Kenny Rossi and Arlene Sullivan, Bunny Gibson and Eddie Kelly, Pat Molittieri, Carmen Jimenez, and Joyce Shafer.

THE ED SULLIVAN SHOW (1955–1971)

Like Scrabble and a solid dinner and dessert, *The Ed Sullivan Show* was a Sunday night staple for many families. The show, which ran for twenty-three years, introduced stars, Broadway acts, and rock groups to Americans. Its famous host, Ed Sullivan, was also a former Broadway performer, bringing his stage talents to television.

When Elvis Presley made his first appearance on *The Ed Sullivan Show* on September 9, 1956, the performance was watched by 60 million viewers—the largest single audience in television history. During the performance of "Ready Teddy," Elvis rocked his infamous gyrating hips, and the camera immediately adjusted to shoot the performance from the waist up to avoid offensive vulgarities.

In his book *All Shook Up: How Rock 'n' Roll Changed America*, Glenn C. Altschuler cited a review from Jack Gould, a journalist and critic of the time: "Presley had 'injected movements of his tongue and indulged in wordless singing that were singularly distasteful.' Over-stimulating the physical impulses of the teenagers was 'a gross national disservice.'"

Later, during Elvis's third appearance on the show in 1957, Sullivan stood next to Elvis as the audience applauded and said to the cameras, "This is a real decent, fine boy. We've never had a more pleasant experience on our show with a big name than we've had with you . . . You're thoroughly all right." A ringing endorsement or a testament to the power of camera censorship? Up for debate.

Since the late '40s, television executives tried to translate the principles of vaudeville to the new medium. Referred to as "vaudeo," this set up combined the skills and entertainment values of sports reporters, gossip columnists, and emcees. Ed Sullivan had this mix down cold. Comedian Alan King once said, "Ed [Sullivan] does nothing, but he does it better that anyone else on television."

THE PERRY COMO SHOW (1955–1963)

Although popular, there wasn't a lot of variety in *The Perry Como Show*. Como would perform his own hit songs as well as invite other artists on as guests. Featured throughout the series were the famous Peter Gennaro Dancers and the Louis Da Pron Dancers.

THE ANDY WILLIAMS SHOW (1958–1971)

As a legendary show host and era-driving show, Andy Williams and *The Andy Williams Show* won three Emmys and maintained a captive audience for thirteen years. In addition to its always rotating guests, the program featured the Good Time Singers and the Nick Castle Dancers.

THE JACKIE GLEASON SHOW (1952–1970)

Slipping on a banana peel or running into the wall have been visual standbys of comedians throughout the years. In the early days of television, these antics were utilized skillfully by the one and only Jackie Gleason. Gleason was a physical comedian who quickly learned to take advantage of the visual connection performers were able to make with an audience through television.

Mixing comedy with variety, Gleason has been called one of the early inventors of television comedy. His show, featuring the June Taylor Dancers in Busby Berkeley–style production numbers, was also specifically designed for the television camera.

THE MICKEY MOUSE CLUB (1955–1994)

Who can pull out jazz hands better than a group of kids mirroring the G-rated tunes of a cute mouse in oversized white gloves? Disney's *The Mickey Mouse Club* was a popular afternoon program that highlighted talented tweens and teenagers. Called "Mouseketeers," the young actors performed weekly singing and dancing production numbers.

THE ARTHUR MURRAY PARTY (1950–1960)

The Arthur Murray Party, which could be considered an early *Dancing with the Stars*, featured Arthur and Kathryn Murray and the Arthur Murray Dancers. Each week, guests, including comedians, athletes, and actors, were taught dance steps or routines to perform for the viewing audience. Unlike *Dancing with the Stars*, no one was voted off; these dancers performed purely for the audience's viewing enjoyment.

THE DINAH SHORE SHOW (1956–1963)

Dinah Shore and her iconic kiss good-bye to the audience made a lasting impact on '50s television in *The Dinah Shore Show*, briefly known also as *The Dinah Shore Chevy Show*. And beyond the memorable smooch, her music style helped shape the "easy listening" genre present today.

THE LAWRENCE WELK SHOW (1955–1971)

Originally introduced as a summer replacement show, the *Lawrence Welk Show* won not only ratings but the hearts of American families for twenty-seven years. The variety format consisted of easy-listening, or what Welk dubbed "champagne" music, performed by a group of family-friendly musicians, singers, and dancers. The show was so clean you could eat off it—and America ate it up.

After the cancellation of *The Mickey Mouse Club* in 1959, it was revived and renewed a couple of times, once in the '70s and again in the '90s. The now famous '90s Mouseketeers included Britney Spears, Justin Timberlake, Christina Aguilera, Keri Russell, and Ryan Gosling.

"In the '50s, television would introduce music to people—which would be increasingly listened to by the eyes and felt by the body." –Hal Malcolm, innovator and leader in vocal jazz education

TOP 10 *BILLBOARD* HITS: 1955

"Cherry Pink and Apple Blossom White"—Pérez Prado
"Sincerely"—McGuire Sisters
"(We're Going to) Rock Around the Clock"—Billy Haley and the Comets
"Sixteen Tons"—"Tennessee" Ernie Ford
"Love Is a Many-Splendored Thing"—Four Aces
"The Yellow Rose of Texas"—Mitch Miller
"The Ballad of Davy Crockett"—Bill Hayes
"Autumn Leaves"—Roger Williams
"Let Me Go Lover"—Joan Weber
"Dance with Me Henry (Wallflower)"—Georgia Gibbs

Hoo·sier [hoo-zher] –*noun*
1. a native or inhabitant of Indiana (used as a nickname)
2. (*usually lowercase*) any awkward, unsophisticated person

TUNING IN AND TUNING UP

The influence of the new electronic box in the living room had started to seep its way into Americans'—particularly teenagers'— lifestyles. Audiences were exposed to pop music artists and their dancing entourages, driving pop record sales to new heights. Entertainment and pop music had moved way beyond Waring and the Pennsylvanians. It was now bigger, more influential, and more central to the lives of Americans.

THE BEAT OF THE NEW DRUM

The music introduced in the '50s was all about fun. The popular tunes of the day contained unchanging tempos and rhythms that didn't require an interpreter and could be enjoyed by a large, general audience. These songs were the toe-tappers and showstoppers that can still be heard at weddings—or covered by pop artists. The bands and their melodies were the beginning of what would later be referred to as rock and roll.

THE SINGING HOOSIERS

The new rhythms and music of the decade introduced a refreshing, caffeinelike energy boost to the airwaves as well as high school dances and university auditoriums. In 1950, George Krueger, inspired by this musical movement, created the first pop-focused glee club at Indiana University, called the Singing Hoosiers.

The group performed with the style of Waring, singing pop music in a semitraditional or formal manner. Although at the beginning they didn't incorporate much movement, they did have staged transitions, or *choralography*, that involved minimal dips and sways.

State by state, they won the hearts of audiences throughout the Midwest and spawned the growth of swing choirs throughout the area.

DANCE FEVER HITS MUSICAL EDUCATION

Recognizing the excitement and obsession that their students had with pop music and television programs, young high school choral directors also started catching '50s fever. One by one, educators began experimenting with choralized pop songs and staged movements for their otherwise-still concerts, adding a little swing. They found this not only helped breathe modern life into the performances, but attracted more student participants than ever before. Swing groups became the cool kids of choir.

Although fun, practical, and timely, this new trend toward swing and pop groups generated serious criticism from music educator associations.

Richard Jaeger, director of choral activities at Jefferson High School in Lafayette, Indiana, remembers putting simple tags, picture changes, step-touch foot patterns, and movement combinations into a concert for the Indiana Music Educators Association (IMEA) in 1958.

> We were going to do a medley from *My Fair Lady*, which included the song "Ascot Gavotte" . . . I added staging for the IMEA performance. When we were done, I had directors coming up to me asking, "What made [you] do that?" . . . They were shocked. They really felt that I had cheapened choral music.

This debate between directors arguing for the betterment of musical education may have started in the '50s, but even now, this dispute continues. There is a resistance to change, and even in an industry built on creativity, this is one area that many associations tend to resist. Traditional choral directors saw, and some still see, emerging styles of trendy, contemporary material as a threat to classical music.

In 1959, to protect the potentially endangered entity of classical music, a group of concerned directors founded the American Choral Directors Association. As described on its Web site, the ACDA's "central purpose [was and] is to promote excellence in choral music through performance, composition, publication, research, and teaching. In addition, ACDA strives through arts advocacy to elevate choral music's position in American society."

Meanwhile, even as that embassy of anti–swing choirs was being created, pop-influenced groups continued to gain popularity, selling out shows, recording music, and entertaining audiences in the Midwest. If change was in the air, these choirs were breathing it all in. They found inspiration from television, their Hollywood idols, and neighborhood trendsetters.

These troupes were creating a new genre of entertainment. Although each performance may have veered further away from classical traditions, it also brought more talented students and performers closer to appreciating and perfecting the art of music.

Swing choirs took their title from the big band era, when traditional bands split into concert and swing bands. It wouldn't be until the late '60s that the word jazz would replace *swing* in this context.

"You have to make yourself a show choir director, because no one is going to teach you how. Show choir offers styles and skills that apply to real life work opportunities. Learning notes and how to sing or play an instrument merely lets you become 'another music teacher.'" — David Fahr, show choir director, Attaché

*The Kids from Wisconsin
Singers in a three-level pose.*

REHEARSAL: POP CULTURE AND CHANGING TASTES

4

I'm going to take care of the discipline. They just need to bring talent and commitment.

—DAVID FEHR, DIRECTOR, CLINTON HIGH SCHOOL'S ATTACHÉ

Practice makes perfect. Every day, people wake up to the sound of an alarm clock, hop into the shower, and begin the day hoping to perfect a part of themselves. Every twenty-four hours may not bring an achievement, but it's the journey that builds character and brings about change.

Rehearsal is about transformation—transforming a habit, a final score, a paycheck.

In the 1960s, change was in the air. Anti–Vietnam War activists exercised freedom of speech with their protests. Free spirits preached peace and love. Artists advanced rock and roll to capture the passionate, history-making decade in song.

There was no denying a shift was occurring. Everywhere. A new generation of Americans started questioning the long-standing traditions held by former generations. A growing commitment for

"Some people tap their feet, some people snap their fingers, and some people sway back and forth. I just sorta do 'em all together, I guess." —Elvis Presley

"The message may not move me, or mean a great deal to me, but hey! It feels so groovy to say . . . 'I did rock & roll music.'" —Peter, Paul and Mary

"It was a wonderful time to be young. The '60s didn't end until about 1976. We all believed in Make Love, Not War. We were idealistic innocents, despite the drugs and sex." —Margot Kidder

"When the power of love overcomes the love of power, the world will know peace." —Jimi Hendrix

FROM WARING TO WARTIME

Inspired by their passions surrounding the Vietnam War and civil rights movement, Americans responded with protests and prose.

"Turn! Turn! Turn!" by Pete Seeger
"Blowin' in the Wind" by Bob Dylan
"Universal Soldier" by Buffy Sainte-Marie
"A Change Is Gonna Come" by Sam Cooke
"I Ain't Marching Any More" by Phil Ochs
"The War Drags On" by Mick Softley
"I-Feel-Like-I'm-Fixin'-To-Die Rag" by Joe McDonald
"With God on Our Side" by Bob Dylan
"Masters of War" by Bob Dylan
"Give Peace a Chance" by John Lennon and the Plastic Ono Band

Television was the main source of inspiration for pop choral singing in the early '60s. Mitch Miller's *Sing Along with Mitch* featured weekly sing-alongs where at-home audiences could follow the lyrics on the bottom of their screen by way of a bouncing ball jumping over each word.

In the movie *Dreamgirls*, the characters create two versions of the song "Cadillac," one suitable for the R & B station and another, more family-friendly, *American Bandstand* version.

social change was on the rise, led by particularly energized groups of young adults and teenagers. Short hair grew longer. Mustaches and unkempt beards replaced the clean-shaven look. Wholesome picnics turned into rallies.

While certainly not a pressing issue of the decade, it became apparent that the teenagers sneaking into clubs and smoking marijuana in school parking lots were not the same as those interested in humming show tunes in the auditorium. They were not in the same cliques, and they were not listening to the same music. The choir-ambitious and electric guitar strummers may have shared the same passion, but the divide had never been larger.

IN TIMES OF CHANGE, THE CRAZIES SHINE BUT THE BRILLIANT SHINE BRIGHTER

Like a teenager in search of a clique, musicians in particular were trying to create and carve out their place and tune within this refreshed society. Many naturally gravitated toward pop music—one of the first genres to start experimenting during this decade with different rhythms, performances, and performers.

As the '60s progressed, pop music became increasingly diverse. The lyrics transcribed everything from politics to sex to drugs, and the music itself was more beat driven and lyrically aggressive than ever. Although it was exciting for those involved, some pop vocalists struggled to make their classically trained voices fit this new sound, defaulting to vocal techniques considered incorrect by traditional standards. They attempted to merge what they knew with what they didn't know, which sometimes resulted in a mess of a sound.

Watching professional performers' difficulties with finding that balance often dissuaded choral music educators from even considering pop arrangements (which weren't being published). Choirs, instead, were encouraged to stick to the safe (respectable) music to avoid embarrassment, as well as to ignore what were dismissed as mere musical fads.

Often, however, safe, noncontroversial songs were yawn-worthy and following the rules was boring. When a director was able to step forward and sneak a pop tune—one that wasn't too racy—into a performance, students loved both the style and the change.

Given this underground demand, specialized '60s pop arrangements were created to focus on family-friendly vocal groups such as the 5th Dimension. Less daring but still progressive, groups employed Broadway renditions in their shows, featuring such tunes as "Aquarius" and selections from *Fiddler on the Roof*. The Broadway tempos and lyrics inherently lent themselves to toe tapping and swaying. Like white doves at a wedding, they just worked.

The only group harmonizing to the Beatles at this point may have been the Beatles, but swing groups were still progressing through the decade with grace and a few grins.

HONING IN ON HARMONY

Although choral instructors of the '60s erred on the safer side of sass, their teaching styles and classroom discussions began to shift. As a whole, traditional vocal teachers continued utilizing formal vocal training techniques when approaching any type of genre—even pop and rock and roll. They focused on how to breathe from the diaphragm, and to enunciate words through diction and Tone-Syllables, the methods of Robert Shaw and Fred Waring.

The newer techniques being introduced to music at this time, such as growls, breathy phrasing, and guttural attacks, were dismissed and disregarded. The idea of using pop recording vocal techniques in live choral performances went against everything Fred Waring, Robert Shaw, and the other choral gods held near and dear to their hearts.

A long time passed before traditional choral groups adapted pop techniques. Acceptance grew with the advancements of microphones and multitrack recording. By the mid-'60s, electric guitars and drums would be required to accompany the pop vocal techniques. During this time, however, the two styles and groups were encouraged to remain separate until further notice.

Despite the hesitation and dismissal of pop vocal trends by seasoned choral directors, young directors were eager to incorporate the new style into their choir concerts. They appreciated the uplifting beats. It was music of their generation. It attracted students to their choir programs. They were curious about the new swing movement. The music industry was undergoing massive change, and they wanted to take part in it.

THE DEVELOPMENTAL DIVIDE

This world of limitless possibilities started creating a

The American Choral Directors organized to protect classical choral music from the on-slaught of pop and rock permeating the air-waves. Shown here is the ACDA steering com-mittee at the founding organizational meeting in Kansas City, Missouri. From left to right are J. Clark Rhodes, Elwood Keister, Curtis Hanson, Harry Robert Wilson, R. Wayne Hugoboom, and Archie Jones. Photo taken by another steering committee member, Warner Imig. (1959).

divide within the community of musical educators.

Generally speaking, the older generation of choral directors, who were legacies of the Fred Waring and Robert Shaw eras, did not connect with the music trends of the '60s. They relied on their generation's choral teachings and maintained impassioned convic-tion in the benefits of classical music traditions.

Next to them stood the younger generation of newly graduated choral teachers who wanted to put their training to use with the current pop music trends. They were excited, edgy, and talented, but equally na-ive. Many newbies lacked the institutional knowledge and choral reputation among the who's who of choral music education to make things happen.

It was the classic battle between those in fine art vs. commercial art. No one, yet everyone, was a winner.

DIVERSIFYING TUNES

As the decade moved on, pop music became more a social statement put to melody than merely a source of entertainment. Music styles also became more diversi-fied, reflecting the more segmented society.

There were no longer just two genres of music, "new" or "old." Artists fresh out of the studio took a more individualistic approach to their tunes. They were labeled "black" or "white," "middle-class" or "poor," "northern" or "southern," "urban" or "rural."

Singers didn't worry as much as earlier genera-tions had about appealing to a larger, general audience, and began creating their own niche and carving out a unique performance style. Many artists dreamed of one day becoming the next Elvis or establishing a new style of rock and roll. And they could if they wanted to. It was a time of musical experimentation and anything felt possible.

DIFFERENCES DISAPPEARING

One of unsung wins that swing choirs achieved in the '60s resulted from the 1964 Civil Rights Act and the racial tension that surrounded that monumental movement. Choral directors across the country were encouraged by their administrations to create musical ensembles that would attract and accommodate the sudden influx of racial diversity that formerly homog-enized schools were experiencing.

Mike Howard, who directed a group called the Showstoppers in Laurel, Mississippi, recalls, "We

Hullabaloo *TV Series on NBC: shown seated, far left, Diana Ross; dancing, far right, Michael Bennett; second from right, Donna McKechnie (1965–1966).*

didn't call it a choir . . . it was a show group. There were a lot of problems with integration at the time, and this was supposed to be a recruitment tool."

Swing choirs, in all their pop culture glory, helped attract diverse crowds. They helped bring common ground to a divided society. And they established commonality despite the differences. They sang through segregation.

THE MELDING POT

Whatever the motive behind the music, the key, many found, to meeting commercial success, whether as a pop vocalist or swing choir, was to mix styles of both pop and classic into a harmoniously melded choral pot. The recipe resulted in attractive vocals, a smart song style, and instant popularity. Once discovered, artists and Broadway composers started eating this immersion style up, one note at a time.

Early swing choirs started adapting this pop-class method because, in addition to the favorable sound, it also helped increase the number of participants. Teenagers were tuning in to this fresh, new version of music performance and stepping forward by the dozens to become more involved.

It made sense.

In a small way, swing choirs allowed students to live out their Hollywood fantasies: singing familiar, popular tunes under the spotlights. And even if performing teenagers didn't have dreams of starring in *The Mickey Mouse Club*, swing choirs still provided a creative outlet that felt more like an adventure and less like school.

Swing choir performances continued to be influenced by the television variety shows of the day—especially when it came to adding dance and movement. Shows such as *The Carol Burnett Show*, *The Dean Martin Show*, and *The Lawrence Welk Show* provided a solid model for how to naturally incorporate some sway into a song.

PIONEERING SWINGERS

As movement, staging, and dance became basic, expected elements in television programming, they started also to become more acceptable in choir performances. These early adapters didn't jump in with all three elements at once, but they did help test the waters. Like the first synthesizer and the first *Rolling Stone* magazine, show choirs were '60s guinea pigs, adding a little more harmony and a heart to the era.

HELLO, BROADWAY!

Utilizing similar techniques, on occasion, led to combustion on the *Billboard* charts and in the industry. The popular musical ran on Broadway from 1964 to 1970, inspiring Louis Armstrong's pop chart hit "Hello, Dolly." The year the musical premiered, the single took the no. 1 spot on the pop charts, making Armstrong the oldest performer to earn a no. 1 hit. For extra bragging rights, he also beat out the Beatles, who had previously held the record position of staying at no. 1 for a consecutive fourteen weeks.

Guinea pig—noun
1. a short-eared, tail-less rodent of the genus *Cavia*; usually white, black, and tawny, commonly regarded as the domesticated form of one of the South American wild species of cavy; often used in scientific experiments or kept as a pet.
2. (*informal*) the subject of any sort of experiment

Indiana University's Singing Hoosiers (1958).

The Young Americans.

The Ball Street Singers.

THE SINGING HOOSIERS

Described as "America's Premier Collegiate Concert Show Choir," Indiana University's Singing Hoosiers was a convergence of both a "concert" and "show" choir. The group was founded in the 1950 as an all-male concert choir. Within a couple of years, a female ensemble called the Hoosier Queens was added. The coed group began incorporating simple synchronized movements, and further enhanced their staging and choreography in 1963, under the direction of Robert Stoll.

The Hoosiers' unique performing style was designed for maximum vocal production while also delivering high-energy choreographic movement. They have achieved this style by varying the level of choreography among the members. The group's elite dancers, called the Varsity Singers, perform action-packed, "full-body" dancing downstage, while those on the risers perform less demanding "choral-ography" behind them. This has been an influential staging technique that allows the Hoosiers, and other groups, to have the best of both worlds—lots of action and great vocals.

THE YOUNG AMERICANS

Billing themselves as "America's Oldest Show Choir," the Young Americans, from Corona, California, introduced the West Coast to show choir love. As the first group to meld pop and show music with extensive choreography, they took their show on the road, performing throughout Southern California, neighboring states, and abroad.

Because of this choir's popularity, Southern California, or SoCal, suddenly became a hub for high school swing choir activities. Groups began to pop up all over the Sunshine State, especially in the surrounding Los Angeles area.

THE BALL STATE SINGERS

In 1964, the Ball State Singers came into the picture, taking Indiana by storm and song. Started by Donald Neuen, this group of twenty-four coed singers featured elements that were cutting edge to college groups at the time.

Neuen and the group used five microphones, a full instrumental section, and, like Waring, singers who doubled as instrumentalists.

Although the ensemble wasn't technically choreo-

graphed, the performers moved with more freedom and were less rigid and stiff than previous college pop choral groups. They were having fun.

UP WITH PEOPLE

Established in 1965 by J. Blanton Belk, Up with People had the goal to act as goodwill ambassadors for young people. Since then, nearly 21,000 young men and women from more than 96 countries have performed with the group—delivering both community service and a message of hope and goodwill to audiences throughout the world.

THE WISCONSIN SINGERS

Because one trendsetting swing choir isn't enough, Arlie Mucks Jr. founded the Wisconsin Singers in 1967 at the University of Wisconsin–Madison. With Don Neuen as director, the Wisconsin Badger-based choir emphasized the combination of singing and communication, creating a revue-style performance marked excellent by swing choir enthusiasts and critics.

THE KIDS FROM WISCONSIN

Another premier choir that brought some "cheese" into their show was the Kids from Wisconsin. The group was formed in 1969 to create a wholesome image of Wisconsin youth for the rest of the nation. The summertime performing group fell under the direction

Milton C. Anderson, a former music supervisor for CBS-TV, formed the college-aged show group, the Young Americans, in the early '60s.

"[When I was in high school], that was the goal: to be like the Young Americans. We had a little show choir of about twenty singers on a flat floor." —Dr. Peter Eklund, director of choral activities at the University of Nebraska, Lincoln

"I did not conduct . . . I did not want to get between the performers and the audience . . . I wanted more show! My emphasis was on singing and great communication." —Don Neuen, director, the Ball State Singers

Up With People.

The fair way to fund: Instead of receiving university sponsorships, the Kids were funded by the Wisconsin State Fair.

of John Clark and Colonel Mark Azzolina, the former conductor for Bob Hope.

SONGS OF THE TIME

By the end of the decade, the world was not the same—and neither was music. Beside the sheer number of swing choirs established, the type of performances, when compared to those of the '50s, was drastically different.

Choirs were singing more than just words and performing more than just songs. Participants considered their group more important to them than a third-period class or just another extracurricular activity. There was passion. There was drama. There was purpose. There were choirs.

. . . And things were about to get competitive.

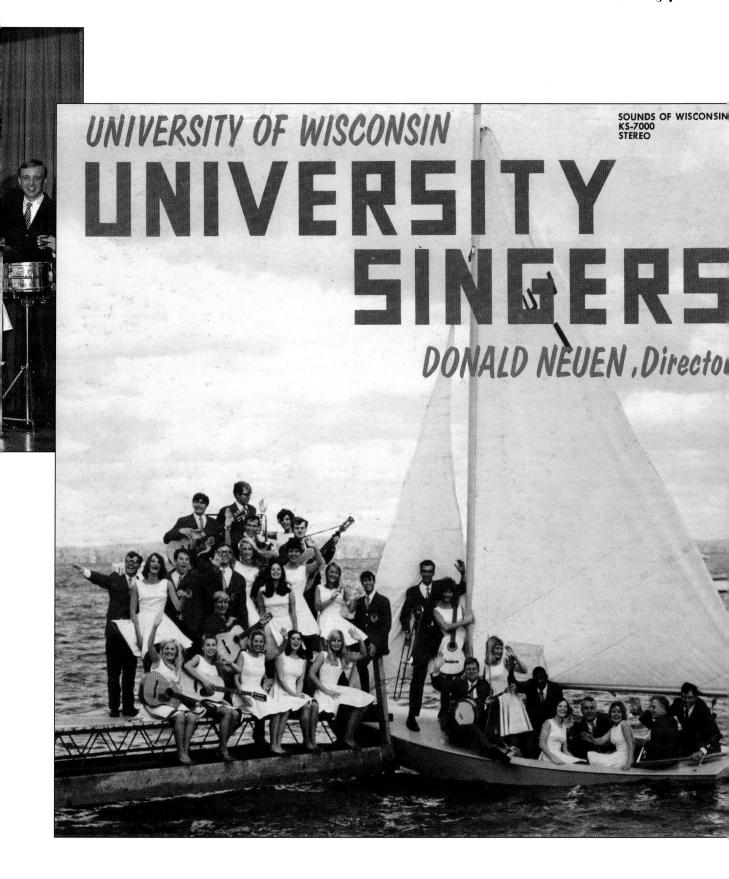

LIGHTS, CAMERA, ACTION: THE INTRODUCTION OF COMPETITION

Competition, for good or for bad, promotes excellence in our art. Many folks think competition is unhealthy, yet the quality of competitive groups versus noncompetitive groups is vastly different, with only a few notable exceptions.

—DAMON BROWN, SHOW CHOIR CHOREOGRAPHER

As humans, we have an innate desire to compete. We compare grades, cars, team scores, lives. We compete with one another and with ourselves. If there are two people working on a project, there is usually a winner and a loser (or second winners, for those in denial). When life throws a tie score in the mix, many are left unsettled.

Let's be honest, even on lazy days, we all want to be better . . . or even the best. But to make that claim, we need someone or something to compare ourselves to, as a benchmark, for both our successes and our shortcomings.

Because of the sudden increased popularity of singing and swaying

The event was referred to as a "swing" festival instead of a "jazz" festival due to the negative connotations of the word *jazz* at the time. Malcolm explained, "I wanted to have a festival that showcased vocal jazz music. But we could not use the word *jazz* in any kind of educational curriculum or event. So I called it the Northwest Vocal Swing Festival . . . with the word *swing* replacing *jazz*."

The word *competition* was also forbidden within the music education vernacular at the time. Perhaps the term was too negative or it created a less-than-positive image of choirs "going at it," but despite the careful wording of its title, within two years the Northwest Choir Festival was absolutely a competition. Choirs traveled hundreds of miles in an attempt to confirm that they were the best. Although some walked away disappointed, they were reinvigorated to up their game for next year.

Hal Malcolm embraced movement in performance and conducted his ensembles with energy and enthusiasm, Mt. Hood College, Gresham, Oregon (1970).

The judging forms were fashioned from the Olympic Stage Band Festival Organization and included the ten judging standards for band: ensemble blend, intonation, balance, rhythm, precision, dynamic, interpretation, concepts, presentation, and arrangements. Then Malcolm substituted "choir" for "band," "voices" for "instruments," and "sing" for "play."

in the late 1960s, more swing choirs were on the scene, ready to judge and be judged. The natural desire to compete, to showcase and compare talents, was settling in, but with one small problem: There were no competitions specific to glee club enthusiasts.

These pop music lovers were not like the choirs of the past and this made them even more ready and eager to strut their stuff.

Lights. Camera. Competition.

COMPETITION SETS IN
THE NORTHWEST SWING CHOIR FESTIVAL

In 1968, Hal Malcolm, former director of choral activities at Mt. Hood Community College in Gresham, Oregon, was looking for a simple way to get young people excited about music again. Growing up with the generation that embraced rock music, Elvis's smooth moves, and the floppy bowl haircuts of the Beatles, Malcolm understood the passion and inspiration that pop culture brought to his impressionable peers. In response, he created the Northwest Swing Choir Festival, featuring both swing and jazz choirs— two emerging styles of the time—in hopes that both students and music educators could learn and be inspired by one another.

The festival, later renamed the Northwest Vocal Jazz Festival, grew significantly within a decade. At its initial showcase in 1968, roughly 250 students representing eleven Oregon and Washington schools showed up to sing their high school hearts out. It was like a traditional choral performance hopped up on 5-Hour ENERGY and Red Bull.

Each of the participating groups had the option whether or not to be judged. Directors were presented with the choice of "Door One" or "Door Two." Door One delivered "comments only" to groups, a safe bet for the newbies to the scene. For the more adventurous choirs, Door Two offered rankings. When rankings were selected, a winner was declared, a first loser was notified, with, subsequently, rivalries following close behind.

Winner or loser, everyone was given the choice.

The festival's equal-opportunity judging system also included a small caveat. Malcolm decided not to include staging and movement categories on the judging sheets. He wanted the festival to be dedicated to rewarding good vocal jazz ensemble singing, but didn't want to inhibit groups from expressing new styles—so although several broke out and "moved," they received no points for it.

Despite a few glitches in this system, Malcolm was the Christopher Columbus of competitive swing choirs. He introduced the new territory of pop choral competitions to American choral performers. It was a start, a beginning.

Malcolm's intentions for the event were to highlight and showcase jazz music and to create an educational opportunity for students and directors who were eager to grasp the emergence of a new genre. While these were honorable objectives, groups had their own motivations beyond wishing to sing jazz. Some came to dance. Some came for the staging. Some just came to experience all the hype.

If a group fit the vocal jazz choir description, the Northwest Swing Choir Festival was the competition to attend. Those choirs that chose to incorporate movement and dance into their shows had to prepare for the judges' criticisms, which weren't necessarily wrong. Coming from traditional choral backgrounds, the adjudicators focused on their area of expertise.

Malcolm understood the struggles jazz choirs faced while they worked to be recognized by the traditional choral community, even without the choreography. Despite those issues, one by one, groups were showing up at the festival, introducing dance to a genre that had barely a foot in the door of choral acceptance. They had guts. They were pioneers, rebelling with rhythm.

Due to its success, the festival continued to take place every spring until 1971.

THE RENO JAZZ FESTIVAL

Dr. John Carrico, head of instrumental music at the University of Nevada—Reno and a force behind Reno Jazz Festival, took notice of Malcolm's success with Mt. Hood's swing choir festival.

Carrico approached Malcolm with the idea of creating a vocal jazz division within the Reno Festival, which, since its inception in 1962, had been devoted strictly to jazz bands and instrumentalists. Together, Carrico and Malcolm not only brought vocal jazz to Reno, but because a growing number of groups were adding staging to their singing, a new category was invented, called *show-pop*. The objective was to identify

The Northwest Swing Choir Competition wouldn't be the first to create a scoring system based on band adjudication forms. Seven years later, the Bishop Luers competition would use its initial scoring system based on that of the Northern Indiana School Band, Orchestra, Vocal Association (NISBOVA).

Author's Note: In review, major influences of show choirs to date include vaudeville, the cigarette industry, media, rock and roll, and the Catholic Church. Yes, it is as amazing as it sounds.

Bishop Luers hosted a folk-pop choral festival in 1973 and 1974. That festival eventually turned into a swing choir contest in 1975, when Father Fred took over the Minstrels—Luers' swing choir. Father Forest McAllister had led the previous pop choral group at Bishop Luers High School. They called themselves Forest and the Trees.

At the first Northwest Festival, students from Fife High School in Tacoma, Washington, performed a three-song program of Broadway music, including "Give a Little Whistle" (*Pinocchio*), "People" (*Funny Girl*), and "Side by Side" (*Side by Side by Sondheim*). Arriving at the festival, they were eager to hear the judges' reactions to their picture changes, step-touch patterns, and jazz squares. To their disappointment, the judges all but ignored these aspects of the show. The only feedback on production included comments such as, "too much emphasis on staging," followed by a low ranking, knocking them out of the finals.

Today the Reno Jazz Festival is the world's largest educational jazz festival.

The first annual Bishop Luers High School Swing Choir contest poster (1975).

Father Fred Link and the Bishop Luers Minstrels on Luers' first "stage"—a tarp-covered gym floor. The audience sat in the bleachers. (1975).

Aware that some audience members might not know the definition of *swing choir*, Father Fred included an introduction in the 1975 contest program:

What is swing choir? As you will discover tonight, it is many things. There are as many varieties of swing choirs as there are directors. Perhaps the simplest definition of a swing choir is that it is a "choir that swings."

This description has two parts. The first is the most basic, and each group shares this in common. The group is a choir. This means that the members sing together, usually in harmony; and if it's a good choir, the different voices are balanced, rhythmically together, expressive, etc. You can see what is expected of a good choir by looking at the different categories on the judging sheet contained in this program.

The second element of the description is that the choir "swings." This is where the variety comes in. For most groups this implies singing a "lighter" type of music, music conducive to movement and special accompaniment. Along with piano or organ, most swing choirs add rhythm and bass guitar and some percussion to their accompaniment. Some directors use extensive choreography, dance routines, special lighting effects and other show-stopping techniques. Other directors choose to have their groups sing a more formal way, concentrating on winning their audiences with good vocal production and very simple movement.

Each is valid if done well.

a niche group of participants who could play together and compete on the same stage.

Consequently, participating groups could compete in one of two divisions: Show-Pop or Vocal Jazz. Different judging sheets were used for each division. Both were based on the National Association of Jazz Educators criteria for instrumental music, but the Show-Pop sheet also featured categories for staging and choreography.

Judges or no judges, given the popular variety television shows of the day, groups that added more visual elements to their set received more enthusiastic applause from the audience.

"The first year in Reno, vocal jazz groups and show-pop groups performed on the same stage, back-to-back," said Malcolm. "Audiences went wild when the show-pop groups performed . . . talented vocal jazz groups would come out and sing six-part arrangements and get just a polite applause."

Malcolm and Carrico quickly realized that not only did these two groups need separate adjudication sheets, they also warranted separate competition venues. The following year, the festival format was changed to place the two different divisions at separate performance venues on the campus. Directors, judges, and audiences appreciated separating church and state . . . and low self-esteem and therapy sessions were avoided.

THE BISHOP LUERS HIGH SCHOOL SWING CHOIR CONTEST

It wasn't until 1975 that the notion of an exclusive swing choir competition would be conceived. At a small Catholic high school in the northeast corner of Indiana, Father Fred Link, known to his students and faculty as Father Fred, was at the helm of both the choir and band at Bishop Luers High School. He became inspired by the camaraderie of marching bands and drum and bugle corps and approached the principal about hosting a contest for swing choirs at the school. A simple yes transported swing choirs into the competition space.

"I saw what was available for marching bands," said Father Fred. "I saw the excitement it created for students and audiences alike . . . I thought, 'There should be something like this for swing choirs.'"

Unlike today's competitions, the Bishop Luers

The Marion High School 26th Street Singers from Marion, Indiana (1975).

High School Swing Choir Contest was not conceived as a fund-raiser or a battle of the bands–style event. Father Fred had clear and distinct goal to bring people together for the enjoyment of music.

Father Fred recalled, "My goal was to create an event with the same thrill of competition but also to make it distinctive. Our first [competition] was just in the gym on a tarp with [groups] facing up into the stands. . . . We had maybe seven groups, and Marion High School won. One judge, Larry Boye, from Ball State University, said to me, 'This has got potential. You have a tiger by the tail.'"

Jim Kress, a Fort Wayne marketing consultant, became Father Link's sounding board and cocreator of what would become Bishop Luers' brand. Kress recalled the shock factor of the first contest: "These kids were singing, nodding, clapping hands, and moving unlike the large choral groups of that time. Their sound and movement would be laughable based on today's standards, but it was a happy innovation when first witnessed thirty-six years ago."

This idea that swing choir could handle more choreography and production started the transition from swing choirs to show choirs. Gone were the days of

F. Ritchie Walton and Father Fred Link Bishop Luers High School gymnasium, February 22, 1975.

The 26th Street Singers should have won Luers! They had been doing show choir before show choir was cool.
The 26th Street Singers, under the direction of F. Ritchie Walton, were, by all accounts, pros. Their shows were designed to accommodate costume changes, and featured boys or girls numbers, before that arrangement became popular. In 1976, the year following the first win at Luers, Walton created a touring group called the Ritchie Walton Review, made up of recently graduated 26th Street Singers. The group toured around the Midwest. Ritchie took a sabbatical leave from teaching during the 1977–78 school year to tour with the show, doing appearances in Las Vegas and California.

The popularity of the contest also helped Father Fred in his recruiting. In one year, the Minstrels went from eight to fifteen members.

"swing and sway with Sammy Kaye"—groups were starting to shake things up, literally.

And Boye was right. In two short months, Bishop Luers High School's swing choir, the Minstrels, recruited seven other swing choirs to participate in their premiere competition. During that time, they also secured judges, drafted rules, ordered trophies, and coordinated the logistics of the show. Although that's completely doable today, as the first competition, they were practically throwing darts blindly onto a wall, hoping something might stick. There were no best practices or key teachings to base many (or any) of the decisions on—especially given the fact that these Hoosiers had never met Hal Malcolm.

Father Fred's Annual Bishop Luers Swing Choir Invitational stood out from the previous festivals, not only for its valiant intentions and ridiculously long name, but also for its concentration on show choirs. It was the first competition created specifically for these groups. Staging, choreography, costumes, and production were not only welcomed, they were strongly encouraged for participation.

The format created by Bishop Luers was later copied by dozens of other competitions. It became the blueprint, the gold standard, for future competitions. Bishop Luers' winners set the bar for swing choirs, and because of that, they improved their performances each year. Staging went quickly from simple step-touch routines to all-out choreographed production numbers.

One of the premiere participants of Luers and swing choir bar-setters, Marion High School's 26th Street Singers, arrived in Fort Wayne, Indiana, in 1975 ready to take swing choirs to a new level. And that's exactly what they did.

Under the direction of F. Ritchie Walton, Marion's set format looked markedly different from those of its competitors. Most groups at the time would stand in standard choral formation on three-tier, foldout choral risers for most of the performance and then move during either the song interludes or transitions between songs. The 26th Street Singers, however, took the movement component a step further, creating a hybrid of a swing choir performance and a Las Vegas revue. Marion visibly paid more attention to choreography and production. As a result, the Bishop Luers inaugural grand champion trophy went home with the

The Bishop Luers High School Swing Choir contest trophies.

First Bishop Luers grand champions—the 26th Street Singers (1975).

The Scott Foods cornucopia sign is a landmark located across the street from Bishop Luers High School and one of the first things that choirs see when they arrive at Luers. Participants have described seeing the sign as an adrenaline rush—"We've arrived!"

DRESSED TO IMPRESS

Large faux gold medallions, embossed with the logo and imprinted "Champion," were attached to ribbons for the winning group. "Swing Choir" was changed to "Show Choir."

Father Fred insisted the Grand Champion trophy be "taller than the one given to the state basketball champions."

Marion 26th Street Singers that year—and the following two years.

Word quickly spread about this "new thing" going on at Luers . . . a swinging show competition. What started off as a little swing choir contest more than doubled in size in just one year.

By 1979, Bishop Luers had made a name for itself. Twenty different show choirs came from various cities, towns, and provinces in the Midwest to sing, dance, and compete, bringing a total of six hundred students and fifteen hundred family and friends. While there were different show sets and themes, everyone arriving wanted to succeed.

To be successful at Luers, groups had to demonstrate skill in five areas: singing, playing (instrumental accompaniment students enrolled in the school), movement, showmanship, and general effect (transitions, pacing, and show design).

Studio-size cameras captured the action.

Carmel High School's Ambassadors performing "Hey There Good Times." Shown from left: Chris Robbins, Cheryl Cord, Andy Spangler, and Gretchen Wachholz (1979).

Larry Bower has been the emcee for Luers since 1976—making him the longest consecutive emcee at any show choir contest in the world!

Carmel Ambassadors winning their first of six Luers Grand Championships. Girl with back to camera: Leslie Reiman; boy facing camera: Bob Sole (1979).

Groups that were named Grand Champion of Luers not only received a six-foot-tall trophy and individual medallions, they were practically crowned Gods of Swing Choir for a year.

"To win at Bishop Luers is to win anywhere," said Ron Hellems, director of the Carmel Ambassadors.

As a testament to its popularity and Kress' marketing skills, in 1976, the contest piqued the interest of a PBS-affiliate in Bowling Green, Ohio. That year, the Bishop Luers Swing Choir Invitational was televised throughout the Midwest, and became nationally syndicated by 1983.

The power of broadcast helped capture the imaginations of choral directors, students, parents, and administrations, novice and seasoned, throughout the United States. It was new. It was (kind of) flashy. And it was coming to families live, in their own home.

Despite the shock and incessant reactions from traditional choral crowds, the sassy students and rebellious directors kept easing down the road. One step-touch at a time.

In retrospect, no one expected this large a tiger at the end of the tail. Seemingly overnight, swing choirs took stiff, robe-wearing choruses into a completely new genre and onto a transformed stage. This arena incorporated choreography, live instrumentalists, and Broadway-worthy production effects into traditional and pop choral singing. No one expected the performances. And certainly no one expected the impassioned cheering sections.

COMPETING IN CALI

Soon after Bishop Luers took the nation by a storm of singing teenagers, a pocket of swing groups in Southern California decided they wanted in on the fun. In the then-late '70s, groups from John Burroughs, West Alamitos, Burbank, and Brea Olinda high schools started organizing regional competitions. Aztec Sing led the way in 1976, soon followed by the Show (1979) at Fullerton College, and the Festival at Colton High School and was Tops in Pop in San Diego at West Covina High School.

AZTEC SING COMPETITION

In 1976, Azusa High School's Aztec Singers, under the direction of John Wilson, began a swing choir contest, called Aztec Sing. The contest would help define

California show choir for nearly a decade, developing many California show choir protocols.

While there were some aspects of the California competitions and choirs that mirrored their Midwestern counterparts, there were differences—especially when it came to competition rules.

Competition rules were originally set to keep the judging fair, but some would argue that, at least for show choirs, many of the rules were put into place to slow down the competition. Either way, because competition at that time was hyper-regionalized, it was the competition rules that separated the West Coast from the Midwest.

The rules were developed throughout the years as experience—and defeats—increased. Early on, large set pieces became forbidden from one choir's competition, after that group had been overpowered by another's elaborate set. Choirs started enforcing time limits on shows after losing to others that had lengthier or shorter sets. When a group won using the chorus as a backup to a particularly talented soloist, rules appeared declaring soloists could not improve the adjudication scores—but could result in a loss of points if they upstaged the choir in any way. And when one group started winning all the competitions by consistently performing an a cappella song, rules were instated to require all competing show choirs to include an a cappella song within their set.

Rules aside, Californians swayed to a different tune when it came to competition, format, and timing. For instance, the typical Midwestern show choir competition would span an entire Saturday, sometimes even dipping into Friday night if there was a middle school division. If lucky, snow or negative windchills wouldn't cause last-minute cancellations or charter buses stuck in snow mounds. But on the West Coast, when it came to show choir contests, their events were, and still are, quick and to the point. They started after school on Friday and ended that night with no finals round. And weather, of course, never seemed to be a factor.

While it might have been a whirlwind of activity for one night, Californians figured out a system that worked for them. In terms of scheduling, the sound checks took place over the dinner hour, and by six or seven p.m., eight to ten schools had started attending one-round judging sessions. At the end of the night, a ranking was announced, a winner was awarded, and

Bishop Luers judges are positioned up high and far back, a vantage point similarly used for judging marching band and drum and bugle corps field shows.

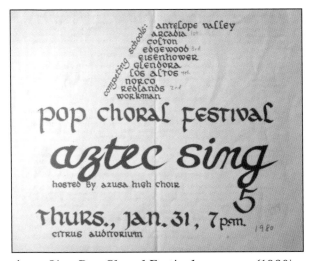

Bishop Luers High School's Minstrels acknowledge their backup band in the 37th Annual Show Choir Invitational. Director Karlene Krouse in the foreground. (March 7, 2011).

Aztec Sing Pop Choral Festival program (1980).

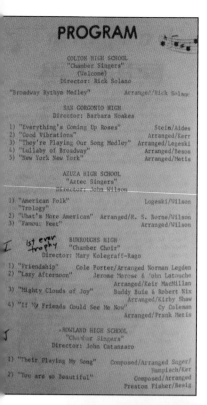

PROGRAM

COLTON HIGH SCHOOL
"Chamber Singers"
(Welcome)
Director: Rick Solano

"Broadway Rythym Medley"   Arranged/Rick Solano

SAN GORGONIO HIGH
Director: Barbara Noakes

1) "Everything's Coming Up Roses"   Stein/Aides
2) "Good Vibrations"   Arranged/Kerr
3) "They're Playing Our Song Medley" Arranged/Legeski
4) "Lullaby of Broadway"   Arranged/Beson
5) "New York New York"   Arranged/Metis

AZUZA HIGH SCHOOL
"Aztec Singers"
Director: John Wilson

1) "American Folk"   Logeski/Wilson
   "Trology"
2) "What's More American" Arranged/R. S. Borne/Wilson
3) "Famous Feet"   Arranged/Wilson

BURROUGHS HIGH
"Chamber Choir"
Director: Mary Kolegraff-Rago

1) "Friendship"   Cole Porter/Arranged Norman Legden
2) "Lazy Afternoon"   Jerome Morose & John Latouche
                                    Arranged/Keir MacMillan
3) "Mighty Clouds of Joy"   Buddy Buie & Robert Nix
                                    Arranged/Kirby Shaw
4) "If My Friends Could See Me Now"   Cy Coleman
                                    Arranged/Frank Metis

ROWLAND HIGH SCHOOL
"Chamber Singers"
Director: John Catanzaro

1) "Their Playing My Song"   Composed/Arranged Sager/
                                    Hampisch/Ker
2) "You are so Beautiful"   Composed/Arranged
                                    Preston Fisher/Besig

Colton Festival program (1982).

Colton Festival show choirs—John Burroughs Chamber Choir, under the direction of Mary Kolegraff-Rago, wins its first trophy (4th place).

Citrus College Performing Arts Center would host Aztec Sing for 34 years. 2010 marked the 35th and final festival.

The California "step-box," popular before risers came onto the stage, was a staging device borrowed from the San Diego Junior Theatre.

choirs parted ways.

The stage setup also had a different look and feel. Before 1995, platforms or risers were not used on California show choir stages. Instead, choreographers would stage half of the group standing (and dancing) on 14 by 14-inch step boxes. To do a picture change, or transition, the singers would hop off their step box, pick it up, move it to a new location and get back on. John Wilson, former director at Chula Vista High School commented, "Kneeling and standing on those boxes . . . we looked like a bunch of seals."

It was between 1986 and 1995 that California groups began deflecting to the world of risers. National competitions underlined the point. Showstoppers, the premier national contest in the '80s and '90s, supplied a three-level riser setup at its events. The contest's rules didn't allow the risers to be moved from the stage. Consequently, California groups that rolled in with step boxes found their boxes to be more cumbersome than cool.

West Coast choreographer Jen Oundjian recalls seeing choirs use risers for the first time in 1994 at the Showstoppers Invitational at Disneyland: "All of these groups from the Midwest were using platforms . . . it was so obvious ... of course the [song] transitions look better when you don't have to carry boxes around. I was saying to myself, 'I want those.'"

Dave Willert commented, "One fallout from the coming of risers [to California] was contest judges [didn't] know how to compare 'riser shows' to 'flat-stage shows.' The risers changed the whole look of the show. It was like comparing apples to oranges. Good singing was good singing, but risers brought a third dimension that made the choreography more dynamic."

By 2000, changes influenced by groups outside of Southern California, such as the implementation of the risers, were becoming more common. The Midwest revolution specifically began to escalate at an uncontrollable speed. Midwest judges started traveling to the West Coast to adjudicate California competitions. They were bringing with them their experience and knowledge of the Midwest's competitive show choir circuits. Many failed, however, to have background on the California state of mind and music.

California choirs couldn't be critiqued under the same spotlight as Ohio, Indiana, Illinois, Iowa, or Wisconsin. They approached show styles in distinctly different ways. The children of the sun did not mirror the children of the corn. California had rules unfamiliar to Midwestern judges. They were, in a way, repeating the mistakes of the Northwest Swing Competition, trying to mix jazz and swing in the same test tube experiment.

Like the British invasion of the Americas, the show choir world on the West Coast was forced to Midwest-ernize themselves to keep up with and compete with the big choirs dominating the country. Many California choirs obliged, taking on then-popular onstage directors, larger backup bands, blowout production–style choreography, and elaborate sets.

The rules also merged with the Midwest. As Willert recalls, "These new regulations benefited [Southern California] groups directly by allowing them to fully-embrace the Midwest style of competitions."

THE SPOTLIGHT BRIGHTENS

As years went on, it became clear there was not one straightforward definition for show choir competition. They were held at high schools auditoriums, college campuses, and community centers throughout the year. They could involve as few as three groups or as many as twenty choirs. They lasted an afternoon or encompassed an entire weekend. Some limited participation based on region, whereas others required qualification to enter and compete nationally.

Competitions, like most valued events, began developing reputations among attendees or wannabe attendees. Technically, any school, organization, or city could organize a multichoir dual fest if they had the funds to support it and followed the proper rules. That wouldn't guarantee success. If you scheduled it, groups didn't always come. There were A-, B-, and C-list competitions molding themselves throughout the country.

Success often relied on the organizers, the chosen participants, and the locations—which were always quite different. The one thing that remained the same, though, was their shared desire to achieve A-status, to parade around with a six-foot trophy and to be the best.

Even if it was a carbon copy of perfection. It shone just as bright.

California competitions could be packed into a night because the actual shows followed a different, faster format. Performances averaged three songs, or about twelve minutes, compared to the eighteen- to twenty-minute sets hitting stages throughout the Midwest. SoCal groups also didn't have large bands, risers, or lavish backdrops to set up. They could be in and out and satisfied in just fifteen minutes.

Regulate: Midwest-influenced Changes to Southern California Rules, an excerpt from Dave Willert's "Unwritten Rules of Competitive Show Choir":

Increased maximum performance time allowance from fifteen minutes to seventeen minutes
Removed prep-time allocated towards construction of their, now large, sets
Allowed directors to conduct from the stage instead of the front seat of the audience
Forbid female choir participants from taking part in more than one competing choir (rule did not apply to male participants)
Limited group size to sixty members
Removed cap from number of accompanying band members allowed
Separated the Advanced Division into AAA and AA

The Young Americans, "America's oldest show choir," used risers only during the first, mostly choral, half of their show. The second half was performed riser free and the entire playing area was fair game for movement.

Joel Grey and cast performing "Willkommen" in the film version of Cabaret—a bawdy take on '30s Berlin variety entertainment (1972).

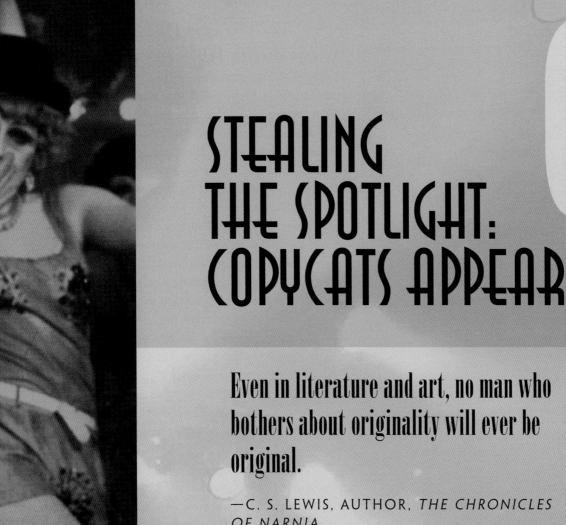

STEALING THE SPOTLIGHT: COPYCATS APPEAR

6

Even in literature and art, no man who bothers about originality will ever be original.

—C. S. LEWIS, AUTHOR, *THE CHRONICLES OF NARNIA*.

Whether in show business or finance, government or marketing, there is one underexposed fact that applies across the board: Originality is nonexistent. What appears as fresh, new thinking is simply variations of old ideas placed inside a hypothetical blender and dished out for taste.

Call it copying or mirroring, admiring or inspiring, but consider it history.

When it comes to creativity, many follow an interesting mathematical approach widely known throughout the entertainment and fashion industries. When it comes to period-focused inspirations, they rely on a twenty-year cycle to keep them ahead of the trends. For instance, the 1970s saw fascination with the '50s, especially on television (e.g., *Happy Days*) and in film (e.g., *Grease*). In the '90s, the '70s tie-dye and hippie-chic came back into the picture. And now, since the end of 2010, there's been a reemerging love for the boy band–style performance groups of the '90s.

Trends fall back on the known and the tried and true. To be the best, one learns from the best.

> Thomas Edison once said, "To have good ideas, have lots of them"—a phrase he, ironically, heard from someone else.

Liza Minnelli performing "Mein Herr" in Liza with a "Z," *her television concert directed by Bob Fosse (1972).*

Fritz Mountford, professor of Music and Director of Choral Activities at Hastings College, gives solid advice to directors in his book, *The Art of Entertainment: A Producer's Sourcebook for Choral Performance:*

As you develop your "producer's eye," you'll begin to find all sorts of ideas that, when approached from a slightly different angle, would work for your project . . . My only defense is that the genesis of each of the ideas I've "collected" was an idea originally swiped from some other thief.

Valerie Lippoldt-Mack, music educator at Butler Community College, choreographer and author of *Ice Breakers: 60 Fun Activities to Build a Better Choir*, commented on stealing inspiration:

Perhaps early on, when I first started out . . . I borrowed choreography that I had seen, but after years of studying many different styles of choreography I came to a realization that you don't have to copy or steal from anyone else . . . If you have a large repertoire of steps and styles, your choreography comes from the song. You have different shows each year and different kids every year and you have to be authentic to the group of kids in that show. It keeps you original.

SHOW CHOIR THIEVES

Show choir was no exception to these copycat rules. After the introduction of Bishop Luers High School's Swing Choir Contest and Aztec Sing, competitions started appearing throughout the country. Suddenly, choirs had more opportunities than ever to meet other show choir geeks, trade ideas, and uncover new choreography and set ideas.

Because the genre was such a new concept, leading groups relied heavily on one another to take turns being the guinea pigs of trial and error. The competition scene skipped over the learn-from-your-own-mistakes process, instead building a culture of borrowing, making it possible for even those creatively challenged high schools to join in on the fun.

Because there were established leaders in the genre, creating a show choir was no longer as daunting a task. Groups could mirror winning show designs, duplicate their favorite arrangements, and analyze top competition scores to create a fifteen-minute show that, to an oblivious audience member, was a completely new concept.

Some groups copied to build entertaining programming or to establish themselves. Others borrowed to steal trophies. But there was no denying, whether big group, small group, new or old, they were all doing it.

The most strategic groups used this sudden increase in competitions to their benefit. They may have found inspiration in other groups' sets or songs, but ultimately, they wanted to figure out what it took to win.

The John Burroughs High School show choir, from Burbank, California, was one of the many groups that became Midwesternized and began taking on a chameleon-like approach in competitions.

"When an adjudicator wanted more choreography or singing, we would look at the competition," commented Brendan Jennings, director of John Burroughs High School show choirs. "We would borrow what was good (or what the judges were rewarding) and work that into what was already unique or special about our show."

Jennings added, "In the contest world, we've become smarter about who we're going up against and who is judging. It absolutely makes a difference in how we prepare for a contest."

A MASTERMIND BEHIND THE MAGIC

Behind the lights of this newly formed show, a few notable front-runners helped define the latest presentational and performance styles. They became the cat that everyone wanted to copy, the ones that perfected the art of drawing inspiration from other groups, performers, and the arts. By setting strong examples in staging, choreography and musical arrangements, they helped groups help themselves and define an undefined musical performance genre.

F. RITCHIE WALTON AND THE MARION 26TH STREET SINGERS

In a classroom filled with show choir entrepreneurs, F. Ritchie Walton would be sitting front row. In 1966, Walton established one of the earliest swing choirs in America at Marion High School in Indiana. Given swing choirs were a new concept, in the choir's formative years Walton continuously drew inspiration from other arts and artists and captured key teachings from similar pioneering choirs to develop a trendsetting team of performers.

Jimmy Walton, unrelated to Ritchie and a senior at Marion in the late 1960s, came into the picture and played a significant role in injecting a much-needed dose of energy and upbeat entertainment into the young choir. As an aspiring (and future) Broadway star, Jimmy, like Ritchie, had a passion for performing and actively encouraged and assisted Walton in setting a modern foundation for the swing group—inspired by pop culture.

In an effort to build his knowledge base and strengthen his choir, every summer F. Ritchie Walton spent time in New York City attending shows, buying recordings, checking out musical scores, and soaking up the spirit of Broadway. He then took his experiences back to Indiana and arranged fresh musical and pop music–inspired scores for the choir to perform.

"F. Ritchie took a lot of his cues from Fred Waring. He was a taskmaster and disciplinarian . . . no talking, no tardiness," recalled Jimmy Walton. "He was feared. He required the singers to have a clean-cut image. The boys had to have their hair trimmed about the top of their ears."

Between 1971 and 1972 the swing choir named themselves the 26th Street Singers. The choir went on to win the first two Bishop Luers High School swing choir contests. They became idols of the swing choir world.

"Rhythm of Life" became a big swing choir hit in 1968 and continued on in its popularity throughout the '70s. For years, the publisher offered choreography techniques for an additional dollar when groups ordered the sheet music.

AMERICAN INSPIRED

In addition to directing the Marion High School swing group, Walton directed two musicals a year. His favorite was *George M!* because, like Cohan, he gravitated toward anything red, white, and blue and patriotic.

Milton C. Anderson, director of the Young Americans, recalls arriving at a Midwest high school concert venue in the late '70s only to find the host choir wearing the same costumes as his choir. It was then that he thought, "There is a movement [occurring]."

"I have also been inspired by seeing other directors and their groups. Show choir, like pop culture, is an ever-changing animal. It has been very exciting to try new twists on songs and make some unique show routines." —Jeff Clark, director of Fairfield High School's Choraliers, Fairfield, Ohio

Jimmy Walton moved from 26th Street to Broadway's production of *42nd Street*; featured in *We're in the Money* (1983), he used the tap skills developed during his days at Marion.

Soon after *Applause* opened on Broadway, Walton bought a ticket for the front row so that he could better hear the instrumentation and be closer to the action.

At Bishop Luers, the setup was timed (groups had to bring their own platforms), so every moment counted. The Ambassadors often made setup part of the show. Here, the band played the "All That Jazz Overture" on front of the stage; traveling to DSC and finally to USC, while the stage crew positioned platforms in front of them. The effect was theatrical, intriguing, and set the pace for what was to come.

The choir was choreographed into place, as well. Here, a soloist (center), sings "All That Jazz" while surrounded by a sea of red gloves.

Stage crews were often integrated into the show. Here, the crew brings on white wooden boards loaded with red his-and-hers tap shoes. Closing their show with "Fabulous Feet", the Ambassadors perform a (hands-only) tap routine.

On a musical cue, the crew lifts the boards up high and the group performs their tap routine overhead—giving the audience a Busby Berkeley–like camera angle. Simple and effective, this was show choir history in the making.

"In 1975, before I got there, the Ambassadors were not sophisticated at all. I wanted them to have the best choral program in the state. The administration and parents—everybody—joined in the cause. Since 1977, Carmel has won more than 100 state athletic championships."
—Ron Hellems, former director, Carmel Ambassadors

RON HELLEMS, ANN CONRAD, AND THE CARMEL AMBASSADORS

Another leader of the jazz hands brigade was Ron Hellems. As a young, first year teacher and director, he led the Norwell High School swing choir to the inaugural Bishop Luers competition. As director of one of the seven inaugural groups, it was easy to take notice of this rising star. Within a year he accepted a position with a neighboring school and began directing its swing choir, the Carmel High School Ambassadors. Under the direction of Hellems and Ann Conrad, the group's codirector and talented accompanist, the Ambassadors became known less for borrowing and more for providing ideas; for being leaders and pacesetters.

Their show, choreographed by Hellems, with assistance from Carla Bush (1975–80), Dwight Edwards (1981–85), and Mary Corsaro (1983–85), mixed the traditions of both a New York City cabaret and revue show. It was calculated. It was systematically designed. And it was executed in a fashion that created an impression of wealth, class, and privilege.

The Ambassadors changed the way show choirs traveled to and from competitions. From the earliest competitions, the group had set rules and standards: They always arrived on charter buses and were required to dress in travel attire: women in skirts and men in jackets and ties. From the minute they stepped off the bus, they looked like winners. Their air of importance was intriguing, and before long, most show choirs were taking charter buses to competitions.

Intentional or not, Hellems, Conrad, and the Ambassadors created a model for strategic show choir branding. Every element, every action—onstage or off—was selected to underline and emblemize the name "Ambassadors" and define the group's persona. They were savvy, well traveled, metropolitan and wealthy—or at least that's what everyone thought. And it helped that they had power vocals.

Carmel came into its own, influencing a vast number of groups between 1978 and 1985. During those years, the Ambassadors won six Grand Championships and were the featured favorites during the televised Luers years.

JIM AND VERDA SAVAGE AND EDGEWOOD'S MUSIC WAREHOUSE

Jim and Verda Savage discovered new ground in Ellettsville, Indiana when developing Edgewood High School's Music Warehouse. Throughout the years, from their success at Luers Competitions and beyond, the show choir earned a reputation as "the cool group." They performed with a nonchalant, confident attitude unlike that of the 26th Street Singers or the Ambassadors. Their choreography was chic, rhythmic, and smooth.

While entertaining, Music Warehouse never seemed to work too hard or sweat too much. They made performing look easy, and they were good. It wasn't long before they attracted wannabe clones.

"Whenever we went to contests, I would constantly have directors tell me they used our choreography [from] old Bishop Luers tapes," said Verda.

Jim Savage's choreography was unique compared with the other show choirs', making the group even more appealing to copycats. He created movements based on simple rocking, weight shifting, and the occasional jazz square. He staged movements that created a constant "bounce" or "pulse" that were then accentuated with hand gestures or dynamic "starburst" effects.

Edgewood's Music Warehouse helped define another early style of show choirs and create another mold that others could follow.

DWIGHT JORDAN

Now a well-known choreographer, Dwight Jordan quickly became a central figure and commonly known name in show choir, leading the genre to a stronger place within the performance industry. Although many mirror his talents now, he, too, took part in creative stealing and borrowing when he first started out.

Jordan joined the show choir world as a choreographer for the Mt. Zion High School Swingsations, after accepting a challenge from the group's director, Roberta Vest, to improve their show. He recalled:

I started choreographing the group my second year of teaching 1977–78. Roberta had just come back from a year off and was starting the mixed group [the Swingsations] my first year of teaching. They met during my free period, and I would often hang out and watch . . . I went with them as a chaperone to their first competition at Western Illinois Uni-

The Ambassadors' elaborate arrangements were orchestrated by Dick Laughlin, a music director, arranger, and pianist for Indiana's Starlight Musicals (a series of summer musical theater productions that operated in Indianapolis, 1940 to 1997).

Fun Fact: Ronald Hellems and Verda Savage sang in the Indiana State University Madrigals together.

Eric Van Cleave, former director of Lafayette Jefferson's First Edition, was a student at Noblesville High School in 1979 when his group competed at Bishop Luers. He recalled:

I will never forget . . . we were on our way to Luers that morning and here comes Carmel, passing us in a chartered coach bus. My group was up against the windows trying to get a glimpse—and the Carmel kids didn't even look up.

Traveling with his own group years later, he settled for nothing less than a charter.

Style Steals: The popular one-shoulder sequined dress (designed by Halston) was introduced by Edgewood's Music Warehouse. Edgewood men were known for wearing black three-piece suits with a classic pocket square.

Cast performing "Dancin' Man" from Fosse's Dancin', a show inspired by Michael Bennett's A Chorus Line (Broadhurst Theatre, New York City).

"I was just an instrumental major who thought [musicals] would be fun and was trying to absorb everything as fast as I could. I will always remember, about a week before we opened, the choreographer stopped the rehearsal, pointed at me, and said to the other dancers, 'Why can't you perform like him?' I thought to myself, 'Hmm, I guess I can do this.'" —Dwight Jordan

Job Stealing—a word from the author, Mike: "The first time I met Dwight was after a performance of Millikin University's show choir, Singing Blue. The show was exciting, the staging was fresh and the singing was impressive. I thought, 'This is something I want to be a part of.' After asking to speak to someone in charge, I was directed to Dwight and boldly introduced myself, saying, "That was a great show. I'd like to choreograph them.' Slightly taken aback, Dwight replied, 'That's my job.' Oops!"

versity. Now that I had some reference, the next year I started making suggestions during rehearsal, and Roberta finally challenged me to choreograph a song. I gave it a shot. You could say I just trusted my instincts, used my musical background and did what came naturally. It went well, and I've choreographed ever since.

As a choreographer, he took dance classes for technical knowledge, observed other groups, and studied film musicals and variety television shows to hone his craft. Jordan was influenced by other show choir, including choreographers Robert Hills (Western Illinois University) and Tom Terrien (Kids from Wisconsin).

Like most professional choreographers, he was a

fast study and learned to adapt his dance knowledge to fit whatever genre or style a performance warranted. Although Jordan's early work included plenty of novelty songs, such as "A Handful of Keys," "Up the Lazy River," and "Splish Splash," it wasn't long before he was a notable trendsetting choreographer in the Midwest.

Throughout his early career, Jordan continued to draw inspiration from such groups as Ron Hellems's Ambassadors or Jim and Verda Savage's Music Warehouse. After watching both groups perform on multilevel platforms, he replaced Mt. Zion's bare floor with a block riser setup. Like the staging style of Music Warehouse, he incorporated more sophisticated, stationary, and pulsing movements within the choreography to keep the show moving but also to ensure the vocals would remain intact.

Following the trends, Jordan may have been inspired by elements from the Ambassadors' popular white-glove number, "Dancin' Man" (borrowed from Bob Fosse), for the well-received Swingsations' 1984 performance of "Salvation Train."

Jordan went on to define many of the primary techniques for staging show choir, encouraging choreographers to set movements with a purpose—not just for the sake of moving. When vocals and lyrics were important, he would add minimal movements to ensure that energy exertion didn't adversely affect the sound. Like other leaders in the genre, Jordan's choreography enhanced the music and put lyrics and vocals first.

THE WEST COAST WAY

In true West Coast fashion, show choirs that appeared in the late '80s and early '90s inspired others throughout the country with their unique styles and distinctive approaches to staging. Just as power ballads gained popularity in the '80s, these power groups had a greater influence than even they knew.

THE BONITA VISTA MUSIC MACHINE

Ron and Reina Bolles, director and choreographer for the Bonita Vista Music Machine in Bonita Vista, California, were the leadership forces behind the group's signature dance-style shows of the '90s. The pair became known for staying true to the style and genre of both the music and choreography within the set. Additionally, audiences and judges came to expect the group's use of humor to entertain; their impressive

Musicals introduced in the 1970s that provided new Broadway material for show choirs included: *Jesus Christ Super Star* (1970), *Company* (1970), *Godspell* (1971), *Pippin* (1972), *Grease* (1972), *Cabaret* (1972), *A Chorus Line* (1975), *The Wiz* (1975), *Annie* (1977), *Ain't Misbehavin'* (1978) *Dancin'* (1978), and *They're Playing Our Song* (1979).

"Everybody was learning from everybody. We were learning from each other." —Verda Slinkard, director, Edgewood's Music Warehouse

A Chorus Line was the first Broadway musical to require triple-threat performers; actors with strong dancing and singing skills.

A SUMMER OF SINGING

In an effort to extend that integrated learning process beyond just competition season, in 1979 Jordan and Susan Moninger cofounded Show Choir Camps of America, the country's leading summer program for choral staging and show choir training.

Basically summer band camp for show choir nerds, the workshop allowed participants to make new friends and talk show choir shop while learning steps and vocal techniques from seasoned choreographers and vocal directors. By the end of the week, participants were inspired, exhausted, and ready to return and share the new insights with their hometown groups.

Since the introduction of *Glee* in 2009, John Burroughs Powerhouse has, in many ways, served as the Hollywood poster child for "real" show choirs. The group has performed on *Oprah* and *Dancing with the Stars*, at a *Glee* cast party, in the British documentary *Gleeful*, and in the Chinese New Year Night Parade in Hong Kong.

blocking, or "stage pictures"; and their overall high-energy performances.

John Wilson, founder of Aztec Sing, once said, "No one changed the face of show choir choreography on the West Coast as much as Reina. She pushed the boundaries of what could be done, staging-wise, with a [group] of singers."

NOGALES HIGH SCHOOL CHAMBER SINGERS

The dynamic director/choreographer pair of Dave Willert and Doug Kuhl came together to lead Nogales High School Chamber Singers in La Puente, California, carving out a unique, Broadway-style show for their performers.

"The energy Dave and Doug brought out of the Nogales kids, and other groups since, was always amazing to us," said Ron Bolles, director of the Bonita Vista Music Machine. "When I think of Dave and Doug's choir, I think of musical finesse, fun and total commitment—leaving everything on the stage."

JOHN BURROUGHS POWERHOUSE

Under the direction of Brendan Jennings, with choreography from Jen Oundjian, John Burroughs Powerhouse, from Burbank, California, created a mash-up style that complemented both the Midwestern-style show and its West Coast traditions.

Founded in 1982 by Mary Rago and choreographed by Debbe Crette and, later, Michelle Jenson, the group was originally called the Chamber Choir. It became Powerhouse in 1997 and developed a show style that can be described as off-beat, innovative, and sometimes dark. Although the group's shows took on a distinctive theatrical approach with a pop-rock soundtrack, its Midwestern influences were evident, utilizing a large instrumental combo and four-tier stage risers.

COSTUME COPIERS

Like other elements of a show choir show, costumes have been subject to copycats throughout the years. Groups have drawn inspiration from other choirs at competitions and festivals. Recorded shows have been passed around to compare and critique. Trends have come and gone.

When the Midwest and the West Coast started playing together in the competition sandbox, copycat trends became as apparent as ever. In 1985, Mt. Zion's Swingsations traveled from their high school in Illinois to California's Young Americans' competition. The women appeared at the competition in full-length, one-shoulder sequined dresses. The Golden State had never seen so much glitter and glam before in their jazz hand–loving lives. The next year, groups, both from the Midwest and West Coast, hit the stage, reflecting sparkle and a little bit of Mt. Zion in their shows.

THE MTV GENERATION

As groups were trading secrets, moves, and best practices like collectible cards, they couldn't help but turn their heads toward the new television programming hitting cable stations. The introduction of Music Television, or MTV, in the '80s suddenly allowed Americans to have more access to music and dance than ever before. Lip-synching artists, their dancers, and film crews began presenting music and dance in different, cutting-edge ways.

From New York to California, suddenly every high school and college choir, whether rural or urban, had access to the latest trends in choreography, fashion, and performance styles. All had their eyes glued to the screen, furiously taking notes and stealing moves whenever and wherever they could.

REACHING TO BE STARS

While some could argue that only a handful of the performers who hit the MTV waves were influential to the early show choir industry, there were a few, in particular, who made show choir nerds almost inappropriately excited. They set new standards for production and commercial choreography. They taunted and inspired the copycats.

THE KING OF POP

To graze the discussion of choreography and pop music requires a mention, if not a tribute to, Michael Jackson. Rising to popularity with the MTV generation, Jackson, and his choreographers Michael Peterson and Vincent Paterson, set countless trends in choreography, film, and production innovation.

Jackson's hit singles, "Beat It" (1982). "Billie Jean" (1983), and "Thriller" (1983), were all credited for taking the medium of music videos, and choreography to the next level. And beyond bringing his unique

"It costs a lot of money to look this cheap," said Dolly Parton, legendary country singer who fully embraces gaudy, flashy, and glitter-fied fashion.

At the Young Americans competition, Dwight Jordan recalls one of the competing groups doing his choreography:

This group did two songs that Mt. Zion had performed the year before, and here was Mt. Zion competing against them! At the time it was pretty strange to see my choreography and arrangements performed by a group that I had never met. It was really the start of groups traveling across country to compete, so the rules of using other people's material had not really been established. I introduced myself to the director as their choreographer. The director was not really fazed by it, but introduced me to the group and was very complimentary. They actually invited be to work with them the next year, which I did.

The Jackson Five (Tito, Marlon, Jackie, Michael, and Jermaine) on the syndicated music/dance variety show Soul Train (1972).

Michael Jackson's *Thriller* transformed the medium of music videos into an art form and promotional tool. When the fourteen-minute-long video aired, MTV ran it twice an hour to meet demand.

In 2009, the year Michael Jackson died, publishers were quick to meet the sudden demand from countless chorus directors and show choirs wanting to pay tribute to the King of Pop. The 2010 contest season saw numerous salutes, with songs such as "Thriller," "Beat It," "Black and White," "Man in the Mirror," "Got Me Working Day and Night," and "Don't Stop Till You Get Enough."

Michael Jackson performing "Smooth Criminal" from Moon-walker (1988).

talents to the table, the success of Jackson and his videos also helped MTV secure and maintain the cable station's early fame.

FAMILY FAME

Jackson's sister, Janet, also helped spark show choir imaginations, with her choreographers Anthony Thomas, Terry Bixler, and Paula Abdul. Her *Rhythm Nation* music video (1989), praised for its probing lyrics and video and production innovation, made her a recognized and respected dancer and performer in the industry. Janet Jackson and her crew's innovative, one-of-a-kind, funk-and-groove choreography was unlike anything seen in the history of pop music.

Choreographers and dancers took notice. By the early '90s, every show choir and every hip-hop dancer wanted to cut and paste parts and pieces of the *Rhythm Nation* production into their set. And some groups were even able to pull it off.

LIKE A VIRGIN

As Madonna rocked out the '80s and '90s with her smash-hit album *Like a Virgin*, show choir groups wanted to rock out right next to her. Although the controversial album received mixed reviews from critics, Madonna made music history. Selling more than 21 million copies worldwide, it is one of the best-selling albums of all time and raised Madonna to icon status.

MUSIC VIDEOS HIT THE BIG SCREEN

The quick-cut editing style used in music videos on MTV and its sister station, VH1, also started to appear in a handful of movies at this time including *Flashdance* (1983), *Staying Alive* (1983), and *Dirty Dancing* (1987). By incorporating the editing techniques and look of music videos, all three became successful and timeless films.

Not long after these movies aired, show choir groups began adding jazzlike *Flashdance* routines, hip-gyrating moves inspired by *Staying Alive* and *Dirty Dancing*–style lifts.

TAPPING INTO TELEVISION

In addition to music videos, concerts, and movies, show choir directors and choreographers found themselves glued to the television, watching several programs and stations beyond MTV for inspiration for their competition sets.

The Rhythm Nation album went on to sell more than 14 million copies worldwide, and the Janet Jackson *Rhythm Nation* World Tour is known today as one of the top, if not the most, successful debut concert tours executed.

Karen Lynn Gorney and John Travolta in **Saturday Night Fever** *(1977).*

Madonna **Like a Virgin** *album cover (1984).*

Patrick Swayze and Jennifer Grey in **Dirty Dancing** *(1987).*

Bonita Vista High School's Music Machine North Sea Jazz Festival, held at The Hague in the Netherlands (1983).

The Solid Gold Dancers on Solid Gold *(1980–1988).*

Throughout the years, many choreographers were involved in molding the moves of the Solid Gold Dancers. One of those, Lester Wilson, a Juilliard graduate, had previously staged and choreographed musical numbers for *Saturday Night Fever*, which during the '70s launched disco dancing into mainstream pop culture.

SOLID GOLD

Saturday nights, viewers often tuned into *Solid Gold*, a syndicated television series featuring a countdown of the Top 40 pop music hits. During its eight-year run, from 1980 to 1988, the show received mixed reviews, its main attraction being the Solid Gold Dancers— a troupe that performed intricate and slightly risqué dances.

The New York Times once described the series as "the pop music show that is its own parody . . . [enacting] mini-dramas . . . of covetousness, lust and aerobic toning—routines that typically have a minimal connection with the songs that back them up."

DONNIE & MARIE

Teenagers throughout the country tuned into the weekly variety show, *Donnie & Marie*, to check out the entertaining performances and the show's heartthrob

The Donny &
Marie Show
(1976–1979).

Cast performing Bob Fosse's "Take Off with Us" from All That Jazz *(1979), using gloves as an expressive prop and focal point of the dance (1979).*

Doh! Whereas Abdul's moves may have inspired new show choir struts, *The Tracey Ullman Show* is most known as the show that led to America's longest-running comedy—*The Simpsons*. Before Bart and Lisa were household names, *The Simpsons* appeared as animation shorts on about fifty episodes of Ullman's series in its first three seasons.

host, Donnie. The ABC show aired from 1976 to 1979 and involved a weekly ice-skating intro performance, musical duets, production numbers, sketch comedy, and celebrity guest appearances.

THE TRACEY ULLMAN SHOW

There was also *The Tracey Ullman Show*, which aired from 1987 to 1989. The series featured weekly performance numbers choreographed by Paula Abdul, the future pop star and American Idol judge. The show helped to advance Abdul's already promising career and built her a credible reputation for incorporating innovative movements within the dances.

AN AWKWARD TRANSITION

While trial and error was shaping the show choir world, errors were becoming apparent and downright awkward at times. As swing choir emerged as an actual genre, few choral directors knew anything about staging, choreography, or directing an instrumental ensemble. One could only learn so much from MTV.

Because this combined skill set was new to music education, there were no established experts to lend advice or teach the skills. Sure, Broadway had plenty of musical theater professionals schooled in crafting vocal production with choreography, but westward, far from Times Square, universities trained vocal music educators only in classical voice and choral conducting, leaving few graduates prepared for the vocal, dance, and sound technology challenges that pop and show production required.

With so many new elements to manage, the quality of the individual practices, especially the vocals, oftentimes slid toward mediocrity. The balance of voice, instrumentals, and visuals was known to go askew. Unstructured, illogical, and/or obstructive staging was common. Audiences could barely understand lyrics of some groups, due to muddy and incomprehensible instrumental accompaniments and problematic homemade arrangements.

And the costumes? Fashion. Assault. TLC's *What Not to Wear* could have created an entire spin-off series devoted to the tragic outfitting that took the stage at high schools and colleges throughout the country. The change from wearing traditional choral robes and tuxedos to contemporary costumes was the opposite of smooth. Fortunately, it was the '80s and the general public fully embraced fashion experimentation and failure. Like mood rings and side ponytails, it was normal teenage fashion to wear three different pairs of mismatched socks at the same time. Enough said.

Regardless of the strong performance traditions that resulted from Luers, this mass of stumbling, disorganized directors fueled traditional choral leaders to view show choirs as a fad detrimental to choral music education.

The arts industry is comprised of passionate, creative people who naturally fuel competition. And competition between those who have similar views or talents typically results in a winner or a resolution. Some battles, however, will never be won. Some arguments are never resolved. Some opposites do not attract.

Republicans and Democrats will never merge into Republicrats. Fast-food restaurants and fine dining establishments won't come together to create fast-fine dining. And it's unlikely that traditional choral music and pop music will ever take the stage for a traditional pop show choir production. These things just will never happen. But, there does come a time when a level of respect settles between the groups. They agree to disagree, and then to focus on winning the battles that they can win. In the 1980s, traditionalists were not quite at that point with show choirs, but they were getting there.

Everyone goes through an awkward phase before coming into his or her own . . . and for show choirs that was the '80s. In the next decade, they would gain their footing, grow a following, and emerge with confidence.

What up, Paula!? The Jackson family was the first to discover Paula Abdul's moves, approaching her after a L.A. Lakers' basketball game. After choreographing one song, "Torture," for the famous Five, she was the chosen choreographer for their Victory Tour.

Spanish Fork High School's Ambassadors on Versalite 3000s— FAME Events, Branson, Missouri.

SHOWSTOPPERS: AN INDUSTRY EMERGES

7

There must be a "wow" moment; something to leave the audience talking.

—ERIC VAN CLEAVE, FORMER DIRECTOR OF
FIRST EDITION, JEFFERSON HIGH SCHOOL

Showstopper. Ironically, this is not the number that stops a show. This is the one that starts it, not literally but emotionally. It awakens the crowd. It draws them to the edge of their seat . . . or out of their seat and into a standing ovation. It creates a memory, a tear, an inspiration. Suddenly for a second, in the darkened theater or auditorium, no one is distracted by a cell phone or thinking about a to-do list for the next day. Like a magnet, a showstopper moment draws all eyes and ears onto the stage and into the performance. This is why music lovers pay $65 for concerts and $100-plus for Broadway performances. People pay in hopes of experiencing a showstopper. An audience wants to be moved.

Every performance, and every performer, doesn't necessarily have a showstopper. But every memorable one does.

As competitions continued to bring communities of singers and dancers together and started identifying experts in the industry, it became apparent that show choir was coming into its own. Its performers now had a focal point and goal.

With all eyes on the coveted competition trophies, an emerging appetite developed amongst both show choir members and their directors to learn, to establish, and to shine—to get bigger and better. Showstoppers were expected in every competitive performance. The elite groups all wanted to be the first to uncover a fresh trend, introduce the coolest new dance move, or coin the next "it" style.

In response, an era of entrepreneurs and leaders began to step onto the stage, organizing national competitions, workshops, businesses, and organizations to further establish show choirs within the performing arts industry. The step-touches and jazz hands were suddenly legitimized. Show choir was becoming its own showstopper.

It was becoming memorable.

NATIONAL COMPETITIONS

By the 1990s, most show choirs attended at least one competition a year; some attended several. The elite choirs used the B- and C-list competitions as grounds to get initial adjudication scores, to perfect their shows, and to see what was working and what could be adjusted. The goal of attending these smaller competitions was essentially practice and preparation for the crème de la crème of high school sing- and dance-offs: the national competition.

Unlike cheerleading or football, show choir didn't—and still doesn't—have just one national competition. Because of the subjectivity of judges' comments and the lack of a standardized scoring system, it was impossible to determine the number one show choir in America. The crowning ceremonies, however, continued.

YOUNG AMERICANS CONTEST

Although the first national competition to draw groups into its lair was the Young Americans Contest in 1985, a handful of other national competitions came onto the scene shortly afterward, having a more long-term impact upon how show choirs competed.

SHOWSTOPPERS

After attending Bishop Luers in 1985, James Dash, travel host with Performing Arts Abroad, was inspired to replicate the successful format of Luers—but make it even better. Dash, as the travel arranger for the Ambassadors, requested Ron Hellems' counsel, knowing the Carmel High School singers were consecutive grand champions of Luers. Beyond suggesting a more open-invite policy and additional competition days, Hellems worked closely with Dash to create one of the

Mt. Zion Swingsations, "Who Put the Bomp,"
Young Americans Competition (1985).

Eisenhower Elite Energy at Showstoppers Orlando American Gardens Pavilion.

largest and most successful show choir competitions in the country.

In the spring of 1986, Keynote Arts Associates presented its first Showstoppers show choir competition with Dash as event producer and Hellems as artistic director. The event, held at Chicago Bismarck Hotel's Palace Theatre, welcomed sixteen groups in its inaugural year.

Hellems commented, "When we started Showstoppers, I wanted show choirs to get better, so that [the genre] would have more credibility."

Over the years, Showstoppers expanded, offering several different competitions focusing on attractive travel destinations, such as New York, Chicago, and Orlando. The travel- and experienced-focused competitions continued through 2010, when they ceased operations due to the decrease in participants and the tight economy.

Beyond establishing one of the first national show choir competitions, Showstoppers and its producers, Keynotes Arts Associates, also attempted to create a national show choir association, to standardize such elements of the genre as competition scoring and curriculum. At the 1996 Showstoppers Chicago competition, Hellems and Dash organized a forum with contest judges and participating choir directors to discuss judging sheets, national contests, and the curriculum of events surrounding them, to improve upon their own events as well as organize the industry.

However, "every time we started the conversation about organizing, the response was lackluster," said Hellems.

FAME EVENTS

FAME Events, the third competition production company to come to the table, hosted their inaugural competition in Branson, Missouri, in spring of 1995.

Unlike Showstopper competitions, the event featured several different types of high school music ensembles, including concert bands, concert choirs, and show choirs. Recalling their first event, Joel Biggs, president and chief executive officer of FAME events, said, "We realized that show choir was its own kind of thing and needed its own venue. That's when we decided to focus our efforts on show choir."

The early judge panel for FAME consisted of well-known and well-established choral education geeks

The Bismarck Theatre, originally called the Palace Theatre, was opened in 1926 as the flagship of vaudeville's Orpheum Circuit. Since, it's been transformed into many different types of performance spaces, including a movie theater, a Broadway tour destination, a rock concert venue, and even a banquet hall. In 1984, it went by the name "Bismarck Theatre" while it hosted such artists as the Cure and Frank Zappa. In the '90s the theater went through an intensive and expensive renovation process, reopening in 1999 under its current name, Cadillac Palace. Its first show was the premiere of Elton John's *Aida*.

"A challenge of working as artistic director for Showstoppers was educating judges to adjudicate objectively. There were judges for whom the adjudication sheet didn't matter. They came in with their own preconceived ideas of who would win. It took a lot of work to change that," commented Hellems.

ASPIRE AWARDS

In April 2011, FAME Events sponsored the first annual Aspire Awards, the show choir industry's top awards ceremony for professionals contributing to the advancement of the genre. Ten awards categories were presented, recognizing individuals who excelled in areas such as directing, choreography, costuming, and arranging. The 2011 winners included:

Brett Carroll (Burbank High School): The Vocal Vanguard Award for outstanding achievement in vocal music instruction
April James (Clinton High School alumni): The Visual Vanguard Award for outstanding achievement in visual presentation and design
Chris Miller (Mitchell High School): Best New Director
Kevin Chase: Best New Choreographer
Eric Van Cleave (former director, Jefferson High School): Best Arranger
Fairfield Classic (Fairfield High School): Best Regional Competition
Mark Myer (Waubonsie Valley): Most Promising New Program
Trojanaires (Jenks High School): Spirit of Service Award
Gail McInnis Production: Best Costumer
Dwight Jordan: Lifetime Achievement Award

Wheaton Warrenville South High School's The Classics from Wheaton, Illinois, are crowned Grand Champion at FAME's 2011 national event. Classics' members pose with their newly acquired hardware.

such as John Jacobson, Don Neuen, Kirby Shaw, and Roger Emerson. Although their names are associated with music education and arranging, these well-known judges were not associated with competitive show choir, which is its own genre. They provided priceless vocal critiques, but lacked useful suggestions regarding the intricacies of competitive show choir.

Participants felt that their innovations were not being recognized. After receiving feedback from participants, FAME shifted to hiring more genre-specific judges—former directors and choreographers—people who worked and understood competitive show choir. They also began to hire seasoned judges from the Midwest and California competition circuits. From then on, FAME events attracted the best groups in the business— solidifying their reputation, credibility, and profits.

Since 1995, FAME Events has produced competitions all over the country in popular travel destinations, including San Antonio, Orlando, Chicago, Hawaii, and New York. In 2004, the company also offered an international contest option in the West End of London. Three show choirs enrolled and took part in what was the first show choir competition in Great Britain. Although all the competitive groups were American, the UK's own West End Kids made an appearance as guest performers at the show.

Given the small number of participants in the UK competition, FAME Events concentrated their efforts within the United States. Biggs commented:

> One of the challenges is convincing school administrations to invest in travel education. Travel, beyond the competition aspect, is a rich opportunity for students to experience other cultures and learn historical facts beyond what comes from books. I've had students tell me that they've learned more about history [on a FAME tour] than in history class. Traveling should ultimately complement what kids are learning in school … they can experience art museums, theater, historical sites . . . live and in person.

The West End Kids was established in September 2001 by Martin-Gwyn Williams, a specialist vocal coach and singing teacher for young voices. The West End Kids Choir served as both a recording and performance group—singing an assortment of highly advanced, popular vocal arrangements.

SHOW CHOIR CAMPS OF AMERICA

Beyond competitions, some performers took active roles during the summer months to advance their skills in show choir by attending Show Choir Camps of America. This weeklong workshop camp, cofounded in 1980 by Dwight Jordan and Susan Moninger, quickly became the country's leading summer program for choral staging and show choir training.

Today, more than twelve hundred students and directors enroll each year, traveling to either Millikin University in Decatur, Illinois, or Heidelberg College in Tiffin, Ohio. Throughout the workshop, students make new friends and talk show choir shop while learning a camp-specific show from choreographers and vocal directors. By the end of the week, participants are inspired, exhausted, and ready to return and share their new insights with their hometown groups.

'99 TERPSICHORE CELEBRITY WORKSHOP LINEUP

Jazz Dance with Tina D'Amato, member of San Francisco Gold Rush and L.A. Laker Girls' choreographer

Audition Techniques with David Friedman, Walt Disney conductor and arranger

Tricks and Lifts with Stacy Walker and Cris Judd, both Michael Jackson tour dancers

Acting Techniques with Heather Headley, Broadway performer in *Aida* and; Tony Award winner

Swing Dancing with Neisha Folkes, choreography for the GAP khaki swing commercial

Improv Techniques with Thomas Greene, Second City National Touring Company

Funk and Hip-Hop with Tim Stevenson, music video and awards show dancer

Voice-over Acting with Norm Woodell, Chicago voice-over actor

TERPSICHORE

Mike Weaver and fellow Millikin graduate David Mathey ran a small company called Show Design, Inc., founded in 1999, which worked to bring entertainment and education together in one forum—but this time in the form of an innovative show choir contest. David had a background in entertainment, as a manager at Disney's Epcot Center, while Mike had the show choir contacts and in-depth industry knowledge.

In 1999, the Terpsichore '99 Show Choir Competition and Performing Arts Seminars, a two-day competitive event, was held at Navy Pier in Chicago. In addition to performing on the impressive ballroom stage, groups participated in seminar sessions with celebrity clinicians who offered insight into swing dancing, hip-hop style, musical theater auditioning, tricks and lifts, voice-over, and the recording industry.

The Terpsichore 1999 contest program booklet with the ultra-cool logo images for listening (learning), acting, singing, and dance.

Masterclass cast rehearsal.

Show Design, Inc. produced three Terpsichore competitions before closing the company. Although they had the connections, the drive, the finances, and the groups, Mike and David lacked travel agent licenses. The top show choir event producers at the time, Keynote Arts Associates and FAME Events, both, at their core, were successful travel companies that also produced music events for their customers. Mike commented, "Producing national level show choir events is harder than it looks, and I have a whole new level of respect for that line of work."

MASTERCLASS CAMP

Although Terspichore wasn't a long-term success, in 2004, a new educational event, developed by Mike Weaver, Linda Pauli, and Kevin Breazeale appeared on the show choir scene—called Masterclass Performing Arts Camp.

Masterclass was built as an intensive seven-day summer camp for advanced singers and dancers, and held at Valparaiso University in Northwestern Indiana. Nearly a hundred performers were selected after a thirteen-site audition tour.

The students were excited to take their show choir training to a new level. Although it wasn't quite show choir, it had familiar elements including soloists, group dances, intricate arrangements, and partner production numbers. This, however, was a step up. It was a camp for students who wanted to explore the world of performing as post–high school graduates. The classes were intended for performers who wanted to take a serious look at the music entertainment industry, from vocal performance to musical theater and pop tour dancing.

Learning from the Terpsichore experience, the founding company, Entertainment Arts Group, partnered with FAME Events to help with promotion and lend credibility to its name. With FAME as a sponsor, the participants not only had a chance to learn from the best and with the best, they also had the opportunity to audition for the newly formed FAME All Stars, a European performance tour group that took place the week prior to the camp.

In June 2005, eight of the Masterclass campers doubled as FAME All Stars, juggling both the FAME European tour and Masterclass camp in one busy summer.

The girls in rehearsal—Natalie Bucey, Allison Douglas, and Erin Cosgrove.

The boys in dress rehearsal—Caleb Mathews, Chase Todd, and Zach Gibson.

Scott Schram rehearses his solo.

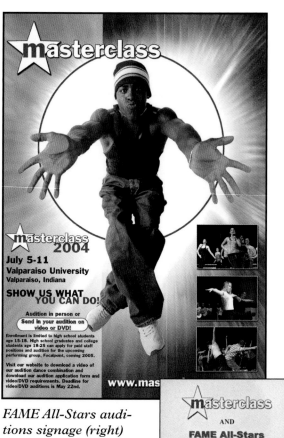

FAME All-Stars auditions signage (right) and Masterclass Camp promotional poster.

The second year wasn't as successful, affected by the recession and tightening budgets. Despite the extra marketing efforts—the cool M-Star logo, slick video trailer, updated Web site, increased number of auditions, and a multitiered advertising approach—the company and Masterclass workshop folded, resting on their two-year success.

COMPETITION SETS THE STAGE

With competitions, festivals, and workshops in full swing around the country, staging and costumes began separating show choirs from just regular, run-of-the-mill choral music ensembles. In the '80s, productions started incorporating the show methods used at theme parks, including costume changes, special effects (fog machines!), backdrops, and large props. It was choir with a little more sizzle and a lot more sass.

MAKING THE STAGE RIGHT

The stage, itself, began to transform. The small risers built for stationary choirs weren't cutting it for anything more than a dip or a sway.

Before long, the Wenger Corporation, makers of staging platforms for professional and educational markets, came to the rescue, offering full stage platforms. One of their most popular items, the Versalite 3000, involved lighter, more flexible platforms that were easily transported, but durable enough to handle a barrage of young performers beating them down every performance. These platforms are still one of the most widely used staging options today.

NATIONAL ASSOCIATION OF SHOW CHOIRS

By 1998, the industry was growing and those involved in the show choir industry were starting to recognize that the genre was slightly disorganized. For-profit companies were forming at a record pace. There were more competitions and festivals than ever before. But no one had direction. There was no standardization in place for infant show choirs, for newly created competitions, or for for-profit companies. Everyone was going rogue.

There had to be a better system.

A meeting took place in 1998 at the Hilton Chicago, with the goal of forming an organization to service the show choir industry. While more than 200 invites were sent out, only twelve participants attended. Over two days, the group accomplished two things: they established a name—the National Association of Show Choirs (NASC)—and created an adjudication sheet and caption-style scoring system for competition show choirs.

The NASC didn't continue to organize annual meetings or collect membership fees. They didn't hire a staff or run an actual office. But that Chicago meeting helped move show choirs in the right direction toward a more recognized and standardized competition performance genre.

According to Biggs, FAME Events participants walked away with a better understanding of what choral directors needed from event organizers. At the top of the list was a desire to create a standardized and consistent adjudication system so that a true national competition could take place.

Showstoppers organizers created a scoring system years before, which they utilized at each of their competitions held throughout the country. When groups attended Showstoppers events, there were no surprises. They came prepared. Groups wanted to feel that secure before every competition.

THE FINALE SHOW CHOIR CHAMPIONSHIP

In April 2011, Mind's Eye Conceptions produced the Finale Show Choir Championships—an event that, from the beginning, was intended to take show choir competitions to a new, more sophisticated level. The competition took place in the Hammerstein Ballroom of New York City's Manhattan City Center. Before this inaugural affair, online banner advertisements, featuring Mario Lopez, were secured on dozens of Web sites to increase awareness and excitement.

While the intentions were noble, the organization of the event was both underwhelming and disappointing to many of the participating groups and judges. The one-day competition experienced a series of budget issues due to elaborate "extras" such as the custom-designed gourmet cake, $7,000 People's Choice Trophy, and A-list spokesperson.

Other organizations may find inspiration in the Mind's Eye Productions marketing techniques; however due to extensive organizational issues, this Finale may not likely see an encore in its future.

SELL ME A STAGE, WENGER!

"[With Versalite] a group's choreography is not limited by the platforms . . . directors can build platform formations that complement the staging . . . Show choirs are very tough on our products. Twenty-four kids dancing is a large load . . . if our platforms can pass the show choir test . . . well, we've accomplished something." Elizabeth Haak, director of marketing, Wenger Corporation.

In 1996, Keynote Arts associates director Jim Dash and artistic director Ron Hellems held a forum during the Chicago Showstoppers weekend. The forum led to the reinvention of the Showstoppers' own proprietary adjudication system. Although that version could have been replicated as the standard in the industry, most show choir contest producers chose to do their own thing—and there was no authority to tell them otherwise.

STAGING PLATFORM HISTORY
STAGERIGHT

StageRight, an all-purpose stage deck that is the latest advancement in risers, become popular in 2003 due to its portability, durability and versatility—and reversible tops. Its Z-frame legs fit neatly into slots in the deck. Show choir performers agree, these babies feel solid, especially during intense dance breaks. However, while the portability helped speed up setup and tear-down, they also caused many pinched fingers when held the wrong way.

THE ENCORE STAGING SYSTEM

Popular in the '80s, the system involved a set of ten triangular boxes designed to fit together to create various formations. The boxes offered enough room for one performer, sometimes two if they stood close together. The system came with a portable sound mixer and amplifiers; two speakers; four microphones; a light control unit; light boxes equipped with bulbs, gel frames, and diffuser (with holders); and stands. Best of all, the shipment also contained the bonus of a miniature model and eighteen plastic "people" to block out where everyone would stand.

THE TROUPER SYSTEM

A staging system made up of heavy 8 by 8-foot folding table–type risers, considered the standard in the 1980s and early '90s. Although they provided a solid base for shows, after a number of years, as expected, the leg braces would weaken and tended to fold up (often during a performance).

VERSALITE 3000

In 1981, the Versalite system introduced relatively lightweight platform risers with aluminum frames and black textured tops. Although the brand name sounds like the latest innovative vacuum or space movie, these platforms were no joke and were all the rage among '90s show choirs. After a short time, however, the leg connectors tended to "strip out" due to the expected wear and tear of thirty performers' stomping on them for several hours each week, and required bungee cords or large C-clamps to hold them together. The new 2.0 model addresses the leg connector issue.

AN INDUSTRY EMERGES

At the end of the day, all of the competitions, festivals, workshops, and companies are put in place to build stronger performers. And the goal of every strong performer is to win.

Winning a national competition gives a show choir bragging rights to coin itself "best in the nation" for at least a year and "nationally recognized" for a solid five years. It is a huge deal—after all, trophies are not given away, they are earned. Winning a national show choir competition requires the same amount of hours, dedication, and premature gray hairs and wrinkles, as winning a national football competition. If not more.

And while there's always an exception, by and large, many groups return to their hometown and maybe receive an announcement over the loudspeaker or a short column in the community newspaper, but not nearly the attention granted of an all-state–winning athlete or team.

Like great athletes, these performers don't dedicate years of their lives to song and dance for a hometown rally or for personal attention and recognition. They don't wake up early on Saturdays or stay up late for a long rehearsal to see their name in print. For the most part, they are driven by their passion, by their commitment, by their team, and by their love for music and dance.

Audiences and judges don't see what was behind the curtain of competitions: groups huddled together practicing and repracticing an especially difficult dance break; the soloists warming up their voice with the pianist; the group sitting on the stairs outside the stage door, listening to a senior performer give one last quick word of encouragement; walking onstage holding hands; tears falling before the lights even hit as performers realize this is their last competition, or their last show. The days, the moments, the seconds before the show begins, some groups, and some individuals, have already won. The resulting score is only a mere formality.

After the competition, show choirs pack up their costumes, their sets, and their instruments. Sheet music is returned to its binder. Banners are rolled up for the next weekend. They leave the auditorium reenergized from a win, or stumble, disappointed by a loss, onto their charter bus. They return to reality.

Oftentimes the reality that awaits them is the question of how they are going to fund the next competition or find the money to replace old instruments or budget new costumes. Beyond the complicated choral arrangements, the intricate accompaniment scores, and advanced choreographed dances, some group's biggest challenge is just to be; to be, despite the budget restraints, cutbacks, and limitations.

Because, as it turns out, passion has a price tag.

Singing and dancing on graduated platforms (risers) came from Broadway and filmed musicals. Center: Cliff Edwards, a.k.a. Ukulele Ike, The Hollywood Revue (1929).

Fred Waring and the Pennsylvanians used risers to not only enhance the look of the staging, but to create a "wall" of sound. The top platform here is nearly twelve feet from the stage floor.

At the 2011 Finale National Show Choir Championship in New York City, the producers worked with Colette Cakes to create a replica of Times Square, customized to include the competition participants.

"Popularity comes and goes, but being good never goes away." —David Fehr, director of Clinton High School's Attaché, Clinton, Mississippi

New York City, Times Square, April 8, 2011.

The size and expense of trophies continued to rise throughout the years. The People's Choice Award at the Finale National Show Choir Championship in New York City in 2011, won by Norwell High School's Knight Moves, cost $7,000.

THE PRICE BEHIND THE PEP: TUITION AND BUDGETS

The connection between music and excellence in academic achievement is undeniable, yet continues to be ignored.

—DAMON BROWN, FOUNDER OF STAGEVISIONS CHOREOGRAPHY, CARMEL, INDIANA

Everything has a price.

Throughout the history of music education, there has been a constant battle for funding. Advocates, such as VH1's Save the Music and its celebrity leaders, including Beyoncé, Jamie Foxx, Gavin DeGraw, Natasha Bedingfield, the Fray, and Venus Williams, have stepped forward, offering the compelling statistics and creating dramatic campaigns and rallying cries for a cause that so many feel passionate about.

Although a few battles have been won, the war continues.

Because of the struggles to financially support general music education, often, in the end, only the students in the more affluent, suburban schools and communities benefit from the show choir experience. It's not because these schools and groups have louder voices, it's just that their supplemental backing becomes possible through other means—such as tuition fees or fund-raising.

As the recent recession hit city after city, affecting families and paychecks throughout the United States, the component of fund-raising became even more crucial to ensuring the survival of these sassy, sequined groups.

There are 244,000 Google search results for the phrase "cow poop."

Cub Scout show choir? Every holiday season since 1960 at the Kings Theatre in Edinburgh, Scotland, there is a scout fundraising event held, called the Edinburgh Gang Show. Much like a show choir, the scouts perform choreographed pop and Broadway songs, and incorporate full costuming.

Many show choirs approach their financial issues with the same inspired energy they use to develop their shows or determine their themes or music. Fund-raising is often seen as the first number in the show, the opener before the opener, the preface of the story.

And when it comes to creativity, in show production or fund-raising, show choirs never fail to impress.

COW PATTY DROP

Culminating all the misunderstood stereotypes of a Midwestern kid into one fund-raising event, the Cow Patty Drop uses cow poop to make a profit.

On the school's football field or another large area of land, the show choir members mark off the ground with checkered squares. Each square contains a number that corresponds to that of a raffle ticket sold for the event.

As the focus of the event, two or more cows are released onto the field to graze. The first cow to eventually "drop a patty" on a numbered square designates the top prize winner, usually of a monetary sum. The event continues until five different squares contain droppings.

Profit Level: $$

BALL DROP

As an alternative to the organic Bingo fund-raising efforts of Cow Patty Drops, another similar event organized by show choirs is the Ball Drop.

This is set up and run exactly like the Cow Patty Drop, with raffle tickets and a checkerboard field. Instead of dramatizing cow defecation, however, groups that organize Ball Drops will partner with the local news station to gain access to their traffic helicopter and, if possible, promotion support.

The night of the event, five beach balls are dropped from the helicopter, landing on the winning squares.

Profit level: $$

FESTIVAL FOR FUNDS

One of the more elaborate, but still traditional, fund-raisers is organizing a show choir competition or festival and charging entry fees for both the participants and audience members. These events, if well planned, well publicized, and well attended (by performing groups and spectators alike), can help raise significant funds and result in minimal lost hairs or headaches.

Because many of these competitions can run an entire day or weekend, host groups normally serve lunch and dinner in the school cafeteria—hot and cold sandwiches, as well as salads, pizza, pasta, and sides, to help cover the event costs and prevent crankiness among the show choir performers. A diva can become destructive without dinner. There are also often concessions, such as popcorn, candy bars, and homemade cookies, to add to the profits.

Local advertisements are included within the program, and event T-shirts line the halls for purchase. Every corner turned is another opportunity to raise a few bucks. Beyond the regular checklist of required or typical activities, some show choirs step up the fund-raising elements and incorporate them into the show. For example, a handful of choirs organize a People's Choice Awards ceremony at the end of the show. Throughout the festival, attendees are encouraged to vote for their favorite show choir—for a voting fee that benefits the host choir.

To keep operating costs down, show choirs rope in volunteer parents, family, and friends to help run the event. And most show choirs can avoid hefty rental fees by hosting in the high school auditorium or low-cost community center.

After organizational charges are taken care of, the remainder of the money goes directly to support the group. The results can be shockingly awesome.

Profit level: $$$$

FOOD FUND RAISERS

Taking a page from the Girl Scouts and Boy Scouts of America, many show choirs fuel their shows with food fund-raisers. These door-to-door-style sales pitch products earn groups about 30 percent of the profits, after the cost of the merchandise is factored in, and include:

CANDY

Whatever the brand, candy bars or other packaged treats can help sweeten the road to singing and dancing. A little.

FRUIT

Oftentimes around the holidays, fruit catalogs will be distributed, offering boxes of navel oranges, grapefruit, and other produce to bite away at the budget.

The orange is the official state fruit of Florida.

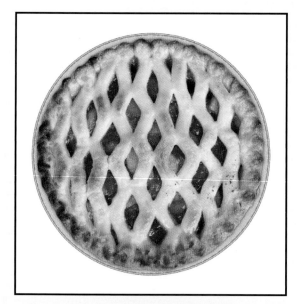

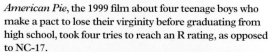

American Pie, the 1999 film about four teenage boys who make a pact to lose their virginity before graduating from high school, took four tries to reach an R rating, as opposed to NC-17.

PIES

Particularly around Thanksgiving, pie sales are all the rage. Instead of home bakers slaving away behind the stove to produce them, the pies can be ordered from a catalog. To maximize profits, some groups do take on the baking themselves, but most do not, given the time and costs involved.

Profit level: $

COOKIE WALK

Merging a love for cookies with a love for music, Greensboro, North Carolina former teacher and social-ite, Josie Gibboney, suggests organizing cookie walks, cousin to the "Bake Sale." With each choir member donating three dozen cookies (sans chocolate chip or oatmeal), a party is organized in a school cafeteria or similar room and attendees are given a bakery box and a plastic glove upon arrival. Attendees walk around the room, selecting their choice of cookies. When their box is full, attendees go to a weighing station to check out and are charged .55 per ounce or $8.80 a pound.

This event is ideal during the holiday season and results in impressive profits amounts.

Profit level: $$$

CUTTING THE COSTS

Groups such as the Petal High School's Soundsa-tions cut out-of-pocket costs by selling Rada Cutlery to family and friends. The knife company offers an attractive fund-raising package and allows groups to make up to a 40 percent profit by dealing directly with the manufacturer. This kind of fund-raiser, held by the Petal High School Soundsations many years in a row, has resulted in well-stocked knife sets in every kitchen in Petal, Mississippi.

Profit level: $$

DUCK RACES

Taking another creative spin to the usual raffle-ticket fund-raiser, show choirs have organized events called Duck Races. Required materials are minimal but not always available for purchase. This list includes a buck-et of five-hundred-plus rubber duckies, a moving river, vivacious organizers, open-minded and enthusiastic participants and, ideally, a rain-free Saturday after-noon in the spring.

Prior to the events, raffle tickets are sold. As with

the Cow Patty or Ball Drops, each duck is branded with a number that corresponds to that of one of the raffle tickets sold.

At the event, the organizer releases the rubber duckies into a shallow creek, river, or pond, and then the crowd watches in anticipation as the duckies move downstream, downriver, or cross-pond. The first five duckies to reach the predetermined destination, such as the other side of the pond or a bridge downstream, win the top prizes of the event. The other duckies are swept up and saved for next year.

Profit level: $$

HAUNTED MANSION

Not appropriate for all, but spooktacular for some, haunted houses can serve as both memorable team-building activities and profitable events.

Every year, Lafayette Jefferson High School's First Edition show choir transforms what used to be the Indiana Knights of Pythian Home into a nightmar-ish Haunted Mansion right out of a Freddy Krueger movie.

Throughout the years, after purchasing the build-ing for just one dollar in the 1980s, the group con-structed secret passageways and applied tricked-out elements that have kept families and haunted house-goers equally entertained and freaked out.

Run much like the Haunted Mansion at Disney's Magic Kingdom, the event features various casts, a wardrobe department, ghoulish guides, and walkie-talkies to keep terrors in check. According to sources involved with the Haunted Mansion, over a six-year period, the attraction brought in more than $1 mil-lion in funding for Jefferson's music department. Scary good.

Profit Level: $$$$

DINNER SHOW

Cabaret-style dinner theater events, not surprisingly, tend to be popular with the show choir–supporting crowd. Instead of catering the event, groups pull to-gether willing cooks to bake up lasagne or make their favorite pasta to serve the masses. Often these events are complemented with a silent auction offering do-nated items from family, friends, and community or-ganizations, to boost the earnings.

Students provide the entertainment: duets, quar-

A spin-off from the dinner show is what's sometimes referred to as a Chocolate Surrey, or "dessert theater." Whether the food is carbs or cocoa, the show is always the same . . .

The Mountain State Apple Harvest Festival takes place in Martinsburg, West Virginia, and crowns a Queen Pomona every year. Victoria "Tori" Shamblin, the 2010 Queen Pomona, served as president of the fellowship of Christian Athletes, and was vice president and dance captain of the Good Times show choir.

The first Oktoberfest festivities in LaCrosse, Wisconsin, took place in 1961. Today, it's one of the few annual authentic old-world folk festivals held in the United States.

tets, solos, and, of course, a headline performance from the fund-raising show choirs. The profits and the performances are standing-ovation material.

Profit Level: $$–$$$

REGIONALIZED-COMMUNITY FUND RAISERS

Whether it's crushing grapes in wine country or hosting whale tours in Maine, show choirs have a solid history of combining their fund-raising efforts with local events or traditions.

OKTOBERFEST

In a state that sometimes feels as German as Germany, Wisconsinites know how to embrace Oktoberfest. Leveraging that love, parents and friends (age twenty-one and older) of the La Crosse Central High School sell beer tickets every year at the festival, earning $8 an hour. All wages help support the show choir.

Profit Level: $$$

APPLE DUMPLING SALE

Martinsburg, West Virginia, is home to both the Mountain State Apple Harvest Festival and the Good Times show choir. Each October, parents and group members get together in the school's cafeteria, for one week, to bake apple dumplings and sell them at the Good Times' stand at the Apple Harvest Festival and in the school's cafeteria. However, "about 80 percent of the dumplings are sold through presales," says Linda Snyder, director of Good Times. Every year, on average, about seven thousand dumplings are sold, resulting in $16,000 and $18,000 for the show choir.

Profit Level: $$$$

BRIDGESTONE INVITATIONAL VALET PARKING

During the Bridgestone Invitational in Akron, Ohio, the freshly licensed teenagers of E.T.C. All Americans work the valet parking area of the renowned Firestone Country Club golf course. In addition to funds provided to the choir for managing the lot, the group also walks away with a bucket full of cash in tips.

Profit Level: $$

AMERICA SINGS

Beyond raising money for their specific group, show

choir performers are also involved in local and national charity organizations. Although these differ from group to group and region to region, there is one organization specifically built around show choir talents: America Sings. This philanthropic organization, founded in 1988 by show choir choreographer John Jacobson, offers young performers the chance to sing and dance to benefit established children's charities. Since its inception, the group has involved more than 200,000 students from two thousand choirs in performances throughout the country, including fifteen Macy's Thanksgiving Day Parades.

MORE THAN MONEY

Since the first costume was purchased and the first set was constructed, fund-raising has been part of every group's DNA. It's expected and necessary, so most try to make it interesting, fun, and creative.

In addition to building revenue, these events and activities create memories, strengthen character, and bond teams that continuously prove to themselves and to their community that they can sparkle both on and off the stage.

In the trenches of show choir, most performers aren't forming picket lines or setting up rallies with music education advocates. They believe in what they do, and they work hard to make ends meet however they can.

And at the end of the day, while everything has a price, show choirs prove that fund-raising can be pretty fun.

Two schools in California, Burbank High School and John Burroughs High School, produce a three-day event called Pop Show, which is equivalent to a series of dinner shows – just no food. Each night is comprised of the group's contest shows along with solos, duets, and featured dance groups. Lighting and video equipment are rented to enhance the production value. California groups usually sell out all three nights.

Burbank In Sync at Show Choir Nationals (2010).

ALL IN THE NAME: THE BRANDING OF A SHOW CHOIR

I think there has always been a perceived formula [for building a successful competitive show choir], but the level and expectations continue to grow, so the formula grows and changes with it.

—DWIGHT JORDAN, CHOREOGRAPHER

Brand loyalty. Although a common marketing term, brand loyalty exists beyond products you can purchase with a credit card. People become brand loyal to their hometown, their high school, their family name, and their culture.

To build a brand is the same as establishing a reputation. It doesn't happen overnight. You can't order it online. And it can't be easily explained and achieved in three steps. These things take time, but if done right, a brand will forge an identity, empower a following, and create a feeling with just the mention of its name.

Establishing a show choir's reputation or "brand" is as much a marketer's job as it is a musician's. Whether through a conscience effort or not, history's leading groups created a palette of distinctive show choir styles. These director/choreographer teams often chose songs that somehow embodied the respective groups' spirit. Early swing choir audiences started to associate groups with their style or performance quality—and developed expectations because of that.

Marion 26th Street Singers, publicity photo (1980).

The Andy Haines version would replicate the style of Fred Astaire and Ginger Rogers, typically ending with a tradition Broadway tap number.

In later years, Andy Haines became the name associated with a choreography style based on ballroom dancing, which kicked the Carmel "dinner show" approach up a notch, adding grandness and a touch of snobbery—all an act, of course.

Carmel High School Ambassadors, "Fabulous Feet," Bishop Luers (1985).

The formal, long gown is best demonstrated by 2010 Center Grove CG Sound System.

TYPE A OR TYPE B?

If every competitive show choir was perfect—all members could sing and dance, and the arrangements and band were flawless—the only way to distinguish one group from another would be the style of their show.

Just as high school students decide which clique they want to eat lunch with—the jocks, the hipsters, the goths—a group needs to carve out its place in the cafeteria before the performers sit down to eat.

From the first Bishop Luers Competition emerged three styles, or brands, of show choirs. The California Clique, which developed quickly afterward, stood apart from these initial three—as its own party.

MIDWEST MEETS VEGAS

The first competitive style was developed in the late '70s by F. Ritchie Walton and Chuck Haley and the Marion 26th Street Singers. This brand took a family-friendly, all-American approach to show choir performances. The productions incorporated brightly colored costumes (and costume changes), tap dancing, and multiple levels of platforms, while delivering Disney-like professionalism. The music ranged from pop and rock to gospel and Broadway-style tap.

CABARET MEETS DINNER SHOW

Another style, employed in the early '80s by Ron Hellems, Ann Conrad, Mary Corsaro, Dwight Edwards, and the Carmel Ambassadors, was a melting pot of Broadway and Off-Broadway theater, film, television, dinner show, and cabaret.

The style was sophisticated and elegant. The women wore conservative attire, usually black or white dresses and pearls, and the men sported multipart tuxedos, dinner jackets, or three-piece suits. Their attitude and costuming provided an appropriate complement to the typically couple-focused choreography and included a ballad conducted by the director.

Throughout the show, no one left the stage to change costumes or grab a prop, allowing the crew members to play a more integral role in the show. The style used a large instrumental ensemble, and novelty numbers were more witty than hokey.

This style also sometimes incorporated character voices within the set, à la Betty Boop, and closed the show with a hat routine and big vocal production.

Edgewood Music Warehouse, in warm-up at Bishop Luers (1982).

URBAN SOPHISTICATED

The urban sophisticated style, developed by Jim and Verda Savage's Edgewood Music Warehouse, created cool, contemporary, and chic show choirs. The most successful performances of this style typically incorporated R & B, funk, and pop arrangements into the show.

Choreography was put into place for a reason—to create a constant rhythmic pulse—with little footwork and few blocking changes. Arms, for instance, were utilized for gestures or dynamic visual effects. Given that the focus lies heavily on vocals, the director conducted the ballad, and performers never left the stage—preventing a loss of sound.

As opposed to the Haines/Hellems style, the Savage/Savage style was stationary gesture based unison movements, little partner dancing and big singing. And they dabbled in dark suits and dinner dresses."

Jim Bales, Cindy Hawkins, David Thompson, Faye Stidd, Anna Kinser, Matt Narey, JD Cowden, and Denise Sanders (1982).

Horizon Step on Stage at FAME (2009).

STYLES CONVERGE

By the mid-'80s, a fourth style arose. Dwight Jordan took on an alias style that combined F. Ritchie Walton's all-American look and attitude with Jim Savage's understated and dynamic choreographic style.

THEME PARK REVIEW

Like an expected theme park performance, the final style to emerge from Luers took its cues from many

Mt. Zion High School's Swingsations performing *"Spirit Song" (1985).*

aspects of pop culture—including television, film, musical theater, and commercial shows.

Sporting bright colors and sequins, groups could be found singing a wide range of selections from rock pop to gospel or novelty. Staging and choreography was clean and uncomplicated—with two primary stage blockings and minimal movements to enhance dynamics and, ideally, they featured soloists or highlighted other talents within the group.

In Sync in their Humans Fighting Back Against Technology show (2010).

While those are still the core styles of show choirs, in recent years, new styles have appeared on the stage.

THEATRICALIZED POP AND ROCK

Groups such as Burbank High School's In Sync, for example, connect pop music, such as Styx's "Mr. Roboto," with stylized costuming and a thematic message, or story, woven throughout the set. Its shows feature contemporary pop and rock titles, but its costuming is of another period. Often utilizing a dramatic video wall backdrop and the latest staging technologies makes for an innovative experience for audience and performers alike.

This style of performance demands triple-threat singer/dancer/actor skills with full commitment to character, both physically and musically. Vocals, beyond a doubt, are at the forefront of the show, with most featuring a particularly talented soloist to drive the story.

Albertville High School's Centerstage! took a similar approach, but in a darker and more dramatic way. This group introduced goth rock to jazz hands with its 2009 "Faces" set, which featured special effects and themed costuming. The backdrop transformed from a street scene to a trio of large mirrors, to finally, a goth underworld of wraiths, ancient drummers, and goddess messengers.

This show aimed to create a journey for the audience through a threaded theme, and incorporated music and fashions from pop culture, film, and television.

SHOW CHOIR-GONE-MUSICAL

Although not necessarily a style, a "show choir–gone–musical" trend started to appear in the late '80s and recently gained popularity with a handful of high school show choirs. Inspired by Broadway, groups created abbreviated versions of the professional shows, adapting the timing and arrangements to meet the requirements of a fifteen-minute show choir set.

Popular with thespian-focused high schools, these choirs choose a musical around which to wrap their annual contest show. One year, they are swirling and twirling as Sharks and Jets in *West Side Story*, and the next, they are belting out tunes as they leave Anatevka dressed as Russian Jews from *Fiddler on the Roof*. This is their key component of their brand—the tone and personality of their shows differ from year to year, depending on the chosen musical.

John Burroughs Powerhouse **Star Wars** *show (2011).*

Powerhouse **Star Wars** *show (2011).*

Golden "wraiths" in the background to lighten the mood.

Albertville High School Centerstage, "Here's Who I Am" (2010).

The Irish band Gaelic Storm dramatically increased its popularity after being featured in the classic dance scene in *Titanic*, starring Leonardo DiCaprio and Kate Winslet.

Without the actual storyline accompanying the song-and-dance numbers, these types of shows often lack context, therefore never reaching their intended emotional potential. It's like catching the last scene of *Titanic* without committing to the first two hours. It's still sad. One might even shed a tear. But there has been no building of character, so there's less of a personal connection to the story.

Current show choir adjudication systems haven't supported or adjusted to this particular style. Although judges find such programs entertaining, judging sheets have yet to offer points for this "CliffsNotes Musicals" format, which is the most prevalent characteristic of such shows. These choirs ultimately get docked points for being too different, for their lack of variety, for their ease of choreography, and/or for the excessive use of solo or dance features. Mini Broadway musical elements certainly stand out in a show choir contest—so much that directors and judges have made the suggestion throughout the years that these types of groups develop their own, niche contest.

ALL IN THE NAME

Seymore Butts. Fatty McGee. Gaylord Focker.

No parents in their right mind would choose to name their children these names, knowing they have to spend their entire lives responding to those syllables. Parents-to-be instead overanalyze baby books and Web sites, envision grade school conflicts, and summon up names they've admired throughout the decades, to select the perfect identification for their offspring. Although they can't control what happens in the world after the birth certificate prints, at least the little ones can start off winners.

In the early days of a show choir, it's important—some would say crucial—to give the group's name substantial thought before embroidering team tote bags and water bottles.

The name should be memorable—something that's not going to get lost. Every group should have a label that stands out, that fits with the personality of the high school or town that will be supporting it. A strong name creates a solid foundation for a winning group.

Young Americans, Attaché, Powerhouse. These names capture the very spirit of the groups they represent. They offer an emotional calling and familiar footing that the performers can lock onto. These are also three choirs that have created a consistent image and continue to build and strengthen that reputation every year. In doing so, they have been nationally recognized countless times throughout the past few decades.

A NAME, A MOTIVATION

To understand the power of a name is to appreciate the science behind team motivation and inspiration.

John Burroughs Powerhouse didn't always have its showstopper title. When this California group started performing in the early '90s, it was known as simply the Chamber Choir.

During a particularly problematic sound check before the famous Aztec Sing competition, the group's choreographer, Jen Oundjian, sat the group down to

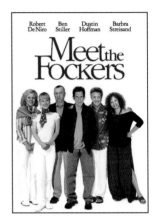

Anderson High School's Singers Unlimited was the first show choir to compete with a musical-style show (*Godspell*) at Bishop Luers in 1977 and 1979, under the direction of Rick Seaver.

WHO'S TO BLAME FOR THIS NAME?

Of the 1000-plus show choirs bopping around the United States, a handful have particularly unique and standout names. Hot or not?

BELLES ET BEAUX
French for "Guys and Girls," this Plainfield, Indiana, show choir is anything but plain and, ironically, their shows are anything but French.

HAPPINESS, INC.
Maybe this group from Cedar Rapids, Iowa, is so happy because it keeps winning.

CORNJERKER CONNECTION
Love. Love. Love. For their community choir name, these Hoopeston, Illinois, showstoppers drew inspiration from the history of the town and high school mascot. However, as many Midwestern high schools, no one ever questioned this name, chalking it up to tradition and to hometown pride.

HURRICANE RED HOTS
Though this Hurricane, West Virginia, show choir doesn't blow into town with sparkly red dresses and black tuxedos, their choreography and vocals always sizzle.

TESTOSTERTONES
As their name implies, this all-male a cappella group attracts attention and estrogen-charged fan clubs to shows in and around Whitman College. The performers' bar attire (jeans and collared shirts), mixed with a solid sound and catchy name, makes these Walla Walla, Washington, singers unforgettable.

Sioux City East's Headliners in classic red and black (2010).

figure out why the sound wasn't meshing and why the performers' vocals and energy were essentially lost. The group had, a year earlier, been diminished by the graduation of a large number of seniors.

Oundjian recalled, "They somehow felt that they weren't as good. And I kept thinking, 'These kids are amazing . . . He's a powerhouse, and she's a powerhouse. These are all powerhouse kids!'"

While she had no certainty this would work, she decided to rename the show choir, right then and there, "Powerhouse." Brendan Jennings, director of the group, wasn't sure whether the rebranding was a premeditated decision or a moment of creative desperation—but it worked. That night, the newly named Powerhouse took home the gold at Aztec Sing for the first time.

MORE THAN JUST A NAME

Once a group has nailed an appropriately motivating name, the style of show, from there, should support that branded selection. The music, the costumes, and the dancing should all align and flatter one another. It's helpful also to reflect the surrounding community, town or high school that supports the show choir.

This complementary equation isn't always easy to solve.

One of the best examples of a choir that's figured out this balance is CG Sound System in Greenwood, Indiana, a suburb of Indianapolis. The choir and its shows, year in and year out, reflect abundance and expense, but in a tactful and professional way. The performers sport expensive-looking costumes, and the productions promise beautiful and grand choreography and high production values. Most important, though, beyond all the glitz and glitter, the group's vocals also live up to its bold name.

When CG Sound System walks onstage, its fans know what to expect. the group's mere presence creates a feeling. Beyond the local standing ovations, the community supports the group in some of the same ways as they cheer on the local football team, with pride and admiration, bumper stickers, and T-shirts. *Show choir* is a common term in town.

Since it first graced the stage in 1973, CG Sound System has spent decades building up its brand. Each year, the group works to come up with a performance set that reflects the town, the parents, the school, and the spirit of its community. In doing so, the performers hone in on the pot at the end of the rainbow: They have supporters who show their appreciation through their applause and their checkbooks, and who are parents, grandparents, and alumni. Their fan club not only arrives for the performance but also invests in the shows, which is invaluable to both the spirit and the sustainability of the choir.

Beyond creating a local name, CG Sound System has achieved national recognition and acceptance as well. As with other well-established and well-branded show choirs, regional judges have come to associate the group with performance excellence, which isn't a bad reputation to have.

TAKE IT TO THE LIMIT

There are limitations to a well-branded show choir, but branding doesn't have to be boring. In a performance genre that is constantly evolving, some choirs see "sticking to character" as limiting or creatively

CG Sound System does its "Matrimony Mega-Mix" (Yes, the bride is on top of a giant wedding cake!). FAME Events, March 15, 2008.

stifling. Groups can, unfortunately, in a weak moment or out of boredom, forget about their once-captivated audience and loyal judges. They want to try out different styles to get a leg up on their competition or simply to attempt something new. But just like Michael Jordan testing out baseball, excelling at one style doesn't always transfer to excelling in another.

When a group veers away from its established style and tries to re-create its reputation, both fans and performers can become confused. A sudden change of character creates a moment of identity crisis, especially for an established show choir. The change has the ability to dilute the performance's "awe factor," which, for the audience of elite choirs, is more of an expectation than a revelation.

The expectation of excellence suddenly becomes an expectation for the unexpected, which is not as sexy as it sounds. No one wants to date someone who is funny one night and completely serious the next, with no explanation or warning. It's difficult to remain faithful to a sports team that goes on a winning streak, followed by a losing streak all season. Moviegoers often walk away disappointed if they think they're going to see a romantic comedy and it turns out to be a drama.

There's comfort in consistency.

An audience wants to connect to a show. It wants to wrap a performance up in a box and place it on the "Broadway" shelf or in the "Mash-Up" aisle. Performances, at the end of the day, should be entertaining—and if a group has discovered an equation that achieves entertainment, it should continue to go with it.

This is not to discourage adding variety and creativity to a show—or advancing beyond what's proven successful. Groups can, and often do, mix varieties together; for example, today's Broadway is pop, which lends well to swing, rock, and/or novelty numbers. It is unlikely, however, that the same group performing Cole Porter will be breaking out Lady Gaga—or at least successfully.

No one consciously decides to commit brand suicide. Before walking up to that ledge, show choir directors should think about the strengths and spirit of their group.

It's important to realize the talents of a particular group before throwing it onstage with an act that may not suit its character. Although middle-class suburban teenagers may listen to hip-hop on their iPod, few have the skills or life experience to effectively perform such material with any amount of believable "street cred."

When a group decides it's time to change styles, instead of opening the dramatic floodgates of change, it should consider making alterations gradually. For example, changing one element at a time, whether that's the name, the style of music, or the type of costumes, might be a more successful strategy than creating a whole new image that risks confusing or alienating established fans.

CHANGE IS IN THE AIR

Sometimes change and advancements are necessary. But to maintain consistency and avoid going overboard, a choir needs to a little strategy behind it to achieve success.

For example, Starbucks might not be dipping its toes into the children's toy market, but it has tried out wine and liquor sales in its test Seattle market. Like other market-leading companies, it is constantly trying to evolve and advance—as should a show choir that wants to stay fresh and become a leader.

In the land of show choirs, change often occurs at the end of a choreographer or director's era with the team. When there's a changing of the guard, new leadership can bring fresh ideas and perspective to a group. It's a good time to reexamine the group's mojo at these crossroads and see if there are areas for improvement that can further set it apart from the competition.

DRESSED TO IMPRESS

Attraction can be judged in less than a minute. And beyond the set, before the group starts singing or dancing, the audience critiques its costuming, its look. A show choir could have award-winning vocals and top-notch dancers, but if its costumes don't reflect the musical content, the audience and judges will be confused. Judges don't like those kinds of surprises, and groups shouldn't have to prove themselves to be better than their appearance.

Costumes should somehow reflect the attitude of the group's musical selection. This elicits the psychology behind colors, which is often underutilized in the outfitting of a choir. For example, for years, red and black was the winning costume color combination in Indiana. Red, representing energy, creates a sexy and exciting feeling for both the performers and the

SHOW CHOIR COSTUMES THROUGHOUT THE YEARS

2000s: Printed fabrics.

1980s: Stock dancewear.

Traditional colors, red and black.

1990s: Jumpsuits and bow ties.

2010: Goth/rock theatrical.

Golden What? "At least since the Renaissance, many artists and architects have proportioned their works to approximate the Golden Ratio . . . believing this proportion to be aesthetically pleasing. Mathematicians have studied the Golden Ratio because of its unique and interesting properties." —Mario Livio

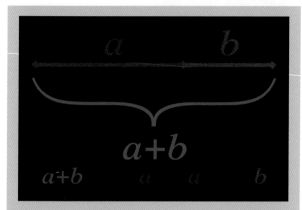

As explained in Mario Livio's book, *The Golden Ratio: The Story of Phi, the World's Most Astonishing Number*:

A straight line is said to have been cut in extreme and mean ratio when, as the whole line is to the greater segment, so is the greater to the lesser.

audience. Black represents luxury, class, and a little mystery. The two colors, red and black, side by side, are intriguing.

That's not to say every director or costume chair should select red and black attire for the performers. In fact, this look has become clichéd and is now associated with traditional, Indiana swing choirs. Today, more fabrics and colors are being incorporated into performances, and more groups are getting creative with their singing suits.

Whether making a creative statement or giving a nod toward traditional wear, a group's show is enhanced if the costumes fit the style of music, the attitude, and outlook of the characters being portrayed in the show. Bottom line: Select costumes based on the music, style, and overall brand of the choir. Own it, then wear it.

FUN + DA + MENTAL SHOW DESIGN

At competitions, audiences and judges will say it all the time: "That choir gets it," or "It really missed the mark." Designing a competitive show choir set isn't as hit or miss as those comments make it appear. Of course, the choral production must be solid. Whether one is singing pop or classical, vowels should be tall and lengthy. The choreography needs to be exciting and cleanly executed. Those elements are basic to the genre. The differentiating factor is show design.

Whereas competition show design requires strategic planning and finding a balance between stagecraft and music production, entertainment design can be attributed to classic artistic ratios.

As a choir steps onto a competitive stage, the spotlight on and the set in place, the odds are already against the performers. Eighty percent of a contest audience, made up of other competing choirs and their cheering squads, does not want them to succeed. It's a unique situation. Groups willingly participate in these competitions and festivals to entertain with a vengeance.

To make sure that vengeance isn't in vain, competitive show design has been developed to capitalize on controlling or swaying the audience's emotional response. Even though only 20 percent of those claps are genuine for the opening lineup, the goal is to woo the rest before the final bow. In the end, despite the uphill battle, this shouldn't be as hard as expected. Everyone, regardless of his or her seat in the audience, wants to be entertained.

One method of taking an audience over to the brighter side of applause is to ensure the program is aligned with the Golden Ratio—a mathematic equation that's been employed by artists throughout the years, from Galileo to Michelangelo—to ensure proper balance to a composition. The Golden Ratio itself is 1.62 with several more irrelevant (for this point) decimal numbers following the 2. The percentage equivalent is 0.618 percent.

What does that mean? For show design, employing Golden Ratio measurements can help determine the ebb and flow of everything from the overall dramatic structure of the show to individual songs.

In a traditional five-song contest show, the ballad is positioned either second or third in the lineup. Why? Because it simply "feels good." Opening with the ballad seems too much, too soon, and closing with the ballad seems like not enough, too late. That leaves slots 2, 3, or 4 for where the ballad could go. Placing the ballad second feels good; so does third. Fourth somehow feels "too late." Employing the Golden Ratio to the overall length of the show, the ballad would ideally peak (be most dramatic) at the golden proportion: 61.8 percent of the way through the show, or its opposite, 38.2 percent of the way into the show. It's not crazy talk. It's mathematics.

In ten minutes' worth of music, the "Golden Moment," or key moment, would occur around 6:18 minutes into the material. In a fifteen-minute performance, the crucial moment to shoot for is therefore 9:27.

It so happens, after years of trial and error, that show choir ballads tend to fall into the program at precisely the golden proportions. And the most successful show choirs, whether they plan it or not, tend to program not only their shows but their musical arrangements in golden proportions, as well. Most directors and choreographers instinctually program shows this way, without realizing it. Programming is so second nature, discussion isn't needed. And Golden Moments don't necessarily have to be associated with the ballad. They can be anything.

Through years of trial and error, musical theater writers have developed formulas to determine when something should happen in a script or score. Act one is always longer than act two in a Broadway show. The

In the 109-page script for the stage play *A Chorus Line* (a ninety-minute show performed without intermission), page 67 (the golden moment) is the Cassie's big dance feature. The dance number provides a show-stopping scene and delivers the theme, "Give me a job and somebody to dance for . . ."

The Golden Ratio made box office gold as well as the *New York Times* Best Seller List, as a prominent character in *The Da Vinci Code*. Both the book and the film have a thriller-style plot based upon the hidden use of golden proportions by Renaissance artist Michelangelo.

cliff-hanging ending or finale number of act one always climaxes with a blackout or the fall of the curtain, which is immediately followed by house lights for intermission. Uncannily, planned or not, that moment tends to fall 61.8 percent of the way through the show.

The Golden Ratio also drives the show's movements. It allows the group to produce emotional thrusts throughout the course of the fifteen-minute show. The best show designs create mini and micro Golden Ratios within the songs themselves. For example, in an eight-measure section (verse, chorus, or dance break), the Golden Moment would happen at measure five. That's where something new, exciting, visually dynamic, or surprising happens. Like tuning the bird to pop out of a German cuckoo clock, these surprises can be planned and timed in the initial stages of show design.

Within most pop music, the most intricate parts follow the center of the piece. In "Rockin' Robin," the 1959 Bobby Day classic–gone–show choir tune, the instrumental break and bridge of the song both occur just past center. The instrumental section then mixes up the otherwise ABAB song formation. To the regular ear, this just makes the song catchy. But it wasn't a random choice. Robin wouldn't be rocking without the Golden Ratio.

Notice where the instrumental break and bridge occur. This seems obvious—aren't all pop songs set up this way—with the dance break or bridge in approximately the same place? Yes. This is the same golden moment or section that appears in most commercial time-based art from pop music on the radio, to Broadway theater to show choir contest shows.

Intentionally or not, the most successful competitive groups manage to hit this classic ratio, not only within their individual songs, but also within the entire length of their shows.

SECONDARY RATIO

There's also a Secondary Ratio that can be considered for a show's "big moment," or spotlight of interest. The Secondary Ratio is the mirror opposite of the Golden Ratio—at the 38.2 percent mark. It's the Golden Ratio's reflective time that allows for an additional statement.

Applied in a fifteen-minute competition show, this Secondary Ratio would fall at 6:49 minutes into the program. Clinton's Attaché fully embraced the Sec-

Verse	Chorus	Verse	Chorus	Instr.	Bridge	Verse	Chorus
A	B	A	B	C	D	A	B

Attaché boys' numbers have often happened just past the midpoint in the competition show, setting up the closing production sequence.

ondary Ratio. For years, their ballad almost always followed the opener. At the Secondary Ratio point, the ballad ended dramatically and the finale production sequence began. The "primary" Golden Moment was reserved for a showstopping men's feature, a dynamic shift in the set pieces, or both.

However, David and Mary Fehr, the creative team behind the Attaché show design, did not credit the Golden and Secondary ratios for the development of the Attaché shows. David commented:

> Math doesn't really come into it. I sit down at the piano and play through the show—I trust my feelings. If I'm bored or something feels like it's going on too long, I think, "Okay, something here has to give . . . needs to change up." There's no math to it— just gut feeling.

Yet, somehow, Attaché shows manage to hit the same classical ratios year after year.

Achieving the Golden Ratio establishes balance with a different sequence. The traditional show choir show structure typically opens with a high-energy number to wake up the audience, followed by a novelty

Leonardo da Vinci's *Mona Lisa* provides an example of the flipped Golden Ratio in classical painting.

Can you spot the two golden sections? Hint: One is in the foreground; the other, in the background.

number to "get them to like you"—something that tells a humorous story through the lyrics or choreography (a stylized number). At that point, both the group and the audience are ready to slow down and connect with the music. This is where the vocal production is crucial. If the ballad peaks at the Golden Ratio, the group has successfully achieved the classical proportions that have intrigued musicians and artists for centuries. It's a quick, easy, and happy ending for everyone.

Both the Golden and Secondary ratios provide a psychological balance unnoticed by most audience members yet subconsciously appreciated. It feels natural, comfortable.

WHAT THE AUDIENCE UNDERSTANDS

Beyond the mumbo-jumbo mathematical equations that can apply to a show choir's success, there are also fundamental factors that are more obvious and that require more creativity than calculators. They are mastered with research, information, and innovation, not mathematics.

THEME

A show's theme is the headline of the performance. It's the decorative ribbon that wraps up all the musical numbers into a comprehensible reason for the season. It's the message a group offers an audience. Ideally, this can be defined by a single, emotionally driven statement. Like a movie, a theme should allow the audience to see through a single character's worldview. The songs and lyrics should demonstrate a scene in the life of a specific character. If they are delivered honestly, the audience becomes more involved in the performance.

Before choosing a theme, the group should consider the audience—just as carefully as when selecting the name. Groups with even the strongest reputations that carry energetic, standout names have alienated audiences after choosing a weird or unrelatable theme. Unlike a classical concert where audiences can enjoy an hour or an evening of music with themes ranging from "colors," to "seasons," to the heavily intellectual (artsy) works of a certain composer or period—show choir competition shows require less abstract themes.

The contest venue presents a timed parade of ensembles back to back, each with about twenty-five minutes to set up, to make a point, to be spectacular, both visually and musically, and hopefully, capture the audience's imagination and respect before striking the set and exiting the stage within their allotted time.

Furthermore, because the show is meant to be competitive—the music chosen must be appropriate and effective for forty to fifty singers and feature dance breaks, transitional material, costume changes, and special effects—in other words, be theatrical. And theater needs thematic structure (no matter how ambiguous) to be coherent.

> You need three things in theater—the play, the actors and the audience—and each must give something. —Kenneth Haigh, British actor

George M. Cohan, a famous vaudeville song-and-dance man, most well known for his role as the "Yankee Doodle boy" was one of the first to coin a personal performance theme. Cohan, who was as Irish as a leprechaun, incorporated the American flag into his staging whenever possible. At a time where there was huge anti-Irish sentiment in America, this brand and theme helped him win over the audience and prove he was a patriotic Irishman— who could sing and dance.

Today there are several different types of themes that show choirs deliver to audiences:

REVUE THEME

In a revue-themed show, all the songs have a like component, such as they all hail from the same musical, are written by the same composer, or are from around the same era. Oftentimes, groups that employ this style select all-Broadway songs or decade favorites (e.g., '60s *Billboard* hits). The key element to maintaining an audience's interest is to create a smooth transition from each song to the next. Costuming and set design can serve as complements but neither should change the overarching style.

STORY THEME

In a story-themed show, all the songs are tied together by an underlying thread or philosophical message such as, "Life is bowl of cherries," or "Freedom is the right of all mankind," or "You can make a difference." The songs are chosen to make a point, take the audience

Famous for his classic hit "Give My Regards to Broadway," George M. Cohan still holds a place on Broadway as the subject of the only statue erected for a performer in New York City's Times Square.

on a journey, and deliver a message. Most show choirs fall into this category. The costuming serves to match the music, and the set design is functional and generic enough to go with any song in the show.

CONCEPT THEME

Like a story-themed show, a concept-themed show communicates an overall message or worldview. This kind of show, however, takes storytelling a step further to incorporate stylized, and often theatrical, costuming, staging, and choreography. Greater attention is placed on set design, on creating an elaborate environment to bring the story to life. The concept musical is by default expensive, because its purpose is to transform the entire stage through illusion. For example, Burbank in 2010 produced a show called *Man vs. Media*, illustrating the concept of the dangers of being overconsumed by technology. Songs included:

> "Mr Roboto" (Styx)
> "Leonardo Dreams of His Flying Machine"
>   (Eric Whitacre)
> "Supermassive Black Hole" (Muse)
> "Hide in Your Shell" (Supertramp)
> "2000 Watts" (Michael Jackson)
> "They Don't Really Care About Us"
>   (Michael Jackson)
> "Life on Mars" (David Bowie)
> "Cloudburst" (Eric Whitacre)
> "Human" (The Killers)

MUSICAL THEATER THEME

Musical theater themes, or as previously referred to as "show choir–gone–musicals," borrow styles from musicals—story- and concept-themed shows. Using music from the same composer (the musical theme), this style sets out to tell a story or underlying message (the story theme), supported by specific theatrical costuming and choreography the (concept theme). Although such productions may not typically win competitions, given the complexities behind mastering all three themes, groups that employ this type of theme hear only positive reviews from performers and their fans.

"Our students love it," commented Karen Luher, director, Sauk Prairie. "Some things never grow old."

THEME COMPONENTS

From vaudeville to VJs, themes have always helped tell the story and create a meaningful performance. Other important elements that communicate to the audience include:

FUNCTION

Function gives purpose to a song, prop, transition, or costume by helping to move the story along or shape the theme. Placing importance on function discourages dancing just to move, choosing a costume strictly because of its color, or making unnecessary transitions to new blocking. Every element of the show has a reason and a purpose behind it.

SIMILARITY

Even without its outwardly shouting a choir's theme, the audience should pick up on the general emotion behind that theme by watching how one element of the show marries the idea of another element; by seeing the similarities between the song choices, costumes, and staging.

CONTRAST

The need for variety is answered when even Grandma and Grandpa sitting in the front row can see how one element differs from a previous element.

REPETITION

Awareness of repetition can be a good or bad thing. A crowd will pick up on a choreographer's favorite dance move, which is often repeated throughout the show in not-so-different ways. They will also recognize an element introduced in the opener that is later thrown back to the audience, creating a storybook feeling. Use repetition with caution. It can strengthen or weaken the show's originality.

VARIATION

Variation allows for repetition with a kick. True show choir fans will be able to recognize when choirs tweak their signature elements over a given period of time. It's a way of doing the same thing every year—only differently.

DEVELOPMENT

Given an audience's inherent need to "get it," to find the connection and to arrive at an understanding, it

Sauk Prairie High Schools Executive Session has become known for its musical-themed show choir sets.

shouldn't be surprising that a crowd will look for a storyline or theme. The audience is searching for a thread of meaning. It's important for a group to introduce the topic or theme and develop it.

UNITY/DISUNITY

Be it cleanly or sloppily done, the faces hidden in the dark auditorium will notice as a choir enacts, or tries to enact, a visual or audible moment. The performance will determine whether it communicates the idea with unity and balance or confusion and randomness. This is a choreographer's tool—but something that audiences notice.

BUT DOES IT WORK?

One of the most overused phrases in marketing is, "You can lead a horse to water, but you can't make it drink." A brand can spend millions of dollars to produce a Super Bowl ad that sweeps all the national advertising awards and is featured on every "Best of" blog review the day after the Big Game. But if the product doesn't live up to its hype, consumers are probably going to lose interest fast.

In a world surrounded by sparkle and spandex, mastering the art of branding will only take a show choir so far. There has to be talent supporting its foundation of creativity, mathematics, and passion.

While it's always good to shoot for the moon, show choirs, as amateur, unpaid extracurricular performing arts groups, shouldn't stress out about being the best at everything. The groups that tend to come out swinging at the stars are the teams who are able to focus and become experts in two of the four elements of show choir: singing, dancing, instrumental ensemble, or production (design, flow, effects, music selection)

Two is an easy and understandable number, and people take notice. A group that can excel at two aspects of the performance will be remembered. As audience members leave the theater, they'll comment on the impressive band or staging or the choral sound. Some may even remember the set pieces or theme of the show. The more memorable the elements, the better chance a group has of creating a brand for itself. Master any two of the four elements and the brand will be remembered.

If a group is able to dig into the details of the genre and style that it has mastered, the horse will drink. Just do it.

WATCH IT

1979 The 26th Street Singers
www.youtube.com/watch?v=4gIZmFJMReo

1980 Edgewood Music Warehouse
www.youtube.com/watch?v=SYCBYDVk5oE

1985 Carmel Ambassadors
www.youtube.com/watch?v=PxFTvswYbIc&feature=related

1986 Mt. Zion Swingsations' "Who Put the Bop?"
www.youtube.com/watch?v=8XpZVp3vBZ4

1996 Cedar Rapids Jefferson West Side Delegation "Laughing Song"
www.youtube.com/watch?v=j_qZ6cUIz-M&feature=related

2006 Happiness, Inc. "Chicago Medley"
www.youtube.com/watch?v=pHYpYigdWJE

2007 Testostertones "Waiting on the World"
www.youtube.com/watch?v=3GOGZO8XH04

2008–2009 Buffalo Grove Expressions Part 2
www.youtube.com/watch?v=qMpiz5aksUw&feature=related

2009 Sauk Prairie Executive Session "Bugsy Malone"
www.youtube.com/watch?v=JEQcspUc46Q

2010 Waubonsie Valley "Black or White"
www.youtube.com/watch?v=5g53H6k0iLk

2010 John Burroughs Powerhouse "Vogue" on Oprah
www.youtube.com/watch?v=ThiidVcHbmg

2010 Hurricane Red Hots "If You're Out There"
www.youtube.com/watch?v=rzlte2Yk55s

2010 Center Grove CG Sound System Opener
www.youtube.com/watch?v=C58OoAWjzCg

The Counterpoints, from North Central High School in Indianapolis, Indiana, are directed by Patricia Wiehe.

THE FACES OF
SHOW CHOIR TODAY
10

> I stayed who I was and therefore, stayed unique in my art.

—DAMON BROWN, SHOW CHOIR CHOREOGRAPHER

As a mature and now well-known performance genre, show choirs are bringing a confident energy and unique sparkle to stages throughout the United States. To illustrate their vast presence throughout the country, the following pages present the faces of show choir today.

ALABAMA

Albertville High School's CenterStage!, from Albertville, Alabama, is directed by Scott Rains and Natasha Tidmore.

Enterprise High School's Encores, from Enterprise, Alabama, is under the direction of John Baker.

Opelika High School's Ovations, from Opelika, Alabama, is directed by Darren Dale. One of the most famous former Ovations members is T. J. Jackson, the former defensive tackle for the Atlanta Falcons and the Kansas City Chiefs.

ARIZONA

Horizon High School's Step on Stage, from Scottsdale, Arizona, is under the direction of Katherine Kouns.

CALIFORNIA

Bonita Vista High School's the Music Machine, from Bonita Vista, California, is under the direction of Roxanne Ronacher.

Masquerade, from Brea Olinda High School in Brea, California, is under the direction of Dave Willert.

In Sync, from Burbank High School in Burbank, California, is under the direction of Brett Carroll.

Powerhouse, from John Burroughs High School in Burbank, California, is under the direction of Brendan Jennings.

The Young Americans, "America's oldest show choir," based in Corona, California, is under direction of Milt C. Anderson.

Los Alamitos High School's Sound FX, from Los Alamitos, California, is under the direction of David Moellenkamp.

Hart High School's SoundVibrations, from Newhall, California, is under the direction of Gail Hart.

COLORADO

Up with People, the international goodwill ambassadors for cultural education and entertainment, based in Denver, Colorado, is under the music direction of Michael Bowerman.

FLORIDA

Syndicated Sound, from Tarpon Springs High School in Tarpon Springs, Florida, is under the direction of Charles Cheeseman.

GEORGIA

Lakeside High School's Soundsation, from Evans, Georgia, is under the direction of Stacy Branch.

ILLINOIS

Crete-Monee High School's Cavaliers, from Crete, Illinois, is directed by Robert Mohr, with assistance from Tamyka Kimbrough.

Elite Energy, from Eisenhower High School in Decatur, Illinois, is under the direction of Scott Hines.

Danville High School's Delegation, from Danville, Illinois, is under the direction of Marty Lindvahl.

Swingsations, from Mount Zion High School in Mt. Zion, Illinois, is under the direction of Michael Winslow.

Great Expectations, from O'Fallon, Illinois, is under the direction of Jamie Lynn Marble.

The Sullivan Singers, from Sullivan High School in Sullivan, Illinois, is under the direction of Connie Checkley Mulligan.

Sound Check, from Waubonsie Valley High School in Aurora, Illinois, is directed by Mark Myers.

The Wheaton Warrenville High School Classics, from Wheaton, Illinois, is under the direction of John Burlace.

INDIANA

The Singing Hoosiers, from Indiana University in Bloomington, Indiana, are under the direction of Dr. Michael Schwartzkopf.

The Carmel High School Ambassadors, from Carmel, Indiana, are under the direction of Lamonte Kuskye and Ann Conrad.

Edgewood High School's Music Warehouse, from Ellettsville, Indiana, is under the direction of Verda Savage.

The Minstrels, from Bishop Luers High School in Fort Wayne, Indiana, are under the direction of Karlene Krouse.

Carroll High School's Minstrel Magic, from Fort Wayne, Indiana, is under the direction of Jill Jeran.

Homestead High School's Class Royale, from Fort Wayne, Indiana, is under the direction Curtis Shaw.

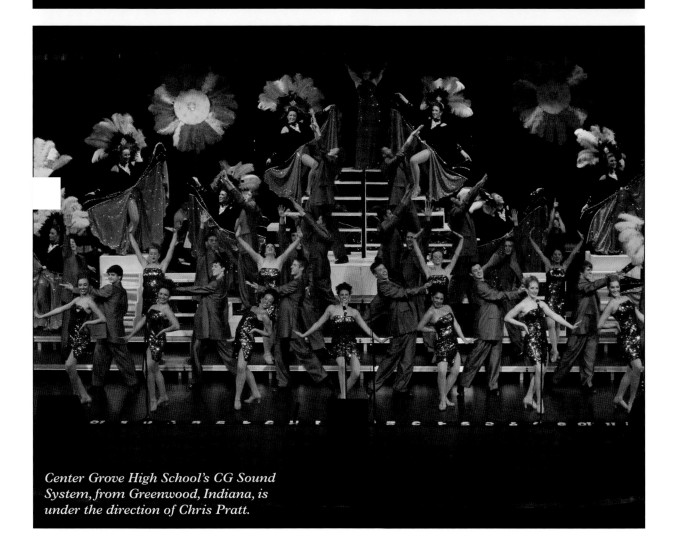

Center Grove High School's CG Sound System, from Greenwood, Indiana, is under the direction of Chris Pratt.

Chesterton High School's Sandpipers, from Chesterton, Indiana, is under the direction of Christopher Brush.

The Franklin Central Singers, from Franklin Central High School in Indianapolis, Indiana, are under the direction of Bradley Gardner.

Dekalb High School's Classic Connection, from Waterloo, Indiana, is under the direction of Shelley Johnson.

The Varsity Singers, from Huntington North High School in Huntington, Indiana, are under the direction of John Wenning.

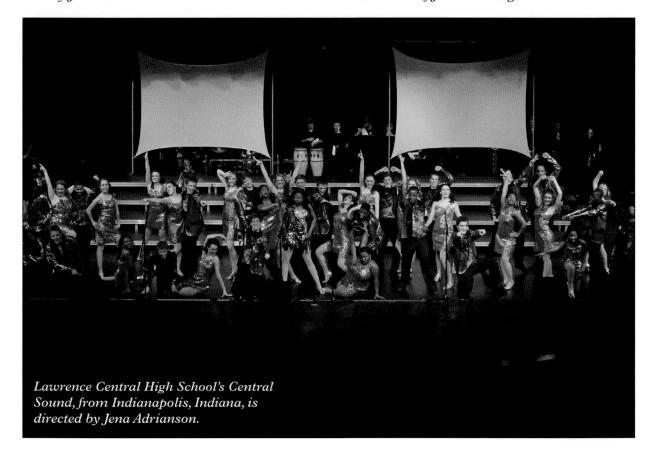

Lawrence Central High School's Central Sound, from Indianapolis, Indiana, is directed by Jena Adrianson.

First Edition, from Jefferson High School in Lafayette, Indiana, is under the direction of David Barnhouse.

The Ball State Singers from Ball State University in Muncie, Indiana, are under the direction of Alan Alder.

Norwell High School's Knight Moves, from Ossian, Indiana, is under the direction of Carla Doles.

Shelbyville High School's Synergy, from Shelbyville, Indiana, is under the direction of Joel Kenemore.

Zionsville High School's Royalaires, from Zionsville, Indiana, are under the director of Aaron Coates.

IOWA

West Side Delegation, from Jefferson High School in Cedar Rapids, Iowa, is under the direction of Byron Schlotterback.

Plainfield High School's Belles et Beaux from Plainfield, Indiana, is under the direction of Jonelle Heaton.

Momentum, from Washington High School in Cedar Rapids, Iowa, is under the direction of Dr, Gerald Kreitzer.

The East High School Headliners, from Sioux City, Iowa, are under the direction of Heath Weber.

KANSAS

The Headliners, from Butler Community College in El Dorado, Kansas, are under the direction of Valerie Lippoldt-Mack.

MASSACHUSETTS

Fantasy, from Shepherd Hill Regional High School in Dudley/Charlton, Massachusetts, is under the direction of Connie Vanco Galli, assisted by Greg "Bubba" Bussiere.

MINNESOTA

Totino-Grace High School's Company of Singers, from Fridley, Minnesota, is directed by Terry Voss.

Hastings High School's Riverside Company, from Hastings, Minnesota, is directed by Lin Warren.

MISSISSIPPI

Clinton High School's Attaché, from Clinton, Mississippi, is directed by David and Mary Fehr. Most notable alumni of the group include Lance Bass ('N Sync), Keith Carlock (drummer for Sting and Steely Dan), Shelly Fairchild (recording artist), and April James (show choir choreographer).

South Jones High School's Company, from Ellisville, Mississippi, is under the direction of Jonathan McKenzie.

MISSOURI

The Hillside Singers, from Pleasant Hill High School in Pleasant Hill, Missouri, are under the direction of Karen Dollins.

City Lights, from Rockbridge High School in Columbia, Missouri, is directed by Mike Pierson.

Troy Buchanan High School's TBHS Express, from Troy, Missouri, is directed by Andre Drinkall, with assistance from Ava Peitzman and Cara Jennings.

NEBRASKA

14 Karat Gold, from Northwest High School in Grand Island, Nebraska, is directed by Dave Sackschewsky, with assistance from Cindy Coe.

The Big Red Singers, from the University of Nebraska in Lincoln, Nebraska, are under the direction of Dr. Peter Eklund and Stephen Todd.

The Amazing Technicolor Show Choir, from Westside High School in Omaha, Nebraska, is under the direction of Doran Johnson.

NEW MEXICO

La Cueva High School's Main Street, from Albuquerque, New Mexico, is under the direction of Deanna Amend.

NEW YORK

Greece Athena Show Choir, from Greece Athena High School in Rochester, New York, is under the direction of Judith A. Ranaletta. The group was featured in the British documentary Gleeful. Dozens of Athena Show Choir alumni have gone on to pursue professional careers in the performing arts, including Donna Lynne Champlin (2007 Obie Award–winner for best actress), Kevin Greene, Rylyn Juliano, Frankie Paparone, and Aaron Serotsky.

Crescendo, from Calhoun High School in Merrick, New York, is under the direction of Sanford Sardo.

OHIO

The Choraliers, from Fairfield High School in Fairfield, Ohio, are under the direction of Jeff S. Clark.

E.T.C. All Americans, from Akron, Ohio, was founded more than thirty years ago by Robert Heid and Robert Carlyon and is currently directed by Carolyn Bagley.

Findlay High School's First Edition, from Findlay, Ohio is under the direction Kevin Manley, with assistance from Dan Wilson.

Swingers Unlimited, from Marysville High School in Marysville, Ohio, is under the direction of Katie Paulson-Silcott.

OKLAHOMA

The Trojanaires, from Jenks High School in Jenk, Oklahoma, are under the direction of Larry Downey and Julie Hester.

TEXAS

Central High School's Voices of Central, from Keller, Texas, is under the direction of Jen Randall.

WEST VIRGINIA

A Touch of Class, from Benton Community Schools in Chantilly, West Virginia, is under the direction of Glenn Cockrell. In 2010, the group was voted "America's Favorite Show Choir" by Parade *magazine.*

Winfield High School's General Admission, from Winfield, West Virginia, is under the direction of Jeff Haught.

WISCONSIN

Center Stage, from Preble High School in Green Bay, Wisconsin, is under the direction of Kevin J. Flogel.

Grand Central Station, from Central High School in La Crosse, Wisconsin, is under the direction of Mike Esser.

The Wisconsin Singers, from the University of Wisconsin-Madison, in Madison, Wisconsin, are under the direction of Robin Whitty-Novotny.

The Kids from Wisconsin, from the Wisconsin State Fair Park Youth Center in Milwaukee, Wisconsin, are produced by Mark Dorn, directed by Taras Nahirniak.

The Hilltoppers, from Onalaska High School in Onalaska, Wisconsin, are under the direction of by Chad R. Lindblom.

Sauk Prairie High School's Executive Session, from Prairie Du Sac, Wisconsin, is under the direction Karen Luher and Susan Holloway.

Bridgwater College Show Choir.

PART 11

FINALE: SHOW CHOIR MATURES, SPARKLES WITH *GLEE*

A love for music and the desire to shine in the spotlight in some small way are things that most of us can share in common. It's this feeling that makes us want to cheer for the underdog characters ... who are brave enough to put themselves on the line and sing with such heart.

—IAN BRENNAN, WRITER/EXECUTIVE PRODUCER OF FOX TELEVISION'S HIT SHOW *GLEE*

Losers. Geeks. Chorus nerds. Stage aliens. Glitter gleeks.

Despite all the nicknames and years of teasing, show choirs have survived. Instead of working against the name-calling, they have embraced those taunting titles and pledged to prove them right at any chance. There is no shame in their game. When groups strut onto stage, an air of pride and an unapologetic confidence follows them.

The chorus nerds have come into their own and heads are turning. People who had previously never heard of show choirs are taking notice.

TEAM OF TALENT

Although portrayed as outcasts in the show, the real-life actors of *Glee* run around with a notably talented team.

Matthew Morrison, a.k.a. the enthusiastic and sensitive high school teacher and glee club director Mr. Schuester, hails from the theaters of Broadway and, even better, the year 2000 boy band, LMNT.

Jane Lynch, otherwise known as Sue Sylvester and coach of the school's Cheerios cheerleading squad, brings to the show an award-winning seasoned past of live theater, television, and movies.

Lea Michele, who plays the overly dramatic but talented spotlight-hogging Rachel, grew up on Broadway, starring as "Young Cosette" in *Les Misérables* when she was eight years old.

Mark Salling, the bad-ass choir kid Puck, came to *Glee* as a classically trained pianist and a man of many musical talents, including guitar, bass, and drums.

Heather Morris, who took on the intellectually challenged character of Brittany, came to *Glee* with an extensive dancing background, and was once asked to tour with Beyoncé's *I Am . . . Sasha Fierce* world tour.

Jenna Ushkowitz, who portrays the timid and insecure Tina, contributes to the *Glee* lineup while also bringing real-life glee club perspective, as the former president of Select Choir, the show choir–like performing group at her high school.

One by one and geek by gleek, show choirs are reviving reputations and converting fans at a record pace.

ALL A *GLEE*

Show choir was in the right place at the right time when it caught the eye of writer, producer, and director Ryan Murphy. In 2009, Murphy and FOX Broadcasting Company took this maturing phenomenon and converted it into a network television comedy series and pop sensation, *Glee*. The mash-up-style dramcom is based on the simple yet intriguing world of high school show choir.

In its freshman season, the cast was presented as group of misfits from William McKinley High School in Lima, Ohio, who came together to form a struggling show choir. As the show progresses, it follows a combination of geeks and jocks as they go about trying to earn respect from their peers, despite the occasional slushie-in-the-face greetings they receive.

For a show that basically launched, "Once upon a show choir," the glee club portion really acts as a supporting role, if not a backdrop, to its drama and weekly production numbers. The focus of the story is a group of very different teenagers, who, while attempting to survive the halls of high school, are brought together by music—and by their Justin Timberlake–look-alike teacher, Mr. Schuester. Each episode's storyline introduces a soundtrack of songs that underscores the plot and emotional state of the characters.

The show features popular songs ranging from Broadway to current top 40 hits. But it doesn't stop there. Instead of simply covering modern pop artists' songs, the show regularly features cameos by the actual artists themselves. The Big Deals of Hollywood are knocking down the doors of *Glee*, hoping for a chance to step onto the auditorium stage of William McKinley High School. In just two seasons, the show has welcomed a series of A-list celebrity guests and walk-ons, including Gwyneth Paltrow, Carol Burnett, John Stamos, Britney Spears, Kristin Chenoweth, Idina Menzel, Jonathan Groff, Molly Shannon, Olivia Newton-John, and Neil Patrick Harris.

It's both completely realistic and wildly unbelievable. The characters on the show are real—not in a "reality show" way, but in a relatable way. And their problems are true-to-life issues faced by teenagers throughout the world. Although the show has brought only positive attention to the amateur performing arts world, every real gleek knows Glee isn't meant to be a documentary on show choirs.

There's a story to show choirs that goes beyond its scripts. This narrative, untold to the audience or FOX viewing network, plays out behind the scenes and away from the camera. The sweat, the ankle sprains, the sore throats, the eight-hour rehearsals, and the sleep-deprived road trips, balanced with schoolwork as well as family and friend obligations, make show choir lives exciting yet hectic. Beyond a love of the stage, performing requires a significant amount of commitment and energy.

Onstage, there are also several drastic differences. As opposed to the no-rehearsal-let's-go style of performing, a show choir spends months perfecting the typically five songs in their set. And while there are many elaborate productions and expensive sets, there has yet to be a show choir that's successfully pulled off a waterfall of rain for a rendition of Rihanna's "Umbrella" mashed with the classic "Singing in the Rain." Yet.

Glee is show choir–gone–fantasy. Although real-life show choirs worked for decades to strike a perfect harmonized balance between pop culture and traditional choral ensembles, in just two seasons Glee figured out a way to nail it every week. The show consumes the most entertaining aspects of Broadway, teenage melodrama, music videos, celebrity, pop culture, and social media . . . and then, unsurprisingly, delivers success

Glee is show choir's idol.

A POP OF CULTURE

. . . And with reason to idolize. Beyond an all-star cast and stellar plot, the show was set up for success from the first note. The pilot strategically aired for the first time after FOX's *American Idol*, offering it a prime-time opportunity to win over not only the show choir–loving counties of Indiana and Ohio, but also the short attention spans of viewers of all kinds.

From the beginning, well-known musical numbers and pop hits were to be included in each hourlong episode. This was a simple yet brilliant idea. Instantly, at the end of each episode, the show's music was available to the viewing audience to download and enjoy. This kept *Glee* top-of-mind and top-of-playlist for its fans and opened up an entirely new revenue stream for FOX Television Network and iTunes.

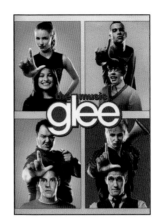

When the Young Americans performed on *The Red Skelton Show* in the mid-'60s, the choir's director, Milton C. Anderson, planned on doing a rendition of "Singing in the Rain." Skelton suggested that they make it rain. Although expensive to do, the show's producers like the idea so much that stagehands were asked to rig the studio so that it could "rain" onstage. During the performance, everyone thought it went off without a hitch, but upon viewing the segment on television, it became clear that the viewing audience wasn't able to see the rain. The crew had used the wrong mixture of coloring in the water to make it visible for the camera. The rain had blended into the background.

I'D LIKE TO THANK . . .

The success of *Glee* shed a brighter spotlight on the show choir genre than ever before, but it also created quite the impression in the larger entertainment industry. Awards achieved by the cast and crew include:

2009 Artios Award from the Casting Society of America for Outstanding Achievement in Casting for a TV Comedy Pilot

2010 Golden Globe Best Comedy Series

2010 Screen Actors Guild for Best Ensemble in Comedy Series

2010 People's Choice Award for Favorite New Television Comedy

2010 Satellite Award Nominations for Best Television Series, Comedy or Musical; Best Actor in TV Series, Comedy (Matthew Morrison)

2011 Golden Globe for Best Television Series, Comedy or Musical; Best Performance by an Actress in a Supporting Role in a Series, Mini-Series or Motion Picture Made for Television (Jane Lynch); Best Performance by an Actor in a Supporting Role in a Series, Mini-Series, or Motion Picture Made for Television (Chris Colfer)

Ian Brennan, screenwriter for *Glee* and former show choir member at Prospect High School just outside of Chicago, wanted to create a show about the unique teenagers who join these groups to express themselves.

In an interview from the book *Gleeful* by Amy Rickman, Brennan said:

I find it interesting that there is something in everybody, a longing for something transcendent . . . there's this desire to shine. That's fascinating and very funny to me, especially when people try to accomplish this through show choir—which, to me, is inherently a little ridiculous.

The show has attracted more than 14 million viewers, spawned 25 *Billboard* Hot 100 hits, resulted in more than 16 million downloaded songs, and converted countless gleeks.

Suddenly, *show choir* was a common term and "Glee" was a top Google search term. Chorus nerds of today and yesterday were stepping out of the show choir closet with the show's symbolic L on their forehead. They had come out loud and proud.

THE *GLEE* EFFECT

Oscar Wilde once said, "Life imitates art far more than art imitates life."

The roots and inspiration of *Glee* can be traced back to high school show choirs and national competitions, but the "*Glee* effect" taking place in the rehearsal halls and competition spaces is an even richer story.

In addition to attracting more participants and making singing and dancing cool again, *Glee* illustrates the power of singing with purpose, of making the show part of a larger story. More show choirs are connecting songs in meaningful ways and finding honest perspectives, relatable to the group and its audience. As on *Glee*, this allows real-life performers to play out the songs more authentically and from the heart.

It's important to note that, even in this *Glee*-obsessed genre, competitive show choirs are not trying to be more than they are. Pre– or post–New Directions, the fact remains the same: Show choir is rooted in the traditions of vaudeville and musical revue shows and was never conceived to be a deep or heavy performance genre. It's always been—and most likely always will be—light and entertaining.

In the words of Hal Malcolm, "It has to swing." To play the game now, given today's *Glee*-savvy audiences, a touch of honesty and a dash of human emotions are required. With that equation set to music, everyone wins.

Sometimes real-life productions are carefully crafted to be based on the choir's brand or style, whereas, other times, groups read between the lines, finding their own personal meaning in the notes and staves.

In 2007, Enterprise High School's Encore show choir filled their fifteen-minute set with a typical mix of pop-inspired songs that included Otis Redding's "I Can See Clearly Now," a mash-up of "A Better Place (9/11 Tribute)" by Michelle Williams and "Life" by Maurice White, "Stand Up for Love," recorded by Destiny's Child, and "DJ Medley," the last of which ironically included the title "You Spin Me Round" by Dead or Alive. For being early in their contest season, it was a solid performance. The show had all the elements needed for success: a theme, strong vocals, and practiced—and nearly perfected—choreography.

Then, tragically, on March 1, 2007, five days after Encore hosted their inaugural show choir invitational, a devastating tornado struck the city. Eight students from the school were killed—three of whom were members of the show choir.

Two weeks after their school was destroyed, Encore headed to Show Choir Nationals competition. What had formerly been five songs became a message the group had come to deliver. The lyrics took on an entirely new meaning. They won the competition that year, dedicating their performance to their friends whom they'd lost.

It is often at these times, when emotions are high and—most important—real, that groups rally to give some of their most heartfelt and energized performances.

PUTTING THE GEEKS IN GLEEKS

To capture these memorable moments, show choirees have relied on their nerd counterparts—computer geeks—to develop technology that allows groups to collect, share, and analyze their performances. And the techies have not let them down. In the past decade, social networks have enabled advancements in show choirs that go beyond sharing links to the latest *Glee* episode.

As YouTube, with all of its video-sharing greatness, has become a common area for the choir community, staging also has become noticeably more eye popping. Audiences are no longer limited to just the fans in the auditorium. Everyone has a camera. Everyone is a star.

Choreographers, at the same time, also have easier and quicker access to music videos, musical numbers, and dance material to gain inspiration for their work. Every show choir performance, whether it has two or two hundred live audience members, now has the potential to have 2 million viewers with a simple point and click. Reputations are both on the line and online.

Parents, performers, and the entire show choir world have become hooked on YouTube for researching new trends as well as critiquing and rehearsing competition sets.

Show Choir Camps of America has incorporated

"The hardest part of *Glee* in particular is that we are singing and dancing on a real stage with a camera right there in your face, following you around while you're dancing."
—Jenna Ushkowitz, cast member (Tina), *Glee*

"The risqué scandals and exaggerated conflicts seen on *Glee* often seem strangely similar to actual events in the show choir world . . . with the overinvolved parents, attention-seeking performers, and controversial administrative or 'judicial' decisions . . . I think the absurd practices of a group like Vocal Adrenaline are even funnier to those familiar with show choir because we know that they aren't terribly far from the truth." — Anna Whiteway, GCS Show Choir at Central High School, La Crosse, Wisconsin

Prior to the pilot episode, Ryan Murphy and the production team for *Glee* spent numerous hours on YouTube, watching and studying the top-ranked show choirs in the Midwest. Eventually, they began to work with Burbank High School's show choirs for counsel and those became the inspiration for *Glee*'s hypothetical rival show choir, Vocal Adrenaline.

The Show Choir Community Web site began as a news and network site for its creator, Häakon Sundry's, own Chula Vista, California, show choir—Bonita Vista's Music Machine—in 1997. Sundry soon expanded the site to include all show choirs in Southern California. In 2002, it grew into to what it is today: Showchoir.com—the online membership-based destination for all things show choir.

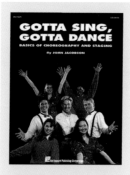

GOING VIRAL

John Jacobson, a choreographer within the show choir world known for his clean-cut image and yellow button-down shirt, gained national recognition after his instructional *Double Dream Hands* video hit YouTube. Originally meant as an instructional video for *Planet Rock*, the 2:47-minute clip, instructing viewers to "rock out," "crank it," and use their "Double Dream Hands," was viewed by more than 3.2 million YouTube users.

The *Glee* Facebook page has more than 15 million fans–and continues to grow daily.

YouTube into its regular curriculum. During the summer camp, instructors set up video cameras to capture the rehearsal and dance instructions. When the participants go back to their rooms at night, they can then review and relearn dance steps by logging onto a private, password-protected YouTube channel. It helps assist those in need of extra instruction and helps move the teaching along as they more quickly perfect their set.

Online communities devoted to show choirs have also popped up on such sites as ShowChoir.com and Facebook, creating more excuses for gleeks to eat, sleep, and breathe show choir. ShowChoir.com, which receives around 3,500 viewers per month, provides this thriving society of singers with a platform for discussion groups, events calendars, and YouTube links.

"My free time is spent improving the site, writing new code . . . all the work [that] people don't see," said Häakon Sundry, creator of ShowChoir.com. "Eighty percent of SCC's visitors are high school students. They're active for two or three years, then they graduate."

Self-created Facebook fan pages offer conversation channels and picture-sharing outlets for individual groups. Usually hosted by either a participant or active parent of the group, the fan pages not only keep current members engaged in discussion, but also help group alumni stay in touch and become virtually active within the group.

THE MOVEMENT TOWARD *GLEE*-TASTICNESS

Even before show choir kids around the country began tuning into *Glee* and spending more than enough time online, a movement toward performance entertainment began before Mr. Schuester and Sue Sylvester came into the picture and the national show choir love fest started. Excitement began brewing as audiences got hooked, season after season, on shows such as *American Idol*, *So You Think You Can Dance*, *America's Dance Crew*, *The Sing-Off* and *Dancing with the Stars*. Each of these series focuses on an essential element that show choirs have delivered to performers for decades: They make ordinary people feel extraordinary. They place contestants on a stage. They hand over a microphone or provide choreography instructions. They perform with confidence. The ordinary become stars.

The blockbuster Disney motion picture *High School Musical* was also a key driver of this singing and dancing phenomenon. The movie took the simple plot line of high school drama and threw in a mix of unrealistic singing and dancing scenes on basketball courts and in cafeterias. It was a ridiculous concept that was ridiculously successful.

Ridiculous or not, it is clear: Gleeking out is both cool and profitable.

PUBLISHERS

Publishing companies and arrangers have found themselves as busy as ever to meet the demand for pop chorals designed for staging.

"Pop arranging has changed," commented Greg Gilpin, choral writer/arranger. "It's not nearly as 'concert choir'–focused. A big reason is the music itself has changed . . . the choir is dancing and singing, which was not going on with pop chorals in the '60's and '70s."

In the wake of *Glee* and these other pop culture sensations, pop arrangements have become less focused on trying to fit into the shape of concert choir formats and instead have created a heavier emphasis on dancing. Pop choral is now written with choreographic considerations, with room for dance breaks.

Arrangements are simplified, given the realities of limited rehearsal times and the possibility that a troupe's performers are stronger dancers than singers. The less complicated compositions allow for the performers to perfect the vocals presented and then maintain the necessary energy and breath control for the choreography.

Not all groups, however, downsize the "choir" part of "show choir." The leading competitive show choirs handle complex and challenging arrangements and create custom-made orchestrations that complement their musical, theatrical, and dancing abilities.

They also take rest time within the performance. Unlike the early days of show choir, when no one entered or left the playing area except the white-suspendered stage crew, today's competitive show choirs remember to breathe. They incorporate offstage costume changes, as well as separate girl/boy and feature soloists to add production value, create visual appeal, and gain a couple minutes, or seconds, of rest time.

DANCE WITH ME

Whether for a high-end competition show choir or community-based group, staging is now an increas-

The national weekly entertainment magazine *Parade* featured Waubonsie Valley's Sound Check on the front cover of its October 3, 2010, issue. "It's nice that people across the country can recognize what we do. But I already thought show choir was cool." —Mark Myers, director

The Emmy Award–winning *High School Musical* (and its spin-offs 2 and 3) was another big hit for director Kenny Ortega, also well known for working on *Dirty Dancing*, *Newsies*, *Cheetah Girls*, and Michael Jackson's *This Is It*.

Ortega, commenting on *High School Musical*: "I really liked the idea of young people coming to know their own voice, regardless of outside pressure from peers, teachers, parents, and society. There's too much bullying that goes on and that causes kids to back off from new ideas they have about themselves."

*Center Grove's CG Sound System
at Fame, Branson, Missouri (2010).*

Each episode of *Glee* requires ten days to shoot, two days longer than other prime-time shows, to account for the extra dance and musical rehearsal time.

The traditional all-men's glee club—in all its stiff-singing glory—actually originated in Britain around the 1700s. The term *glee* referred to the specific two-or-more-part voice format carried out by these groups. This particular musical format remained popular in the United Kingdom until around the Victorian era, when newer forms of music distracted, overshadowed, and eventually pushed glee clubs out of the picture. But it didn't push them too far. In 1858, Harvard University adopted the "glee" style and created the first—and now oldest—glee club in America.

ingly critical part of the performance. Choreography was optional at the Reno Jazz Festival or Aztec Sing. Today, however, it is required. Simply implementing a sway or a step-touch into a number doesn't qualify a group as a show choir.

With an increased emphasis on dance, it makes sense that the type of choreography has also shifted, becoming more complex and requiring a higher energy level. Because members' dance experiences often vary, groups will often share the task of creating energy by separating the boys from the girls, or by featuring the more advanced dancers on risers from the floor. In this way, the choreography can play off everyone's strengths.

In the early '80s, both Carmel High School's Ambassadors and Edgewood High School's Music Warehouse often blocked five-star couples on the floor. These featured performers executed more advanced techniques, while behind them, on the risers, the rest of the group performed less complex but complementary movements.

The carefully crafted combination creates visual excitement, while still allowing for a strong vocal production.

As more groups have incorporated advanced dance moves into their shows, the unfortunate trend of overchoreographing followed. Luckily, with *Glee* and the elite groups leading the way, more show choirs are starting to understand the importance of branding and connecting the music with a purpose. When it comes to choreography, however, there's often a disconnect. The less strategic groups often fall into the trend of dancing for dancing's sake because movement is expected, required, and fun. Because adjudication sheets don't address overchoreography, most guilty choirs aren't even conscience of their faux pas. And there is at least one blameworthy party at every competition.

Bottom line: Good choreography makes a point. Better choreography tells a story.

TAKING *GLEE* ACROSS THE POND

Glee has helped show choirs cross many boundaries by just being the media maven that it is—showing up on award shows, being featured in every major magazine, appearing on *Today*, *The View*, *Oprah*, and *Ellen*. But one of the most interesting, and unexpected, developments from the "*Glee* effect" took place across the pond—in the United Kingdom.

Before the show, show choirs were virtually unknown in Great Britain. Even in rural towns and countrysides, British kids stuck to traditional musical activities such as theater and band, and the athletic classmates took up football (soccer), cricket, rugby, golf, and tennis.

When asked why show choirs never caught on in the United Kingdom as much as they have in the United States, Peter Ling, professor of American Studies at Nottingham University, commented, "They are uniquely American . . . American schools and colleges have always had a hugely competitive element. They like things that tap into something climactic, that could end in triumph or disaster—hopefully triumph."

Mind-sets began to change, however, when *Glee* began airing in Great Britain in January 2010. The show became an instant hit, and its music quickly spiked to the top of the British pop charts. It was apparent *Glee* fever had spread. Before long, copycats started popping up everywhere.

In January 2010, British journalist John Walsh observed a show choir–like glee club in London. He commented, "It's singing by brute force rather than any real technique. You are just grabbing a tune and going for it. Forget book clubs, glee clubs are the future."

In July 2010, Emma Bunton, former member of the Spice Girls, launched a UK talent show contest called *Don't Stop Believing*. Described as a hybrid of *The X Factor* and *Glee*, and televised live, it took on a search for the UK's best new musical group. They extended the competitiveness of the show not long after it started by adding a Supergroup component. The Supergroup, made up of thirty performers, regularly competes with the other choirs on the show —serving as the ultimate challenge to beat.

The two-hit punch of *Glee* plus the popular reality show *Don't Stop Believing* helped put show choir on the UK map. But prior to these hit shows, only a few British groups had already embraced the love of singing and dancing. They just didn't necessarily call themselves show choirs. Like their jazz hands, show choirs continue to spread far and wide. One Brit at a time.

WEST END KIDS

One of the first show choirs formed in the United Kingdom was the West End Kids, created by Martin-

> "Glee clubs are extremely exportable and kids over here have taken to other such exports, like the school prom. It's only a matter of time before we have them here, and they will be the all-singing-and-dancing version."
> —Professor Ling, Nottingham University

> "I came to realize that music is an international language of emotions. It connects people. During the time of riots and desegregation, music was the thing that brought my students together. It didn't matter about race or economic background—my kids took pride in what they were doing, became friends, and racial lines didn't matter." —Michael Howard, director of Laurel High School's Gold Horizons, Laurel, Mississippi

Gwyn Williams in 2001. Still the best-known choir in the country, the West End Kids perform at high-profile events and locations throughout the year, including on the BBC and ITV.

After being named UK's Brightest Star Within Youth Music Theatre in 2010, the group performed for Prime Minister David Cameron and five hundred additional governmental attendees at the Commonwealth State Banquet.

BRIDGWATER SHOW CHOIR

In 2007, Kathryn Stevens established the Bridgwater Show Choir to create a positive but competitive musical offering at the Bridgwater College Performing Arts Academy.

Its show style comes inspired by Mississippi's Attaché, containing confident choreography and impressive vocals. The choir's set, however, differs from the American format in that it is slightly shorter—lasting between seven and fourteen minutes—and involves significantly fewer members. The 2010 choir totaled just sixteen performers.

Bridgwater continues to receive high acclaim from critics around the country. In August 2010, the group was recognized on *Don't Stop Believing*, which introduced its talents to millions of audience members. In that same year, the choir was officially crowned the UK's Best Glee Club by Lee Mead, of the UK cast of *Wicked*.

MAIDSTONE SHOW CHOIR

Post-*Glee* and *–Don't Stop Believing* swinging choirs have become more common in UK high school stages and auditoriums—and community theaters. In 2010, Maidstone Show Choir was founded under the direction of Jess Walter. The community-based show choir, set in Kent, splits into a junior and senior group, welcoming participants of all ages and talents. Stone finds inspiration through researching U.S. groups on YouTube, but then puts the majority of control in the members' hands to ensure it's an enjoyable experience for everyone.

MATURED MANIA

In just a year, the all-American kids of William McKinley High School have created an international performing arts movement causing kids and adults

Bridgwater taping for BBC Channel 5's *Don't Stop Believing*.

After they won as Youth Choir of the Year at the prestigious Bournemouth Festival of Music and Drama, the adjudicator, Kathryn Stevens, commented that Bridgwater Show Choir had "terrific panache and confidence . . . with excellent harmony singing, full of verve and energy."

from New York City to London to raise their L-shaped hands with pride.

There is no doubt that *Glee* provided the spark that helped show choirs mature. After finding comfort and gaining solid reputations in their niche, rural areas of the United States, show choirs seemingly became Hollywood stars overnight.

Show choirs have achieved shelf space in the entertainment industry. They gained respect, found acknowledgment and established a voice.

And they don't seem to be getting quieter.

"Here's how I see it: the choir kids are always going to get tormented. But the guys in choir, when they're done with high school, if they want a lady, they can sing to her. And that is going to get a lady. You're not gonna get a lady after high school by throwing a football." —Matthew Morrison, cast member (Mr. Schuester), *Glee*

Dan Miller [Center], musician, O'Town.

THE ENCORE: LIFE AFTER SHOW CHOIR— THE MUSICIANS, THE ACTORS, THE SUCCESSFUL

12

I feel lucky to have had a career in the show choir world. I have come to know a family and friends who have made for a fulfilling life.

—VERDA SAVAGE, DIRECTOR, EDGEWOOD HIGH SCHOOL'S MUSIC WAREHOUSE

The encore. One last song—one last performance—before the show is over. Many times, especially at concerts, the encore is the most coveted performance. It's the song that made you buy the ticket, suffer through the crowds, and justify the $10 hot dog. It leaves the audience with a memory. With a moment. With closure.

But after the encore, the curtain closes. And sometimes, when it's over, it really is over. There's not always a second performance or a new show to bring the students back onto the stage. The audience has left the theater. The performers have packed up their costumes and gone home. Sometimes the end really is the end—especially for those graduating from show choir.

So what happens after the final curtain of show choir has fallen? After students have devoted years of their adolescent and teenage lives to memorizing sheet music, perfecting dance moves, and learning the value of facial expressions? After they have created a close network of friends who they consider family? What happens when it's time to walk away?

Life happens.

Just as some people become depressed after their big wedding or having a baby, some performers may go through a period of post–show choir depression. Luckily, this is typically only a mild form of the blues and can be easily cured by discovering new passions. It is recommended that show choir graduates concerned about their mental stability and limp jazz hands avoid show choir video benders, shower every day, and strive to pull it together.

Because there *is* life after show choir.

Though show choir alumni have gone on to create famous careers in music, the purpose of show choir is not to train performers to become professional show choir performers. Show choir is a unique extracurricular activity; it's a small chunk of a person's young life that can provide a solid base of life lessons. These experiences can help lead former members in the right direction toward a successful future—whether that be on the stage or in a cubicle, in a three-piece suit or in a military uniform.

Show choir participants usually walk away with a solid appreciation for music education, teamwork, creativity, and theater. They have a better sense of self and a strong network of support. They are set up for success. They are set up for life.

SUCCESS AFTER SHOW CHOIR
THE FAMOUS

Many famous Hollywood and Broadway performers spent notable time on the show choir stage. This star-studded cast includes:

"Show choir isn't a real thing! It's a training ground . . . Show choir offers education on styles of music and communication skills that apply to real like work."—David Fehr, director for Clinton High School's Attaché.

WHERE ARE THEY NOW? WRITE-INS FROM SHOW CHOIREES OF THE PAST

Lydia Moes, from the Sioux City East Headliners, is now a high school English teacher in Sioux City, Iowa.
Megan Brienzo, from the Sioux City East Headliners, became a cosmetologist in Sioux City, Iowa.
Bethany, from the Sioux City East Headliners, practices neurologic music therapy in Phoenix, Arizona.
Colton A. Burke, from the Sioux City East Headliners, joined the U.S. Navy and is stationed in Pensacola, Florida.
Andrew Allen, former member of E.T.C. All Americans, works as an actor, singer, and dancer in Los Angeles, California.
Lindsay Mauldin, former performer with E.T.C. All Americans, is a firefighter and medic in Washington, D.C.
Christine Goff, former member of Vermillion Soundsation, teaches fifth grade in Kent, Ohio.
Lauren Fuller, former member of E.T.C. All Americans, is an early intervention specialist and teacher of children with multiple disabilities, in Kent, Ohio.

Blake Lively, actress, Gossip Girl, The Town.

Christopher Spaulding, Broadway performer, Curtains.

Jim Walton, Broadway performer, 42nd Street, Guys and Dolls, Bye Bye Birdie, The Music Man.

Kevin Greene, Broadway performer and television actor, Gabelle in A Tail of Two Cities, Gossip Girl.

Frankie Paparone, Broadway performer, White Rabbit in Shrek, The Musical.

Lance Bass, musician, 'N Sync.

Larry Raben, actor, director, and Broadway performer, Forever Plaid, The Producers.

Corey Mach, Broadway performer, Wicked.

Aaron Serotsky, Broadway and TV actor, August: Osage County, Guiding Light, Law and Order, All My Children.

Nia Peeples, dancer, choreographer, and television actress, Fame.

Sarah Litzsinger, Broadway's longest-running Belle in Beauty and The Beast.

Jenna Ushkowitz, actress, Tina Cohen-Chang in Glee.

Chris Kirkpatrick, musician, 'N Sync.

Gavin Creel, Broadway performer, 2009 Tony Award nominee for best actor, Hair; 2002 Tony Award nominee, best actor in a musical.

Heather Headley, recording artist and Tony Award–winning actress in Broadway's Aida.

Marc Cherry, executive producer of Desperate Housewives.

Eden Espinosa, Broadway performer; Elphaba in Wicked *and Maureen in* Rent.

Clay Aiken, musician.

Joe Reid, Broadway performer, Catch Me If You Can, Chicago, Curtains.

Donna Lynn Champlin, Obie Award–winning stage, TV, and film actress and recording artist. Broadway's Billy Elliot, Sweeney Todd, By Jeeves, *portrayal of Carol Burnett in* Hollywood Arms.

Jason Mraz, musician.

Kye Brackett, actor, singer, and choreographer, Five Guys Named Moe, *and Barry Manilow's Emmy Award–winning Ultimate Music.*

Rylyn Legit, national touring company as Cassie in A Chorus Line.

Tiffany Blanchard.

Ashton Kutcher, producer/director, film and television star.

Christina (Slangen) Reinerman.

Chad Coudriet.

THE FAMILIAR

While there are several stars on Hollywood Boulevard that can pay tribute to the box steps and chasse's of their past, most graduates of show choir find their spotlights off the stage.

Ten years ago, a close group of friends and performers in E.T.C. stood together onstage in Akron, Ohio. It was their final encore. Singing "What Would I Do Without My Music," they looked at one another and at the audience, unsure of where their lives would take them, unsure of life beyond show choir. But as it turned out, they were in for some of their most interesting shows yet.

Tiffany Blanchard, the thin and vivacious front-row dancer and audience grabber, went off to Washington, D.C., to become a program manager at the U.S. Department of Energy. Recently engaged, she's in the process of planning a wedding back in the Akron area.

Christina (Slangen) Reinerman, the gorgeous ballad soloist who was too nice and talented to hate, went on to study marketing at the University of Cincinnati—where she met her husband, Rob. At their 2006 wedding, in addition to a dedicated performance from a fellow E.T.C.er, more than half of her bridesmaids were friends from show choir. Christina and Rob currently live in Walmart land (Fayetteville, Arkansas), where Christina works as a PR girl at Mitchell Communications Group and is involved in local community theater.

Chad Coudriet, the dramatically hilarious guy who constantly juggled high school part-time jobs, musical theater, and intramural sports with show choir rehearsals and competitions, graduated from Baldwin Wallace College with a bachelor's degree in musical theater. He spent six years working different shows, Off-Broadway and regionally, and now is currently touring with the Tokyo Philharmonic Orchestra as Gaston in *Beauty and the Beast* in Japan.

Katie Bishop, the peptastic and popular high school girl–gone–show choiree, took her talents to St. Louis, where she is now working as a successful medical device sales representative. When she's not traveling for the J.O.B., she spends her free time with her vast network of St. Louis friends and her energetic Labrador retriever named Jack.

Helen (Rotnem) Vivian, the quiet but incredibly sarcastic soprano, quickly broke out of her shell after high school and became president of her sorority for three years in college. Postgraduation, she led the Ohio State University Sorority and Fraternity Life program for two years. Now, in addition to being a full-time nanny, she spends her time with her daughter and husband in Columbus, Ohio.

CALLING OUT FOR COMMENTS

Famous or not, what these performers took away from show choir was more than a brain filled with lyrics and a body ready to dance at any given beat.

When asked to share lessons and key teachings from their show choir experiences, gleeks from around the United States answered with different, yet similar, responses. As opposed to drilling down to specifics, such as learning a difficult lift or mastering the art of a cappella, they focused on the lessons that would or did take them beyond show choir. Their comments speak for themselves.

"The lesson [I learned is] to not miss rehearsal; that you are important and will be missed. It's evident when someone misses rehearsal, their absence affects the group." *—Jessica Hauger, Lakeside High School Soundsation, Augusta, Georgia*

"It showed me that if you want to do something, you have to earn it. By earning it, you'd have to give it your all and see how it goes." *—Chue Keng Moua, Grand Central Station, La Crosse, Wisconsin*

"I've learned to always give 110 percent in what I love to do and to always work as a team." *—Phebe Tisdale, Gold Horizons, Laurel, Mississippi*

"I am not very much of a team player, but I have learned in show choir how important teamwork is." *—Rachel, Greenbrier High School Show Choir, Evans, Georgia*

"I learned how to truly express myself through performance in show choir. Socially, it helped me to open up and not be shy when it comes to meeting new people . . . It taught me to work hard at whatever I do, no matter how difficult or stressful (or dramatic)." *—Alex Calderone, E.T.C. All Americans, Copley, Ohio*

"[I've learned that] if things get tough, just break it up and work it out individually." *—Michael Rich, Greenbrier High School Show Choir, Evans, Georgia*

"Watching others have their moment is just as important as having your own." *—Erin Davis Dwyer, Elan Show Choir, Indianapolis, Indiana*

Katie Bishop.

Larissa Shukis Allspaugh, Broadway performer, Little Women, *National touring company:* Disney's Beauty and the Beast.

Helen (Rotnem) Vivian.

Seychelle Gabrielle, actress, Fallen Skies, The Spirit.

"I have learned how hard work and dedication pay off eventually." —*Hannah Fields, Greenbrier High School Show Choir, Evans, Georgia*

"I've learned that you can't always win, but you can always have fun. When I look back in twenty or thirty years, I won't remember the trophies or the places, but I will remember how much fun I had with my best friends doing what we love most." —*Bryan Detweiler, E.T.C. All Americans, Cuyahoga Falls, Ohio*

"[I've learned] to not judge people because they sing and dance" —*Anonymous, Greenbrier High School Show Choir, Evans, Georgia*

"It taught me how to take constructive criticism and produce positive results and how to deal with stress in a positive way. It gave me a great work ethic. And show choir also taught me that you don't have to be blood related to be family." —*Molly Halpin, E.T.C. All Americans, Monroe Falls, Ohio*

"I can dance better now, so my women enjoy it quite thoroughly." —*Nikolai Russo, Greenbrier High School Show Choir, Evans, Georgia*

"We're like a family and, no matter what happens, we'll always be there for our fellow show choir members." —*Lauryn, Gold Horizons, Laurel, Mississippi*

"I learned how a group of people can become as close as a family and that music brings people together in a way that few other things can. E.T.C. really is my second home." —*Steven Palmieri, E.T.C. All Americans, Akron, Ohio*

"Coming from a show choir with a weak program, I learned leadership skills to try to motivate and encourage others to be the best they can be . . . The emotional tears that flow during a touching ballad rarely happen in any other school activity." —*Micheal Walley, Wayne County High School, Orange Sensations, Waynesboro, Mississippi*

"Management of time." —*Quinn Mihalovic, Grand Central Station, La Crosse, Wisconsin*

"I learned to work as a team and understand the importance of every member . . . I learned to not just focus on improving myself, but on improving the team as a whole. As I've moved past my show choir days into my university days, these lessons have helped me gain leadership positions." —*Caroline Linden, E.T.C. All Americans, Chicago, Illinois*

"I have learned a lot about choosing priorities and how this can affect a lot of things in your life." —*Cassie Isaacs, Grand Central Station, La Crosse, Wisconsin*

"Show choir has taught me that you don't always have to be front and center in order to get noticed or have that one solo to be the best. If you believe in yourself and work hard, great things can come your way. It's not about winning or losing, it's about leaving it all on the floor and the journey getting there. And when life gets you down, no matter what, a simple song, dance, some glitter and, of course, jazz hands can make everything better, every time." —*Lauren Nervo, E.T.C. All Americans, Stow, Ohio*

"I learned that there are politics in everything especially in music. It was a great lesson to learn early in my singing career. [Sometimes] I would forget that it's not about the results but the communication of live performance." —*Nicholas Anderson, Sioux City East Headliners, Sioux City, Iowa*

"It taught me how to deal with a lot of different [types] of people. We all have different personalities." —*Nikki Kimball, Grand Central Station, La Crosse, Wisconsin*

"I learned team work, dedication . . . [Specifically,] I learned how to be dedicated to something while having other obligations." —*Frederick Reed, North St. Paul Northern Lights, Chicago, Illinois*

"I learned how exciting it was to be part of something that was bigger than myself." —*Lydia Moes, Sioux City East Headliners, Sioux City, Iowa*

"When I was young, I went to private, Catholic schools with not a lot of diversity. Being in a community show choir helped me realize that there is a melting pot of individuals in this world and that we don't all look or act the same—or come from the same economic situation. It's helped me appreciate and understand how to work with people from all walks of life." —*Christina (Slangen) Reinerman, E.T.C. All Americans, Fayetteville, Arkansas*

"I was always pushed to be the best that I could possibly be in show choir. Now, I can't imagine doing things any differently." —*Megan Brienzo, Sioux City East Headliners, Sioux City, Iowa*

"I think all of us would agree that this group really taught commitment, persistence and support of each other. I was nowhere near the most talented of

Spanish Fork High School's Ambassadors preparing for their final performance at Fame's Show Choir Cup. Tri-Lake Center, Branson, Missouri. (2008).

the group. We all came with different gifting and abilities. We all learned to support each other, highlight on individuals strengths, and together pursue excellence." —*Lauren Fuller, E.T.C. All Americans, Kent, Ohio*

"I learned that extreme frustration and anger doesn't help in getting things done in life." —*Blair Remmers, Sioux Center Satisfaction, Sioux City, Iowa*

"I definitely learned how to be a leader. Being a dance captain taught me how to take control of a group of people. It's a talent in itself to be authoritative while being engaging and relatable. And with a bunch of high school students, you have to be all of those, especially when they are your peers." —*Katy Alberti, E.T.C. All Americans, Chicago, Illinois*

"[I learned] how to deal with egos and divas and parents of divas. Also, how to fix and clean a show without hurting anyone's feelings." —*Cheryl Boigegrain (director), E.T.C. All Americans, Tallmadge, Ohio*

"I've learned that in life, you don't always get what you want, but it will still work out in the end." —*Megan Calderone, E.T.C. All Americans, Copley, Ohio*

> "A good show must reach a point where it delivers a big finish. You want the other directors to think, 'Damn, I should have thought of that!'" —Eric Van Cleave, former director for Lafayette Jefferson High School's First Edition

Our high school was the only competitive show choir in the state of Utah. I have had four children participate and in each instance it has been the highlight of their schooling if not, a life changing experience.

In 2008 the theme for our show was, "You Can Make a Difference." To help . . . "feel" what they were singing about, the kids organized service projects. The emphasis within the group was on giving of yourself and making a difference for others. The students loved that experience. The "practice" pep talk we had right before the final performance was sweet beyond words. The entire group was in tears. The picture of the boy embracing Mr. Lunt, their director, was heartrending. He broke down in tears and told Mr. Lunt what a difference he had made in his life and he would be a different person because of his experience in show choir. —*Pat Frandsen, Ambassador parent, Spanish Forks, Utah*

THE BEGINNING

In the end, show choir is surprisingly . . . more. It's more than just a fifteen-minute performance or the validation of a competition trophy, more than the star soloist or the standing ovation.

The show choir genre is edutainment. It takes lessons outside of the classroom and brings them onto the stage. It's all the history, the pop culture influences, the competitions, and the branding—wrapped in a package of sweat, tears, and jazz hands.

Whether it's a performer, a director, a band member, or a parent, being part of the show choir experience is unforgettable—from the first practice and the awkward icebreakers to the last bow and click of the drums. Whether one stays involved for eight years or eight minutes, it promises to make an impression.

There will always be a story to tell.

GLOSSARY
TALK THE TALK: SHOW CHOIR LINGO

The time to sing is when your emotional level is too high to just speak anymore, and the time to dance is when your emotions are just too strong to only sing about how you feel.

—BOB FOSSE

Adjudicators/Judges: The only three or four audience members who really matter during a competition; selected to rate and critique the performance and award a winner.

Ex. "We thought we had a good chance of winning the competition until we found out who the judges were."

Adjudication Sheet: A nonstandardized judge's checklist used to determine the strength and quality of a group, which usually includes the categories of vocal, choreography, and general effect.

Ex. "We usually check out the adjudication sheet before deciding which competition we're going to attend."

Ballad: The tearjerker of the show, created to please the moms and the judges in the audience; typically a nonchoreographed, but sometimes staged, moment where the emphasis is on vocal production and not on the choreography.

Ex. "As we were singing the ballad, I looked out into the audience, and they were as still as we were."

Blade: Sharp like a knife, this movement can be described as the opposite of a jazz hand with closed but straight fingers; very karate chop–like.

Ex. "When reviewing the tape, the choir noticed half of the group was using jazz hands, when the choreographer had instructed them to use blades."

Blocking: The act of arranging positions onstage for each song and performance, to ensure the person who refuses to smile never ends up front and center—in addition to other strategic considerations.

Ex. "After blocking the song, Stephen wondered why he was always placed in the back row."

Bow: A traditional theatrical moment where the performer acknowledges and thanks the audience and the combo before ending the show.

Ex. "As soon as we saw the group before us bow, we knew we had to line up backstage for our performance."

Boys' Number: A tough, testosterone-driven song, typically labeled either "cool" or "physically acrobatic."

Ex. "The boys' number reminded me of an N'SYNC performance!"

Buffer Number: A song in the show designed to buy time for a costume change or a shift in the performance; a transitional number that allows for resting time, typically vocal focused.

Ex. "After the production-heavy opener, the group incorporated a buffer number to allow the performers to catch their breath."

Caption Scoring: Set in place to judge each of the performance elements with separate score. Groups walk away with scores for choral, choreography, instrumental ensemble, and overall general effect.

Choreo: A nickname for *choreography*: premeditated and planned movements, spasms, jumps, and/or jitters set to music
Ex. "The singing was kind of pitchy, but the choreo was hot!"

Choreographer: Toe-tapping teachers who wear many hats and hold several positions within a show choir organization, such as a visual designer, motivator, choral enthusiast, and creator of energy.
Ex. "You could see our choreographer get frustrated when no one was picking up what he was throwing down."

Closer: The final song in the performance, usually a production number, involving bows, excessive smiling, and the falling curtain.
Ex. "The closer, like the final chapter of a book, helped sum up the show's 'story' nicely."

Combo: The band geeks who accompany the gleeks; typically can include a combination of the following instruments, piano, bass, drums, keyboard, percussion, winds, and brass.
Ex. "At the end of the performance, we acknowledged the combo before our final bow."

Crew: Usually made up of laymen (i.e., boyfriends and girlfriends of the show choirees); the "cool" crew is responsible for operating set movement and/or setup, striking props, and organizing costumes.
Ex. "Although the show started at 8 p.m., the crew had to be there at noon to unload the truck."

Contrast: The recognition that one element differs from a previous element.
Ex. "The contrast between the bright and cheery songs and the dark costumes threw me off a bit."

Costume Change: Formerly a novelty, now an unwritten requirement of a competitive show choir, which provides a visual change, complementing the vocal or tempo shift of the performance.
Ex. "The group that won incorporated four costume changes into its set."

Critique Session: A constructive workshop, led by an expert in either music, choreography, or overall show design, which tends to take place in a festival or contest setting and is created to help groups improve on elements in their show.
Ex. "It wasn't until the critique session that we realized we actually weren't as good as we thought."

Dance Break: Often referred to as "the fun part of the show," where the singing stops and the focus is placed on the dancing.
Ex. "E.T.C. totally rocked out its dance break."

Dancers in Front (or Floor): A strategic staging technique that highlights the strengths of the performers by placing the strongest dancers in front, allowing for a more visual performance, and choreographing minimal movement on the risers to create a strong wall of sound.
Ex. "I went to a year of dance class before being asked to join the front-row dancers."

Development: The route a show takes to arrive at its theme or message.

Ex. "The choir's theme of 'happiness' didn't mean much at the end of the show, due to the lack of development."

Director: The head honcho and designated senior leadership of the group; often responsible for giving grades, collecting participation fees or dues, organizing concerts, serving as a family psychologist, and, in his or her spare time, teaching choral notes.

Ex. "The director saw each of the show choir students as her family, for better or for worse."

Feature: The moment in the show when a group gets to flex its muscles and highlight a particular talent, which could be its combo, the dancers, a soloist, and so forth; commonly used as a distraction during transitions, to focus the audience on a particular moment.

Ex. "Tia was hoping her solo could be the feature in between the ballad and the closer, but the combo beat her out."

Finals: Designated time during a competition when the highest-scoring groups are invited back onstage, after hearing the judges' comments and seeing the audience's reaction, to fight it out for the Grand Championship.

Ex. "We would've won the competition, but during finals our backdrop caught fire."

Function: The purpose of a song, prop, transition, or costume to help move the story of a show along.

Ex. "I was confused as to the intended function of the Chinese dragon costuming in the song 'Staying Alive.'"

Girls' Number: This estrogen-filled performance alludes to either sassiness or sexiness, with the recent trend of highlighting songs that empower and highlight women's independence and strength.

Ex. "That girls' number was very 'Rihanna'!"

Grand Champions: As the BMOCs (Big Man on Campus) of the weekend, these overall winners of a particular competition outperformed the other show choirs and left with a bigger ego and, often, an oversized trophy.

Ex. "When we were named Grand Champions of Showstoppers last year, the choir dumped Gatorade on the director."

Invitational: A festival where most participants are invited in an *American Idol*–like fashion, by way of a videotape audition. Other invites are distributed to highly sought-after choirs with a reputation for winning. Although judging might not take place, groups often receive feedback or participate in workshops.

Ex. "We hosted the invitational to raise money for the show choir but also to build relationships with neighboring groups."

Jazz Hands: Unofficial gang symbol of show choirs; a wide display of fingers, sometimes moving back and forth (*see* Shimmering), typically incorporated into a movement to elicit energy through the fingertips.

Ex. "I wasn't sure if Sarah would be okay with the fact that I was in show choir, but when she flashed a couple shimmering jazz hands my direction, I knew we'd be friends."

Mash-ups: More traditionally referred to as a *medley*, the term became more popular with the rise of such artists as Girl Talk.

Ex. "My favorite mash-up on *Glee* was when they mixed 'Singing in the Rain' with Rihanna's 'Umbrella.'"

Nationals: A slightly inaccurate or misconstrued term that generally refers to a competition involving show choirs from various states; there are several national competitions throughout the year.

 Ex. "We've been working all year to get ready for nationals!"

Novelty Number: A prop or character-driven song, inspired by musical theater, pop music, or other influences, which allows a show choir to pull out a witty, humorous, or clever gimmick.

 Ex. "Their novelty number looked a lot like STOMP."

Olympic Scoring: Aimed at maintaining a fair score, the Olympic system takes scores from a panel of judges and "throws away" the highest and lowest scores. The final tallies are then based upon the median-scoring judges.

Overall Scoring: Built to allow judges an opportunity to provide general subjective feedback on the overall show. A way to score a performance's final impression—a general level of quality or ranking.

Participation Plaque: Perfect for the entitlement generation, this standard awards recognizes everyone as a winner, just for showing up.

 Ex. "Though we have yet to win a competition, our participation plaques line the rehearsal hall for inspiration."

Poison Box: A figure of speech or a figure of the stage. This taped-off area in front of the risers—between the microphones—can make or break show choirs during competitions. Performers who stepped out of the box would lose points for the team.

 Ex. "I woke up this morning in a cold sweat after having a dream that I stepped out of the poison box."

Production Number: Usually the grand finale of the performance; oftentimes a mash-up of two or three songs meant to wrap up the show; can involve new costumes, new feature-soloist dance breaks, and/or multiple transitions. All the stops are pulled out and all the tricks are uncovered to leave the audience speechless.

 Ex. "It was clear they were wrapping up the show when they came out in different costumes, performed two dance breaks, and broke out the pyrotechnics."

Repetition: To utilize an element of the show more than once.

 Ex. "It was clear we were watching an amateur show choir, when its dances repeated the same eight counts for the entire fifteen-minute show."

Rip-away: Refers to a Velcro- or snaps-rigged costume that can be removed within a beat; created for quick costume changes, abused in miscellaneous show choir pranks and Super Bowl performances (e.g., J.T. and Janet Jackson).

 Ex. "Although we didn't have enough time to run offstage, the rip-aways helped make time for a costume change and created a cool visual effect."

Risers: Platforms used to create three-dimensional staging and an extra couple of feet for the prepubescent boys that have yet to hit their growth spurt.

 Ex. "I could finally see Brian once he moved to the top riser."

Rock Out: Also referred to as freestyle, break down, breakout moment; several beats of nonchoreographed moments, allowing the performer to be as weird and as much of an individual (or an individual based on a celebrity idol) as his or her ego allows.

 Ex. "During the rock out, Caitlyn broke out some Beyoncé moves onstage."

Rubric Scoring: Geared toward defining and identifying "quality" shows and show choirs, this point system uses rhetorical descriptions and point spreads based on level of quality.

Set: Elements of a backdrop or stage design that create a theatrical setting, an environment for the show, and a need for a road or backstage crew.
>   Ex. "The waterfall set in *Glee* was completely unrealistic, and made our backdrop look amateurish."

Shimmering: Movement that adds caffeinelike energy to a regular set of jazz hands; the act of moving fingers back and forth in a quick fashion.
>   Ex. "The Tone Rangers ended their set with jazz hands that kept shimmering until the audience gave them a standing ovation."

Show Design: This is the strategic development of elements that form the overall concept and impression; the choice of music, transitions, costumes, and colors; cohesion.
>   Ex. "The show design presented a modern twist on 1950s fashion and music."

Similarity: The recognition that one element of the show or an entire show mirrors another.
>   Ex. "The similarities of the two choirs make sense, given they share a choreographer."

Staged Ballad: A ballad on dramatic steroids that focuses on the choral elements of the song, but unlike a regular ballad, involves minimal movement with purpose, such as walking or staging.
>   Ex. "When the group performed "Eleanor Rigby," they set the song to movement, creating a dark and dramatic rendition of the Beatles' cover."

Step-touch: A simple, weight-shifting foot pattern where one foot steps (in any direction) and takes weight, and the free foot touches nearby, bringing the feet together. The pattern then reverses. For example:

>   Step R, L foot touches next to R— beats 1 and 2
>   Step L, R foot touches next to L—beats 3 and 4

Tricks and Lifts: Couple-oriented moves incorporated into a number to create a more visually appealing show and introduce surprises into the performance; makes the girls feel light and airy and the men feel masculine.
>   Ex. "That group reminded me of a mash-up between Cirque du Soleil performers and the cast from *Step Up*, they had so many tricks and lifts."

Unity/Disunity: The way in which a visual or audible moment communicates its idea through the use of unison, harmony, or counterpoint; the opposite of randomness.
>   Ex. "The ballad brought unity and clarification to the message the group was trying to convey."

Variation: The need to incorporate element changes over a period of time.
>   Ex. "We would've been more impressed with the newbie group had it added more variation into its show, even if it was easier to perform."

Windows: The space between staggered blocking that allows Grandma to see her little one without straining a neck muscle.
>   Ex. "Grandma slipped a disk due to Fabian's ignorance of his stage windows."

ACKNOWLEDGMENTS

Colleen Hart

I've been fortunate in my life to have an amazing network of support around me, and my name would not be on the cover of this book without them.

My family, the people who have heard *all* of my "this one time in E.T.C." stories, deserve the first acknowledgment. So thank you, fam. Thanks to my mom, who was and always is, my number one fan. She took me to my first E.T.C. show; drove my friends and me to limitless rehearsals and shows all over Ohio; was costume mom and backstage mom and winter gala mom and poinsettia mom; and who, offstage, continues to cheer me on daily. And to my dad and brother who I don't think ever really "got" show choir, but still came and supported me, sitting through eight years of four-hour Spring Gala shows and other "obviously important" performances that they were under family obligation to attend. Although I'm sure they enjoyed every minute (insert sarcastic intonation), I still feel I owe them at least thirty-two hours of their lives back. To my cousin, Lauren Nervo, a.k.a. Mini-Me, who is continuing on the family tradition in E.T.C., and to my Aunt Mary who is my number one unofficial book publicist.

I would have no experience to write about without E.T.C. I will always have great appreciation for Bob Heid and Cheryl Boigegrain, my E.T.C. parents for nearly a decade. They built me up from the awkward four-foot-something fifth grader, who couldn't quite reach the microphone during her first show to the seventeen-year-old singing Christina Aguilera's "What a Girl Wants" in a pastel triangle tank top. While I may regret that particular song selection and the Rave-purchased costume choice, I will always cherish the time spent growing up at Canal Place.

Throughout both my school and work life, many mentors along the way have stepped in with insight and inspiration and ultimately taught me the tricks of the typewriter. A thank-you is overdue to Mr. Storad, my junior year colloquium teacher at Walsh Jesuit High School, for showing me that even the most boring research and writing assignments can have a little life when injected with creativity; that every paper and story should be supported with "bookends." And also to my most recent professional role models at Burson-Marsteller and Edelman who taught me to think larger than myself, whether that's training a turkey-cooking monkey to get a product on late-night television or developing an international marketing campaign from a cubicle in Chicago. And to the staff at Applause Books and, of course, Mike, for his endless knowledge of show choir history and positive can-do attitude throughout this process. Thank you. Thank you. Thank you.

But I'm not sure I would have even considered writing a book if not for the encouragement from my CITY girls: Christina Reinerman, Katie Bishop, and Helen Vivian. If I had a word for every time one of the three of you told me to write a book, I would have a sizable dictionary. Although it's been a lifetime since we performed together in E.T.C. and while we are scattered throughout the country from Arkansas to Ohio, you are still my "persons," my emotional emergency contacts, and my reality grounders. From Disco Ball eye shadow to road trip mixed CDs to years of e-mails and trips down to Sanibel, this book would not be written without your years of support. We've come a long way since the sequins.

Mike Weaver

The thank-you list could truly go on and on—and I already know I'm going to hear from those friends, both old and new, that I forgot to mention. Your exclusion was not intentional, really.

Let me start by thanking my writing partner Colleen Hart, for her relentless pushing, no . . . shoving me along this process. It's hard to catch a moving target! She is perky, witty, and brilliant, and I couldn't have had a more committed and creative writing partner. Hey, woman! We did it!

This book could have never been written without countless conversations, phone calls, e-mails, and sharing from my friends and colleagues. Many of the people listed have been around long enough to witness each other's triumphs and challenges. Thank you for your time and advice and intentional or not, mentorship.

Joel Biggs; Bert Johnson and the staff at Fame; Kye Brackett; Damon Brown; J. Kevin Butler; Michael Esser; Peter Eklund; David Fehr; Andy Haines; Ronald D. Hellem; Dwight Jordan; Kim Malone; Gail McInnis; Linda McEachran; Fritz Mountford; Linda Pauli; Scott Rains; Tara Tober; Eric VanCleave; Dave Willert, Jeff Thorne, Karlene Krouse, Kirk Wolf at Indy Action Photos, Ron Mendlebaum and Derek at Photofest, Eric Van Cleave, Brett Carroll, Carla Doles, Adam Miller and Nick McGraw for their outstanding research, Haakon Sundry, Ron Bolles, Mary Rago, Johanne McIvor.

A special thanks to Emily Crocker, John Cerullo, Carol Flannery, Marybeth Keating, and the staff at Hal Leonard Performing Arts Publishing Group for your guidance, hand holding, and trust as we embarked on creating a book.

Those friends, though not directly related with the compiling of information for this book, who have offhandedly made an impact on me and my work:

Stephen Barefoot, Roger Emerson, John Fricke, Jane Marshall, Chet Walker, Bill Hastings, Niesha Folkes

And those mentors that left the world a better place than how they found it: Robert Hills, Hal Malcolm, Judith Meeks, Jim Savage, Roger Schueler.

And special thank yous to my extended family, Tom and Helen Potakis and Kevin Breazeale, for their loving support.

And I give a special thank-you to my two mothers, Charlene Williams, for being so dedicated to my future that she once drove me to an All-State choral convention wearing shoes, a nightgown, and an overcoat . . . and stayed all day to watch me sing. And to my other mother, who changed so many people's lives for the better with her single decision. Thank you both for giving so much of yourselves not only to me, but to everyone.

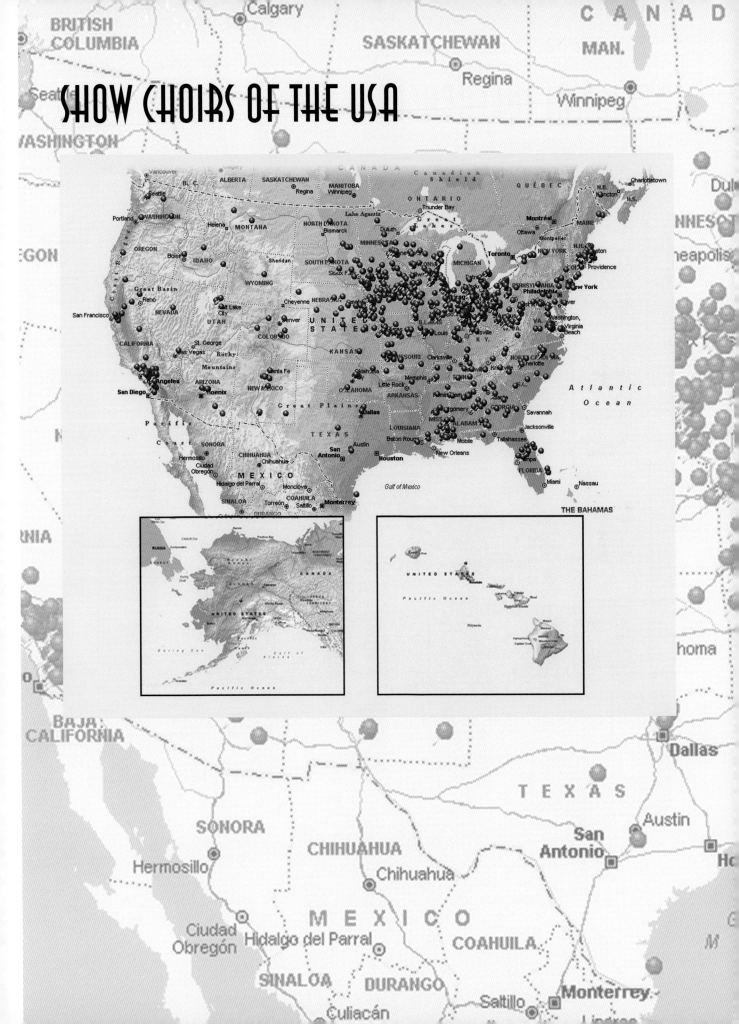

SHOW CHOIRS OF THE USA

REGIONAL INFLUENCES

Midwestern to Eastern Influences

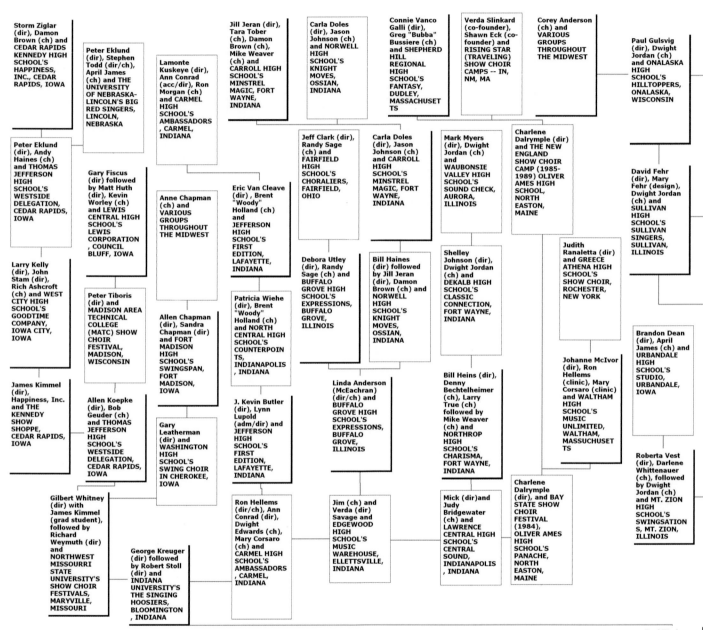

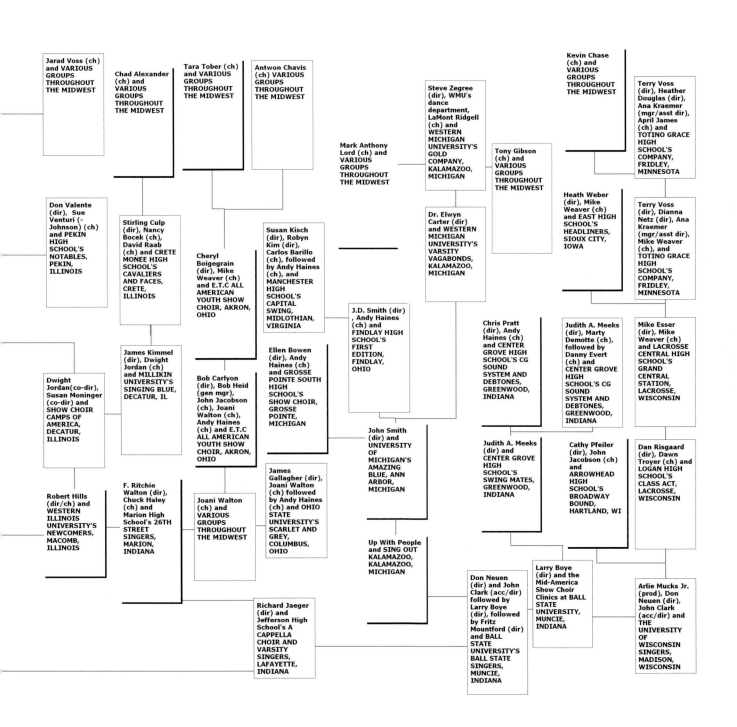

Jarad Voss (ch) and VARIOUS GROUPS THROUGHOUT THE MIDWEST

Chad Alexander (ch) and VARIOUS GROUPS THROUGHOUT THE MIDWEST

Tara Tober (ch) and VARIOUS GROUPS THROUGHOUT THE MIDWEST

Antwon Chavis (ch) VARIOUS GROUPS THROUGHOUT THE MIDWEST

Mark Anthony Lord (ch) and VARIOUS GROUPS THROUGHOUT THE MIDWEST

Steve Zegree (dir), WMU's dance department, LaMont Ridgell (ch) and WESTERN MICHIGAN UNIVERSITY'S GOLD COMPANY, KALAMAZOO, MICHIGAN

Tony Gibson (ch) and VARIOUS GROUPS THROUGHOUT THE MIDWEST

Kevin Chase (ch) and VARIOUS GROUPS THROUGHOUT THE MIDWEST

Terry Voss (dir), Heather Douglas (dir), Ana Kraemer (mgr/asst dir), April James (ch) and TOTINO GRACE HIGH SCHOOL'S COMPANY, FRIDLEY, MINNESOTA

Don Valente (dir), Sue Venturi (-Johnson) (ch) and PEKIN HIGH SCHOOL'S NOTABLES, PEKIN, ILLINOIS

Stirling Culp (dir), Nancy Bocek (ch), David Raab (ch) and CRETE MONEE HIGH SCHOOL'S CAVALIERS AND FACES, CRETE, ILLINOIS

Cheryl Boigegrain (dir), Mike Weaver (ch) and E.T.C ALL AMERICAN YOUTH SHOW CHOIR, AKRON, OHIO

Susan Kisch (dir), Robyn Kim (dir), Carlos Barillo (ch), followed by Andy Haines (ch) and MANCHESTER HIGH SCHOOL'S CAPITAL SWING, MIDLOTHIAN, VIRGINIA

Dr. Elwyn Carter (dir) and WESTERN MICHIGAN UNIVERSITY'S VARSITY VAGABONDS, KALAMAZOO, MICHIGAN

Heath Weber (dir), Mike Weaver (ch) and EAST HIGH SCHOOL'S HEADLINERS, SIOUX CITY, IOWA

Terry Voss (dir), Dianna Netz (dir), Ana Kraemer (mgr/asst dir), Mike Weaver (ch), and TOTINO GRACE HIGH SCHOOL'S COMPANY, FRIDLEY, MINNESOTA

James Kimmel (dir), Dwight Jordan (ch) and MILLIKIN UNIVERSITY'S SINGING BLUE, DECATUR, IL

J.D. Smith (dir), Andy Haines (ch) and FINDLAY HIGH SCHOOL'S FIRST EDITION, FINDLAY, OHIO

Chris Pratt (dir), Andy Haines (ch) and CENTER GROVE HIGH SCHOOL'S CG SOUND SYSTEM AND DEBTONES, GREENWOOD, INDIANA

Judith A. Meeks (dir), Marty Demotte (ch), followed by Danny Evert (ch) and CENTER GROVE HIGH SCHOOL'S CG SOUND SYSTEM AND DEBTONES, GREENWOOD, INDIANA

Mike Esser (dir), Mike Weaver (ch) and LACROSSE CENTRAL HIGH SCHOOL'S GRAND CENTRAL STATION, LACROSSE, WISCONSIN

Dwight Jordan(co-dir), Susan Moninger (co-dir) and SHOW CHOIR CAMPS OF AMERICA, DECATUR, ILLINOIS

Bob Carlyon (dir), Bob Heid (gen mgr), John Jacobson (ch), Joani Walton (ch), Andy Haines (ch) and E.T.C ALL AMERICAN YOUTH SHOW CHOIR, AKRON, OHIO

Ellen Bowen (dir), Andy Haines (ch) and GROSSE POINTE SOUTH HIGH SCHOOL'S SHOW CHOIR, GROSSE POINTE, MICHIGAN

John Smith (dir) and UNIVERSITY OF MICHIGAN'S AMAZING BLUE, ANN ARBOR, MICHIGAN

Judith A. Meeks (dir) and CENTER GROVE HIGH SCHOOL'S SWING MATES, GREENWOOD, INDIANA

Cathy Pfeiler (dir), John Jacobson (ch) and ARROWHEAD HIGH SCHOOL'S BROADWAY BOUND, HARTLAND, WI

Dan Risgaard (dir), Dawn Troyer (ch) and LOGAN HIGH SCHOOL'S CLASS ACT, LACROSSE, WISCONSIN

Robert Hills (dir/ch) and WESTERN ILLINOIS UNIVERSITY'S NEWCOMERS, MACOMB, ILLINOIS

F. Ritchie Walton (dir), Chuck Haley (ch) and Marion High School's 26TH STREET SINGERS, MARION, INDIANA

Joani Walton (ch) and VARIOUS GROUPS THROUGHOUT THE MIDWEST

James Gallagher (dir), Joani Walton (ch) followed by Andy Haines (ch) and OHIO STATE UNIVERSITY'S SCARLET AND GREY, COLUMBUS, OHIO

Up With People and SING OUT KALAMAZOO, KALAMAZOO, MICHIGAN

Larry Boye (dir) and the Mid-America Show Choir Clinics at BALL STATE UNIVERSITY, MUNCIE, INDIANA

Arlie Mucks Jr. (prod), Don Neuen (dir), John Clark (acc/dir) and THE UNIVERSITY OF WISCONSIN SINGERS, MADISON, WISCONSIN

Richard Jaeger (dir) and Jefferson High School's A CAPPELLA CHOIR AND VARSITY SINGERS, LAFAYETTE, INDIANA

Don Neuen (dir) and John Clark (acc/dir) followed by Larry Boye (dir), followed by Fritz Mountford (dir) and BALL STATE UNIVERSITY'S BALL STATE SINGERS, MUNCIE, INDIANA

Southern Influences

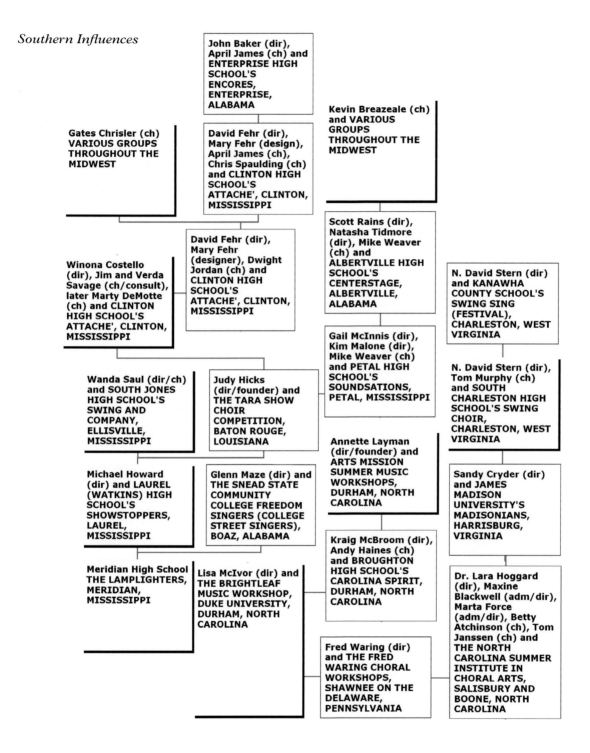

Western Influences

Brett Carroll (dir), Joshua Greene (writer), April James (ch), Damon Brown (ch) and BURBANK HIGH SCHOOL'S IN SYNC, BURBANK, CALIFORNIA

Brendan Jennings (dir), Jen Oundjian (ch), Jon King (ch), Marie Christine (ch), Dan Scoville (dir) and JOHN BURROUGHS HIGH SCHOOL'S POWERHOUSE, BURBANK, CALIFORNIA

Rollie Maxson (dir) and ARCADIA HIGH SCHOOL'S CHANTEURS, ARCADIA, CALIFORNIA

Roger Duffer (dir) and REDLANDS HIGH SCHOOL'S CHAMBER SINGERS, REDLANDS, CALIFORNIA

Rick Solano (dir) with COLTON HIGH SCHOOL'S CHAMBER SINGERS AND THE FESTIVAL (FESTIVAL), COLTON, CALIFORNIA

Mary Rago (dir), Debbie Crette (ch), Michelle Jenson (ch) and JOHN BURROUGHS HIGH SCHOOL'S CHAMBER SINGERS, BURBANK, CALIFORNIA

Dave Willert (dir), Doug Kuhl (ch) and BREA OLINDA HIGH SCHOOL'S MASQUERADE, BREA, CALIFORNIA

Bruce Bishop (dir) and UNIVERSITY OF WYOMING'S CENTENNIAL SINGERS, LARAMIE, WYOMING

Jim Cusack (dir), Jack Tygett (ch) and MT. CARMEL HIGH SCHOOL'S THE MAIN ATTRACTION WITH TOPS IN POPS (FESTIVAL), POWAY, CALIFORNIA

Tom Kessler (dir) with WEST COVINA HIGH SCHOOL'S CHAMBER SINGERS AND THE SHOW (FESTIVAL) AT CITRUS COLLEGE, WEST COVINA, CALIFORNIA

Ron (dir) and Reina (ch) Bolles and BONITA VISTA HIGH SCHOOL'S THE MUSIC MACHINE, CHULA VISTA, CALIFORNIA

Randy Boothe (dir) and BRIGHAM YOUNG UNIVERSITY'S AMBASSADORS, PROVO, UTAH

John Wilson (dir), Johnny Mann (dir) and THE GREAT AMERICAN CHORAL FESTIVAL, SAN DIEGO, CALIFORNIA

John Wilson (dir) and Aztec Sing (festival) with AZUZA HIGH SCHOOL'S AZTEC SINGERS, COVINA, CALIFORNIA

K. Gene Simmonds (dir) and THE SOUTHERN CALIFORNIA YOUTH CHORALE, LOS ANGELES, CALIFORNIA

Milton C. Anderson (dir) and THE YOUNG AMERICANS, CORONA, CALIFORNIA

Doug Anderson (dir) and MCMINNVILLE HIGH SCHOOL'S TWILIGHTERS, MCMINNVILLE, OREGON

Dr John Carrico (prod), Hal Malcolm (dir) and SHOW POP CHORAL DIVISION AT THE RENO JAZZ FESTIVAL, RENO, NEVADA

Don Large (dir), The Wayne King Orchestra and chorus on RADIO STATION WJR, DETROIT, MICHIGAN

Milton C. Anderson (dir) and THE GREATER CINNCINATTI YOUTH CHORUS ON TV STATION WKRC, CINNCINATTI, OHIO

Hal Malcom (dir) MT. HOOD SWING CHOIR FESTIVAL, MT HOOD COMMUNITY COLLEGE, GRESHAM, OREGON

DIRECTORY OF SHOW CHOIRS

V= Varsity	JV= Junior Varsity	V-W= Woman	V-M= Men

Albertville High School	CenterStage! (v), CenSations! (jv)	Albertville	AL
Auburn High School	Varsity Singers (v), Elan (u-w)	Auburn	AL
Benjamin Russell High School	Traditions (v), Women's Chorus (u-w)	Alexander City	AL
Boaz High School	Show Choir (u-w) 2009	Boaz	AL
Booker T. Washington High School	Paradigm (v) 2004	Tuskegee	AL
Brookwood High School	Synergy (u-w)	Brookwood	AL
Dothan High School	Show Choir (v)	Dothan	AL
Enterprise High School	Encores (v), Esprit (u-w)	Enterprise	AL
Eufaula High School	Vibe (v)	Eufaula	AL
Homewood High School	The Network (v), The Legacy (u-w)	Homewood	AL
Hoover High School	Chamber Choir (v)	Hoover	AL
Jefferson Davis High School	Starburst (v)	Montgomery	AL
Jess Lanier High School	***Listed on SC.com but no record of an actual show choir***	Bessemer	AL
Lee High School	***Listed on SC.com but no record of an actual show choir***	Huntsville	AL
Mars Hill Bible School	Celebration (v)	Florence	AL
Oak Mountain High School	Con Brio (v), Chanter (u), Craftsmen (u-m)	Birmingham	AL
Opelika High School	Ovations (v), Impressions (u-w)	Opelika	AL
Pelham High School	Show Choir (v)	Pelham	AL
Pell City High School	Showstoppers (v)	Pell City	AL
Prattville High School	Spotlight (v)	Prattville	AL
Spain Park High School	Park Singers (v) 2007 , Park Singers (u-w)	Hoover	AL
Tallassee High School	Divas (u), Gold Edition (u-m), New Image (u-w)	Tallassee	AL
Vestavia Hills High School	Singers (v), Trebles (u-w) 2004	Birmingham	AL
Chugiak High School	Chugiak Show Choir	Chugiak	AK
Lathrop High School	Lathrop Show Choir	Fairbanks	AK
Valdez High School	Valdez Show Choir	Valdez	AK
Horizon High School	Step on Stage (v), Show Divas (u-w)	Scottsdale	AZ
Ironwood Ridge High School	Encore! (v), Glitz! (u-w)	Oro Valley	AZ
Nortre Dame Prepatory	Saints Alive (v)	Scottsdale	AZ
St. David High School	Anthem (v)	St. David	AZ
Willow Canyon High School	Evolution (v)	Surprise	AZ
Sloan-Hendrix High School	Show Choir (v)	Imboden	AR
Sylvan Hills High School	Sylvan Sound (v) 2004	Sherwood	AR
Abraham Lincoln High School	Varsity Gold (v)	San Francisco	CA
Alta Loma High School	Sound Sensations (v) 2005	Alta Loma	CA
Antelope Valley High School	Anteleers (v), Treble Show Choir (u-w)	Lancaster	CA
Apple Valley High School	SunSations (v), Vocal Motion 2005	Apple Valley	CA
Arcadia High School	Chaunteurs (v), New Spirit (u-w)	Arcadia	CA
Azusa High School	Aztec Singers (v)	Azusa	CA
Bear River High School	Starlite Express (v)	Grass Valley	CA
Bonita Vista High School	The Music Machine (v), Sound Unlimited (u), Barontones (u-m) 2004	Chula Vista	CA
Brea Olinda High School	Masquerade (v), Spellbound (u-w), Thundercats (u-m), Tiffanys (u-w)	Brea	CA
Burbank High School	In Sync (v), Impressions (u-w), Sound Dogs (u-m), Out of the Blue (jv), Sapphire (u-w)	Burbank	CA
Carlsbad High School	Sound Express (v), Encore (u-w)	Carlsbad	CA
Chula Vista High School	Main Attraction (v), Dreamgirls (u-w) 2004	Chula Vista	CA
Claremont High School	***Listed on SC.com but no record of an actual show choir***	Claremont	CA
Cypress High School	Sensation (v), Choir Ensemble (u-w) 2005	Cypress	CA
Davis Senior High School	DHS Jazz Choir (v)	Davis	CA
Deer Valley High School	Show Choir (v)	Antioch	CA
Diamond Bar High School	Marquis (v), Solitaire (u-w), Notorious (u-m) 2005, Diamondtones (jv), Diamondaires (u-w)	Diamond Bar	CA
Diamond Ranch High School	Stylus Singers (v) 2004	Pomona	CA

Eastlake High School	Center Stage (v), Spotlight Ladies (u-w)	Chula Vista	CA
Eisenhower High School	Finale (u-m) 2005, Ike Singers (v), Ikettes (u-w)	Rialto	CA
El Modena High School	Chamber Singers (v) 2004, Harmonia (u-w) 2004	Orange	CA
El Rancho High School	Choraleers (v), Song and Dance (u-w) 2005, Legacy of Men (u-m) 2005	Pico Rivera	CA
Encore High School	Song Burst (v)	Hesperia	CA
Enterprise High School	Starship (v)	Redding	CA
Esperanza High School	Vivace (u-w)	Anaheim	CA
Fairmont Prepatory Academy	Show Choir (v)	Anaheim	CA
Gladstone High School	Dynamic Divas (u-w)	Covina	CA
Glendora High School	Royal Stewart Singers (v), Tartan Silhouettes (u-w)	Glendora	CA
Golden Valley High School	Solid Gold (v)	Santa Clarita	CA
Granada Hills Charter High School	Highlander (v)	Granada Hills	CA
Hart High School	Sound Vibrations (v), Hartbreakers (u-w), Unleashed (u-m), Hart 'n Soul (jv), Sweetharts (u-w)	Newhall	CA
Helix High School	Show'n Off (u-m) 2004, Guys & Dolls (v) 2004	La Mesa	CA
Jame Logan High School	Show like Whoa (v)	Union City	CA
John A. Rowland High School	Infusion (v), Enchantment (u-w), Acapella (jv) 2005	Rowland Heights	CA
John Burroughs High School	Powerhouse (v), Sound Sensations (u-w), Men@Work (u-m), Sound Waves (jv), Decibelles (u-w)	Burbank	CA
John F. Kennedy High School	***Listed on SC.com but no record of an actual show choir***	La Palma	CA
Junipero Serra High School	Show Choir (u-m)	San Mateo	CA
Jurupa Valley High School	***Listed on SC.com but no record of an actual show choir***		CA
La Puente High School	***Listed on SC.com but no record of an actual show choir***	La Puente	CA
Lancaster High School	Vocal Motion (v)	Lancaster	CA
Los Alamitos High School	Sound FX (v), Soundtrax (u-w), Xtreme (u-m), Connexion (jv) 2004, Axcent (u-w)	Los Alamitos	CA
Los Altos High School	Production Choir, (v)	Haciendo Heights	CA
Los Amigos High School	***Listed on SC.com but no record of an actual show choir***	Fountain Valley	CA
Madison High School	Rhapsody in Blue (v) 2005, Women's Jazz (u-w) 2005	San Diego	CA
Mark Keppel High School	Aztec Singers (v)	Alhambra	CA
Martin Luther King High School	Vocal Jazz (v)	Riverside	CA
Mayfair High School	Mayfair Showtime (v) 2004	Lakewood	CA
Mesa Grande Academy	Voices of the Heart (v)	Calimesa	CA
Monrovia High School	Camerata Singers (v) 2004	Monrovia	CA
Los Alamitos High School	Sound FX (v), Soundtrax (u-w), Xtreme (u-m), Connexion (jv) 2004, Axcent (u-w)	Los Alamitos	CA
Monte Vista High School	Sound Odyssey, Giltterama, Soundtrax, Xtreme, Rennaisance, Dream Street Singers	Monte Vista	CA
Mount Eden High School	Monarch Mirage (v)	Hayward	CA
Nogales High School	Singers (v)	La Puente	CA
Oceanside High School	Sound Waves (v), Sea Notes (u-w) 2006	Oceanside	CA
Ontario High School	Show Choir (v)	Ontario	CA
Orange Glen High School	OPUS (v), Center Stage (jv) 2007	Escondido	CA
Otay Ranch High School	Full Effect (v)	Chula Vista	CA
Oxford Academy	***Listed on SC.com but no record of an actual show choir***	Cypress	CA
Pacifica High School	Encore (v), Pearls (u-w)	Garden Grove	CA
Portola High School	Portola H S (v) 2004	Portola	CA
Ramona High School	Encore (v) 2004, Melody Express (u-w) 2004	Ramona	CA
Rancho Buena Vista High School	Silverado Showcase (v) 2005, Silver Ensemble (u-w) 2005	Vista	CA
Rancho Verde High School	Scarlet Rhapsody (v), Scarlet Rhapsody (u-w) 2006	Moreno Valley	CA
Redlands East Valley High School	Sweet Sensations (u-w) 2005, Revaliers (u-m) 2005	Redlands	CA
Redlands High School	Les Chanteuses (u-w), Ambassadors (u-m) 2004	Redlands	CA
Rio Mesa High School	***Listed on SC.com but no record of an actual show choir***	Oxnard	CA
San Pasqual High School	Showtime (v)	Escondido	CA
Santa Susana High School	Show Choir (v)	Simi Valley	CA
Saugus High School	Blue Heat (v), Blue Heat (u-w) 2004	Saugus	CA
Serrano High School	Vocal Point (v), Bedazzled (u-w), Forte (u-m) 2006	Phelan	CA
Tehachapi High School	Treble Ensemble (u-w) 2004	Tehachapi	CA
Temecula Valley High School	Show Choir (v), Company B (u-w) 2005	Temecula	CA
The Kings Academy	Knightshine (v)	Sunnyvale	CA
Vista High School	Showcats (v), Treble Cats (u-w) 2004	Vista	CA

School	Choir	City	State
Walnut High School	Show Choir (u-w) 2004, Rhapsody in Blue (u-w)	Walnut	CA
West Covina High School	Westcovaires (v)	West Covina	CA
Western High School	Vocal Motion (v)	Anaheim	CA
Westlake High School	Vocal Ensemble (v), Treble Makers (u-w) 2005	Westlake Village	CA
Wilson High School	Wilson Singers (v)	Hacienda Heights	CA
Woodbridge High School	Entertainers (v), Encore (u-w)	Irvine	CA
Battle Mountain High School	High Notes (v)	Edwards	CO
Canon City High School	Encore (v), Tiger Ladies (u-w)	Canon City	CO
Cheyenne Mountain High School	Moonlight Metallics (v) 2004	Colorado Springs	CO
Delta High School	Starmakers	Delta	CO
Hotchkiss High School	Show Choir (v)	Hotchkiss	CO
West High School	***Listed on SC.com but no record of an actual show choir***	Denver	CO
Canton High School	The B-Sharps	Canton	CT
Coginchaug Regional High School	Show Choir (v)	Durham	CT
Daniel Hand High School	VIBE (v)	Madison	CT
East Hartford High School	Jazzapella (v)	East Hartford	CT
Mercy High School	Choralations (v)	Middletown	CT
Metropolitan Learning Center	Originality (v)	Bloomfield	CT
South Windsor High School	Choral Spectrum (v)	South Windsor	CT
Tourtellotte Memorial High School	Genesis (v)	North Grosvenordale	CT
Windsor Locks High School	Vocal Motion (v)	Windsor Locks	CT
Caesar Rodney High School	C R Show Choir	Camden	DE
Christiana High School	Viking Visions	Newark	DE
Bayside High School	***Listed on SCIndex.com but no record of an actual show choir***	Baysdie	FL
Bloomingdale High Schools	Ambassadors	Valrico	FL
Brandon High School	***Listed on SC.com but no record of an actual show choir***	Brandon	FL
C. Leon King High School	Pride (v)	Tampa	FL
Eau Gallie High School	Encore	Eau Gallie	FL
Ft. Myers High School	Sound Wave	Ft. Myers	FL
Graceville High School	Prodegy (v)	Graceville	FL
Hernando High School	Spot Lites (v)	Brooksville	FL
J.R. Arnold High School	***Listed on SC.com but no record of an actual show choir***	Panama City Beach	FL
Lake Gibson High School	Audio (v) 2005	Lakeland	FL
Leesburg High School	Innovation (v) 2005, Illusions (u-w) 2005	Leesburg	FL
Marianna High School	Powerhouse (v), Decibelles (u-w)	Marianna	FL
Merritt Island High School	Island Singers	Merritt Island	FL
Oasis High School	Ovations	Cape Coral	FL
Olympic Heights Community High School	***Listed on SC.com but no record of an actual show choir***	Boca Raton	FL
Royal Palm Beach High School	IMPACT! (v) 2005	Royal Palm Beach	FL
Satellite High School	Ten Tones (v)	Satellite Beach	FL
Seminole High School	Destiny (v) 2009, Pizazz (u-w) 2009	Sanford	FL
Tarpon Springs High School	Syndicated Sound (v), Sophisticated Ladies (u-w)	Tarpon Springs	FL
Timber Creek High School	Show Stoppers (v) 2009	Orlando	FL
Wellington High School	Wellington Choirs	Wellington	FL
Americus-Sumter County High School	Front and Center Singers (v) 2005, Divas (u-w) 2004	Americus	GA
Appling County Comprehensive High School	Applause (v)	Baxley	GA
Bremen High School	***Listed on SC.com but no record of an actual show choir***	Bremen	GA
Dekalb School of the Arts	Highleit (v)	Avondale Estates	GA
Fitzgerald High School	Encore Unlimited (v) 2004, Women's Show Choir (u-w) 2004, Men's Show Choir (u-m) 2004	Fitzgerald	GA
Lakeside High School	Soundsation (v)	Evans	GA
Spalding High School	***Listed on SC.com but no record of an actual show choir***	Griffin	GA
Sprayberry High School	Gold Company (v)	Marietta	GA
Tift County High School	Eighth Street Singing Company (v), Ladies Choice (u-w)	Tifton	GA
Washington County High Schools	Show Choir	Sandersville	GA
Kahuku High School	Vocal Motion (v) 2004	Kahuku	HI
Declo High School	Trendsetters	Declo	ID
Ridgecrest Alternative High School	***Listed on SC.com but no record of an actual show choir***	Nampa	ID
Shelly High School	Horizons (v) 2006	Shelley	ID

Adlai Stevenson High School	Syncopation	Lincolnshire	IL
Alan B. Shepard High School	Nova (v)	Palos Heights	IL
Althoff Catholic High School	Crusader Innovation (v)	Belleville	IL
Arthur High School	High Energy	Arthur	IL
Argo Community High School	Ebullience (v)	Summit	IL
Belleville East High School	Blue Revolution	Belleville	IL
Buffalo Grove High School	Expressions (v), New Vibes (u-w)	Buffalo Grove	IL
Cary-Grove High School	Swing Choir (v)	Cary	IL
Centennial High School	Expressions (v)	Champaign	IL
Central A&M High School	Cameo Appearance (v) 2004	Moweaqua	IL
Clifton Central High School	New Impressions (v)	Clifton	IL
Crete-Monee High School	Cavaliers (v), Faces (u-w)	Crete	IL
Danville High School	Delegation (v), Contemporaires (u-w)	Danville	IL
Dunlap High School	Forte (v)	Dunlap	IL
Durand High School	Northern Lights (v), Here Comes Treble (u-w)	Durand	IL
Dwight D. Eisenhower High School	Eisenhower Express (v), Swing Street (jv) 2004	Blue Island	IL
Eisenhower High School	Elite Energy (v)	Decatur	IL
El Paso-Gridley High School	Modulations (v), Hi Fidelity (u-w)	El Paso	IL
Elk Grove High School	Town Criers (v)	Elk Grove Village	IL
Freeport High School	Showtime (v) 2006	Freeport	IL
Glenwood High School	Titan Fever (v)	Chatham	IL
Harold L. Richards High School	Encore (v)	Oak Lawn	IL
Herscher High School	Class Act (v)	Herscher	IL
Hinsdale Central High School	Encore (v)	Hinsdale	IL
Hoopeston Area High School	New Direction (v)	Hoopeston	IL
John Hersey High School	On Stage (v), Ladies First (u-w)	Arlington Heights	IL
Joliet Central High School	Show Steelers (v)	Joliet	IL
Lake Zurich High School	Blue Notes (v) 2004	Lake Zurich	IL
Lanphier High School	Lion's Pride (v)	Springfield	IL
East Leyden High School	LHS Swing Choir (v) 2005	Franklin Park	IL
Lutheran High School	Revelations (v)	Springfield	IL
Mateno High School	Magic (v)	Manteno	IL
Maroa-Forsyth High School	Rhythm Riders (v)	Maroa	IL
Mendota High School	***Listed on SC.com but no record of an actual show choir***	Mendota	IL
Momence High School	Midwest Melodies (v), Girls Show Choir (u-w)	Momence	IL
Monmouth-Roseville High School	Velocity (v)	Monmouth	IL
Morton High School	Vocal Motion (v) 2005, Survivors (jv) 2004	Morton	IL
Mt. Zion High School	Swingsations (v), Les Femmes (u-w)	Mt. Zion	IL
Mundelein High School	Sound (v), Lights (u-w), SoundFX (u-m)	Mundelein	IL
Normal Community High School	New Dimension	Normal	IL
O'Fallon Township High School	Great Expectations (v)	O'Fallon	IL
Oswego High School	Commotion (v), Ambiance (u-w)	Oswego	IL
Palatine High School	Forte (v)	Palatine	IL
Paxton-Buckley-Loda High School	Unlimited (v), Unlimited (u-w) 2005	Paxton	IL
Pekin Community High School	Noteables (v), Intuition (u-w), Advance Notice (jv) 2004	Pekin	IL
Peotone High School	Powerhouse (v), Decibelles (u-w)	Peotone	IL
Prospect High School	Company (v), Mixed Company (jv)	Mount Prospect	IL
Quincy Senior High School	QHS Show Choir (v), Varsity Singers (jv)	Quincy	IL
Riverton High School	Dynamics (v) 2005	Riverton	IL
Rockridge High School	Show Choir (v)	Taylor Ridge	IL
Rolling Meadows High School	New Directions (v), Trebellious (u-w)	Rolling Meadows	IL
South East High School	Spartan Sensations	Springfield	IL
Springfield High School	Scarlet Harmony (u-w)	Springfield	IL
Sullivan High School	Singers (v), New Generation (u-w)	Sullivan	IL
Thornton Township High School	***Listed on SC.com but no record of an actual show choir***	Harvey	IL
Ursuline Academy	Supersonics (v) 2004	Springfield	IL
Watseka High School	Sensations (v)	Watseka	IL
Waubonsie Valley High School	Sound Check (v), Girls in Heels (u-w)	Aurora	IL
Wheaton North High School	Flight (v)	Wheaton	IL
Wheaton Warrenville South High School	The Classics (v), Esprit (u-w)	Wheaton	IL
Wheeling High School	New Dawns (v)	Wheeling	IL
Woodruff High School	Great Expectations (v) 2004	Peoria	IL

Anderson High School	Singers Unlimited (v), 2005, Class Act (u-w)	Anderson	IN
Austin High School	Dimensions (v)	Austin	IN
Avon High School	Accents (v), Attraction (u-w)	Avon	IN
Batesville High School	Singers (v)	Batesville	IN
Bedford-North Lawrence High School	Starlets (u-w)	Bedford	IN
Beech Grove High School	Jubilaires (v), Elan (u-w)	Beech Grove	IN
Bellmont High School	Brave Generation (v), LEGS (u-w)	Decatur	IN
Ben Davis 9th Grade Center	Preview (jv)	Indianapolis	IN
Ben Davis High School	Premiers (v), Sounds (u-w)	Indianapolis	IN
Bishop Dwenger High School	Summit Sound (v), Elegance (u-w)	Fort Wayne	IN
Bishop Luers High School	Minstrels (v), Knight Stars (u-w)	Fort Wayne	IN
Bloomington High School North	***Listed on SC.com but no record of an actual show choir***	Bloomington	IN
Bloomington High School South	***Listed on SC.com but no record of an actual show choir***	Bloomington	IN
Bluffton High School	Musical Entourage (v)	Bluffton	IN
Brown County High School	Elegance (v)	Nashville	IN
Brownsburg High School	Spotlight Singers & Company (v), Starlight Voices (u-w)	Brownsburg	IN
Carmel High School	Ambassadors (v), Accents (u-w)	Carmel	IN
Carroll High School	Minstrels (v), Select Sound (u-w), JV Singers (jv)	Fort Wayne	IN
Castle High School	Knightsensations (v), Knightengales (u-w)	Newburgh	IN
Center Grove High School	Sound System (v), Debtones (u-w), Surround Sound (jv)	Greenwood	IN
Chesterton High School	Sandpipers (v), Drifters (u-w)	Chesterton	IN
Churubusco High School	New Era (v)	Churubusco	IN
Columbia City High School	City Heat (v), City Lights (u-w)	Columbia City	IN
Columbus East High School	Center Stage (v)	Columbus	IN
Columbus North High School	Debuteens and Music Men (v), North Stars (u-w)	Columbus	IN
Concord Community High School	Singers (v)	Elkhart	IN
Crawfordsville Senior High School	Show Choir (v)	Crawfordsville	IN
Decatur Central High School	Goldenaires (v)	Indianapolis	IN
Dekalb High School	Classic Connection (v), Sound Sensation (u-w), Guy in the Spotlight (u-M	Waterloo	IN
East Noble High School	Knight Rhythms (v), Premiere Edition (u-w)	Kendallville	IN
Eastbrook High School	Panther Edition (v), Panther Kittens (u-w)	Marion	IN
Edgewood High School	Music Warehouse (v), Sophisticated Ladies (u-w), New Edition (jv)	Ellettsville	IN
Fairfield High School	Fusion (v), Expressions (u-w)	Goshen	IN
Fishers High School	Silver Streak (v), Silver Sound (u-w)	Fishers	IN
Frankfort High School	Fortissimo (v)	Frankfort	IN
Franklin Central High School	F.C. Singers (v), High Voltage (u-w)	Indianapolis	IN
Franklin Community High School	Heritage Singers (v), Sensations (u-w)	Franklin	IN
Garrett High School	Encore (v), Rhythm Connectoin (u-w)	Garrett	IN
Hamilton Southeastern High School	Royal Sound (v) 2004	Fishers	IN
Highland High School	Highland Singers (v), Starliters (u-w), Impulse (jv) 2005	Anderson	IN
Homestead High School	Class Royale (v), Elite (u-w)	Fort Wayne	IN
Huntington North High School	Varsity Singers (v)	Huntington	IN
Jefferson High School	First Edition (v), Expressions (u-w), CSN (u-m), A Cappella (jv)	Lafayette	IN
Kokomo High School	Karisma Singers (v)	Kokomo	IN
Lakeland High School	Vocal Motion (v)	LaGrange	IN
Lawrence Central High School	Central Sound (v), Sweet Sensations (u-w), Sound Connections (jv) 2004 New Expressions (jv) 2004	Indianapolis	IN
Lawrence North High School	New Dimension (v), Hip Street (u-w)	Indianapolis	IN
Lebanon High School	Charisma (v)	Lebanon	IN
Marion High School	Innovations (v) 2004, Sweet Inspirations (u-w) 2004, 26th Street Singers (jv)*	Marion	IN
Martinsville High School	Flash'n Fascination (v)	Martinsville	IN
Monrovia High School	Shooting Stars (v)	Monrovia	IN
Mooresville High School	Spotlighters (v), Finesse (u-w), Millenium (jv)	Mooresville	IN
New Castle Chrysler High School	Red Hot Blues (v), Dynamiques (u-w)	New Castle	IN
New Haven High School	Sound Edition (v) 2005	New Haven	IN
New Palestine High School	Crimson Heat (v), Diamond Sensations (u-w)	New Palestine	IN
Noblesville High School	NHS Singers (v), New Dimensions (u-w)	Noblesville	IN
North Central High School	Counterpoints (v), Descants (u-w), Varsity (jv), Accents (u-w)	Indianapolis	IN
North High School	Northernaires (v) 2005, Aurora (u-w) 2004	Evansville	IN

School	Choir(s)	City	State
North Side High School	Wave of Distinction (v)	Fort Wayne	IN
North Ridge High School	Northern Lights (v), Starlights (u-w)	Middlebury	IN
Northrop High School	Charisma (v), Allure (u-w)	Fort Wayne	IN
Northwood High School	Dawning Generation (v) 2006	Nappanee	IN
Norwell High School	Knight Moves (v), Knight Stars (u-w)	Ossian	IN
Owen Valley High School	Soundwaves (v)	Spencer	IN
Pendleton Heights High School	Pendletones (v)	Pendleton	IN
Pike High School	Encores (v), Mystiques (u-w)	Indianapolis	IN
Plainfield High School	Belles et Beaux (v), Femmes Fatales (u-w)	Plainfield	IN
Princeton Community High School	Varsity Singers (v), Innovations (u-w)	Princeton	IN
Rensselaer Central High School	Show Choir (v)	Rensselaer	IN
Roncalli High School	Rebel Rhapsody (v)	Indianapolis	IN
Seymour High School	Show Choir (v)	Seymour	IN
Shawe Memorial High School	Encore! (v) 2004	Madison	IN
Shelbyville High School	Synergy (v), Soundwave (u-w) 2004	Shelbyville	IN
South Dearborn High School	Opening Knight (v)	Aurora	IN
Southern Wells High School	Raider Rhythm (v)	Poneto	IN
Southmont High School	Panache (v), Sudden Impulse (u-w), Young Originals (jv)	Crawfordsville	IN
Southport High School	Simply Chic (u-w)	Indianapolis	IN
Southwestern High School	Esprit (v)	Hanover	IN
Taylor High School	Glitz and Glamour (v)	Kokomo	IN
Tipton High School	Young Originals (v) 2004	Tipton	IN
Triton Central High School	TC Singers (v)	Fairland	IN
Twin Lakes High School	Sound Wave (v), Singsations (u-w)	Monticello	IN
Warren Central High School	Connection (v), Hi-Lites (u-w), Vivace (jv)	Indianapolis	IN
Washington High School	Impulse (v) 2005, Accents (u-w) 2005	Washington	IN
Wayne High School	***Listed on SC.com but no record of an actual show choir***	Fort Wayne	IN
Whiteland High School	Rhythm Masters (v)	Whiteland	IN
Woodlan High School	Warrior Ambition	Woodburn	IN
Zionsville High School	Royalaires (v), Choralaires (u-w)	Zionsville	IN
Algona High School	Algona Swing Choir (v) 2004	Algona	IA
Anamosa High School	Sadie Street Singers (v)	Anamosa	IA
Ankeny High School	Visual Adrenaline (v), Perpetual Motion (jv), Intensity (u-w)	Ankeny	IA
Atlantic High School	Ambassadors (v), Sensations (u-w), Fresh Look (jv)	Atlantic	IA
Audubon High School	Show Choir (v)	Audubon	IA
Ballard High School	Remix (v)	Huxley	IA
Bcluw High School	Fire & Ice (v)	Conrad	IA
Bedford High School	Touch of Class (v) 2005	Bedford	IA
Benton Community High School	Celebration Co. (v), Jubilation, Inc. (jv)	Van Horne	IA
Bettendorf High School	Surround Sound	Bettendorf	IA
Bishop Heelan Catholic School	Harmonia Mundi (v), Magnifique (u-w), Starlights (u-w) 2005, Genesis (jv)	Sioux City	IA
Bondurant-Farrar High School	***Listed on SC.com but no record of an actual show choir***	Bondurant	IA
Boyden-Hull High School	Show Choir (v)	Hull	IA
Brooklyn-Guernsey-Malcom High School	Dynamics (v)	Brooklyn	IA
Carroll High School	Swingsations (v),	Carroll	IA
Kennedy High School	Happiness, Inc. (v), Protégé (jv), Chanteurs (jv)	Cedar Rapids	IA
Center Point-Urbana High School	Summit Street Singers (v), Illumination (u-w)	Center Point	IA
Central Lee High School	CENTRifugAL Force (v)	Donnellson	IA
Columbus Catholic High School	Sound Coalition (v), Sound Connection (jv)	Waterloo	IA
Council Bluffs Jefferson High School	Jefferson Edition (v), Second Edition (jv)	Council Bluffs	IA
Council Bluffs Lincoln High School	Jazz Connection (v), Lady Lynx (u-w), Young Design (jv)	Council Bluffs	IA
Dallas Center-Grimes High School	Rhythm 'n Red (v)	Grimes	IA
Danville High School	Vocal Chords (v)	Danville	IA
Davenport Central High School	Central Singers, Inc. (v), Blue Vibrations (jv), Rhapsody in Blue (u-w) 2004	Davenport	IA
Davenport North High School	Northside Establishment (v), Center Stage (jv)	Davenport	IA
Davenport West High School	West Connection (v), This Just In! (jv)	Davenport	IA
Denison High School	Singing Ambassadors (v), Sixteenth Street Singers (u-w)	Denison	IA
Des Moines Christian School	Light, Inc. (v), Destination Excellence (jv)	Urbandale	IA
Des Moines Lincoln High School	Infinity (v), Sound Attraction (u-w)	Des Moines	IA

Dike-New Hartford High School	***Listed on SC.com but no record of an actual show choir***	Dike	IA
Dowling Catholic High School	Dimensions (v)	West Des Moines	IA
East High School	Headliners (v), New Sound (jv), Impulse (u-w)	Sioux City	IA
Emmetsburg High School	High Voltage (v), Black and Gold (u-w)	Emmetsburg	IA
Fort Madison High School	Swingspan (v), Crimson & Black (jv) 2004	Fort Madison	IA
George Washington High School	Momentum (v), Celebration (jv), Sensation (u-w), Vivace (jv)	Cedar Rapids	IA
Glenwood High School	Titan Fever (v)	Glenwood	IA
Griswold High School	GT Thrillers and The Rubber Band	Griswold	IA
Guthrie Center High School	Center Stage (v)	Guthrie Center	IA
Hamburg High School	Show Choir (v)	Hamburg	IA
Hinton Community School	Soundwaves (v), Sound Explosions (jv)	Hinton	IA
HLV High School	Pizzazz (v)	Victor	IA
Holy Trinity High School	Commotion (v)	Fort Madison	IA
Hudson High School	First Edition (v)	Hudson	IA
Indianola High School	Side One (v), Flip Side (jv)	Indianola	IA
Iowa City High School	4th Avenue Jazz Company (v), City Lights (jv), NiteLites (u-w) 2005	Iowa City	IA
Iowa City West High School	Good Time Company (v), Showtime (jv)	Iowa City	IA
Jefferson-Scranton High School	J-Town Singers (v)	Jefferson	IA
Johnston High School	Innovation (v), Synergy (jv)	Johnston	IA
Keokuk High School	Purple Harmony (v), Vibrations (jv)	Keokuk	IA
Keota High School	EagleRock! (v)	Keota	IA
Kuemper Catholic High School	Show Choir (v)	Carroll	IA
Laurens-Marathon High School	Impulse (v)	Laurens	IA
Lawton-Bronson High School	Momentum (v), Vocal Effect (jv)	Lawton	IA
LeMars Community High School	Crimson and Black (v)	LeMars	IA
Lewis Central High School	Corporation (v), Company (u-w)	Council Bluffs	IA
Linn-Mar High School	10th Street Edition (v), In Step (jv), Hi Style (jv)	Marion	IA
Manson Northwest Webster High School	Quantum (v)	Manson	IA
Maquoketa Valley High School	***Listed on SC.com but no record of an actual show choir***	Delhi	IA
Marshalltown High School	Southside Transit (v), Encore (u-w)	Marshalltown	IA
MFL MarMac High School	The Young Americans (v)	Monona	IA
Mount Pleasant Community High School	InMotion (v)	Mt. Pleasant	IA
Muscatine High School	River City Rhythm (v), Encore! (jv) 2010, Encore (u-w)	Muscatine	IA
Nevada High School	Starburst, Inc. (v) 1990, Music in Motion (u-w) 1990	Nevada	IA
New Hampton High School	Main Street West (v)	New Hampton	IA
New London High School	Black & Gold Company (v)	New London	IA
Newton High School	Midnight Express (v), Jubilation (jv) 2004	Newton	IA
North Polk High School	Vivace (v)	Alleman	IA
North Sentral Kossuth High School	Coda Blue (v)	Swea City	IA
Norwalk High School	Sound Revolution (v)	Norwalk	IA
Ogden High School	Bulldog Beat (v)	Ogden	IA
Osage High School	Show Choir (v)	Osage	IA
Ottumwa High School	Sudden Impact (v)	Ottumwa	IA
Pella High School	AcaPella (v), Dutch Divas (u-w)	Pella	IA
Pocahontas Area High School	Showstoppers (v) 2010	Pocahontas	IA
Prairie High School	The Ambassadors (v), Focal Point (jv)	Cedar Rapids	IA
Prairieview High School	***Listed on SC.com but no record of an actual show choir***	Waukee	IA
Ruthven-Ayrshire High School	Raider Rhythm (v)	Ruthven	IA
Sheldon High School	Show Choir (v)	Sheldon	IA
Sioux Center High School	Satisfaction (v)	Sioux Center	IA
South Hardin High School	Cabaret (v)	Eldora	IA
South O'Brien High School	Show Choir (v)	Paulina	IA
Southeast Polk High School	RAMification (v), Southeast Celebration (jv) 2004	Pleasant Hill	IA
Spirit Lake High School	Music Factory (v)	Spirit Lake	IA
Sumner-Fredericksburg High School	Sensations (v)	Sumner	IA
Theodore Roosevelt High School	Varsity Show Choir (v)	Des Moines	IA
Thomas Jefferson High School	West Side Delegation (v), Ovation (jv)	Cedar Rapids	IA
Tri-Center High School	T-C Sensations (v)	Neola	IA

School	Choir	City	State
Union High School	Union Station (v)	La Porte City	IA
Urbandale High School	Studio (v), Vitality (jv)	Urbandale	IA
Valley High School	Choralation (v), Vertigo (u-w) 2004, Rhythmic Ignition (jv)	West Des Moines	IA
Vinton-Shellsburg High School	DanSing Corp. (v)	Vinton	IA
Wahlert High School	Impulse (v), Impact (jv), Intuition (u-w) 2004	Dubuque	IA
Walnut High School	Singers (v)	Walnut	IA
Waterloo West High School	West High Story (v)	Waterloo	IA
Waukee High School	Millenium (v), Spirit (jv)	Waukee	IA
West Branch High School	Christopher Jive and the Uptown 45 (v)	West Branch	IA
West Burlington High School	DyNAMix (v)	West Burlington	IA
West Delaware High School	WD Forte (v), Crescendo (jv)	Manchester	IA
West Liberty High School	Voices Unlimited (v)	West Liberty	IA
Western Dubuque High School	5th Avenue (v), Aristocats (u-w)	Epworth	IA
Westwood High School	Rebelaires (v), Voices in Motion (jv)	Sloan	IA
Williamsburg High School	Sound Attraction (v)	Williamsburg	IA
Winterset High School	Vocal Explosion (v)	Winterset	IA
Woodbury Central High School	Showstoppers (v)	Moville	IA
Xavier High School	Xhileration (v), Xuberance (jv), Xcitement (u-w) 2006	Cedar Rapids	IA
Belle Plaine High School	Singers (v)	Belle Plaine	KS
Junction City Senior High School	JC Singers (v)	Junction City	KS
Manhattan High School	Pops (v), Sugar n' Spice (u-w)	Manhattan	KS
Ottawa High School	Cytones (v)	Ottawa	KS
Sabetha High School	Odyssey (v), Chantee (u-w)	Sabetha	KS
Seaman High School	Show Choir (v)	Topeka	KS
St. Thomas Aquinas High School	Swingin' Saints (v)	Overland Park	KS
Bluegrass United Academic Center	Show Choir (v)	Nicholasville	KY
Bowling Green High School	***Listed on SC.com but no record of an actual show choir***	Bowling Green	KY
Greenwood High School	***Listed on SC.com but no record of an actual show choir***	Bowling Green	KY
North Oldham High School	Northern Lights (v)	Goshen	KY
Owensboro High School	Encore! (v)	Owensboro	KY
Shelby County High School	Blast (v)	Shelbyville	KY
Comeaux High School	Magic Moods (v) 2005	Lafayette	LA
Franklinton High School	Demonaires (v)	Franklinton	LA
Northeast High School	Southern Harmony (v) 2005	Pride	LA
Northshore High School	Silvertones (v) 2004	Slidell	LA
Tara High School	Show Choir (v)	Baton Rouge	LA
Woodlawn High School	Entourage (v)	Baton Rouge	LA
Ellsworth High School	Show Choir (v)	Ellsworth	ME
Hampden Academy	***Listed on SC.com but no record of an actual show choir***	Hampden	ME
Houlton High School	***Listed on SC.com but no record of an actual show choir***	Houlton	ME
Fort Hill High School	***Listed on SC.com but no record of an actual show choir***	Cumberland	MD
Patapsco High School	Great Expectations (v)	Baltimore	MD
Quince Orchard High School	***Listed on SC.com but no record of an actual show choir***	Gaithersburg	MD
Walter Johnson High School	Popfly (v)	Bethesda	MD
Winston Churchill High School	Showstoppers (v), Simply Irresistible (u-w)	Potomac	MD
Andover High School	From Start to Finish (v)	Andover	MA
Auburn High School	Contrary Motion (v)	Auburn	MA
Beverly High School	Vitality (v)	Beverly	MA
Boston Latin School	Pizzazz (v)	Boston	MA
Dracut High School	Show Choir	Dracut	MA
Shepherd Hill Regional High School	Fantasy (v), Illusion (u)	Dudley	MA
Everett High School	Pop Vox (v)	Everett	MA
Tantasqua High School	Encore (v)	Fiskdale	MA
Gateway Regional High School	???	Huntington	MA
Lowell High School	Spindles (v)	Lowell	MA
New Bedford High School	Pure Energy (v), Charisma (u) 2004	New Bedford	MA
Oliver Ames High School	Panache (v)	North Easton	MA
Converse Middle School	CONVERSation	Palmer	MA
Somerset High School	Electrify (v)	Somerset	MA
South Hadley High School	Adrenaline (v)	South Hadley	MA
Stoughton High School	Knight Moves (v) 2004	Stoughton	MA
Joseph Case High School	Showcase (v)	Swansea	MA

Waltham High School	Music Unlimited (v), Music Express (u),		
	Music Odyssey (jv) 2004	Waltham	MA
Bartlett Junior-Senior High School	Impressions (v) 2004, New Attitude (jv) 2004	Webster	MA
Whitman Hanson Regional			
High School	High Frequency (v)	Whitman	MA
Worcester Acedemy	WA Harmony (v) 2004, Harmony On The Hill (jv) 2005	Worcester	MA
Lakeview High School	Spartanaires (v) 2008	Battle Creek	MI
Chelsea High School	Company C (v)	Chelsea	MI
Coopersville High School	Main Event (v) 2008	Coopersville	MI
University of Detriot Jesuit			
High School	Show Choir (v)	Detroit	MI
Oakland Early College	Glee (v)	Farmington Hills	MI
Grosse Pointe South High School	The Point Singers (v)	Grosse Pointe Farms	MI
Ludington High School	Sound Explosion (v)	Ludington	MI
Saint Joseph High School	***Listed on SC.com but no record of an actual show choir***	Saint Joseph	MI
Henry Ford II High School	***Listed on SC.com but no record of an actual show choir***	Sterling Heights	MI
Tecumseh High School	The Company (v), Women's Show Choir (u)		
	The Testostertones (u)	Tecumseh	MI
Bedford High School	Soiree Singers (v)	Temperance	MI
Adrian High School	Gragon Fever (v), 2005	Adrian	MN
Albert Lea Senior High School	Cat'aclysmic (v), Sass (u)	Albert Lea	MN
Pacelli High School	***Listed on SC.com but no record of an actual show choir***	Austin	MN
Bemidji High School	Vocalmotive (v), La Voce Ballo (u)	Bemidji	MN
Jefferson Senior High School	Jefferson Connection (v), Jive (u)	Bloomington	MN
Kennedy Senior High School	Rhythm in Gold (v), East Side Swingers (u),		
	East Side Rhythm (jv)	Bloomington	MN
Brooklyn Center High School	Field of Fire (v) 2005	Brooklyn Center	MN
Denfeld High School	Steppin' Up (v)	Duluth	MN
International School of Minnesota	Show Choir (v) 2004	Eden Prairie	MN
Totino Grace High School	Company of Singers (v), Encore Singers (jv),		
	Testostertones (u-m)	Fridley	MN
Hastings High School	Riverside Company (v), Upstage Revolution (jv), Divaz (u)	Hastings	MN
Jackson County Central High School	Encore (v)	Jackson	MN
Madelia High School	Centerstage (v)	Madelia	MN
Maple Grove Senior High School	Crimson Chorale (v)	Maple Grove	MN
Marshall High School	Tiger Drive (v)	Marshall	MN
Westonka High School	Pop Singers (v)	Mound	MN
North High School	Northern Lights (v), Soundsations (jv) 2005	North St. Paul	MN
Rush City High School	New Horizons (v)	Rush City	MN
Sauk Rapids-Rice High School	Storm Singers (v)	Sauk Rapids	MN
South St. Paul Secondary	SouthSide Sensation (v)	South St. Paul	MN
St. James Secondary High School	Limited Edition (v)	St. James	MN
Waconia High School	Power Company (v), The Current (jv)	Waconia	MN
Waseca High School	State Street Singers (v)	Waseca	MN
McDonald County High School	Rhapsody 'n Rhythm (v)	Anderson	MO
Carrollton High School	9th Street Singers (v), Touch of Crimson (u)	Carrollton	MO
Carthage Senior High School	Soundwave (v), Suite Sounds (u)	Carthage	MO
Cassville High School	Center Stage (v), NBA (u)	Cassville	MO
Marquette High School	Center Stage (v)	Chesterfield	MO
Parkway Central High School	Pizzazz (v), Razzle Dazzle (u), Encore (jv)	Chesterfield	MO
Cole Camp High School	Encore (v), Impressions (u)	Cole Camp	MO
Rock Bridge High School	City Lights (v), Satin 'n Lace (u)	Columbia	MO
El Dorado Springs High School	Sound Collage (v), Sound Investment (jv)	El Dorado Springs	MO
Eureka High School	Onstage! (v) 2005	Eureka	MO
Fulton High School	Sting (v)	Fulton	MO
Grain Valley High School	Exclamation (v)	Grain Valley	MO
East Newton High School	Patriot Singers (v)	Granby	MO
Green Ridge High School	***Listed on SC.com but no record of an actual show choir***	Green Ridge	MO
Hannibal High School	River City Revue (v)	Hannibal	MO
Harrisonville High School	Music Makers (v), Forefront (jv)	Harrisonville	MO
Holden High School	Into the Blue (v)	Holden	MO
Hollister High School	City Lights (u)	Hollister	MO

Helias High School	Parallel in Motion (v)	Jefferson City	MO
Jefferson City High School	Riot (v)	Jefferson City	MO
Joplin High School	Sound Dimensions (v), Touch of Class (u)	Joplin	MO
Oak Park High School	Oak Street Singers (v)	Kansas City	MO
Park Hill High School	Park Avenue Singers (v)	Kansas City	MO
Parkway South High School	Showstoppers (v), Southern Belles (u-w), Southern Gentlemen (u-m)	Manchester	MO
Maryville High School	Spectrum (v)	Maryville	MO
Mount Vernon High School	Vocal Motion (v)	Mount Vernon	MO
Neosho High School	Choraleers (v), Sugar and Sprice (u)	Neosho	MO
Nevada High School	Soundsational Singers (v), Treble Effects (u)	Nevada	MO
North Kansas City High School	***Listed on SC.com but no record of an actual show choir***	North Kansas City	MO
Odessa High School	Ovation (v)	Odessa	MO
Pacific High School	Pizzazz (v)	Pacific	MO
Raymore-Peculiar Senior High School	Rush (v)	Peculiar	MO
Pleasant Hill High School	Hillside Singers (v), Hilltop Harmony (u) Hillsound (jv)	Pleasant Hill	MO
Smith-Cotton High School	New Score Singers (v), Cabaret (u)	Sedalia	MO
St. Joseph Central High School	Encore (v)	St. Joseph	MO
Mehlville High School	Adrenaline (v)	St. Louis	MO
Bayless High School	Expression (v)	St. Louis	MO
Ladue Horton Watkins High School	Footnotes (v)	St. Louis	MO
Stover High School	Showtime (v)	Stover	MO
Troy Buchanan High School	Express (v), Soundwave (jv)	Troy	MO
Warrensburg High School	SoundWave (v), Prism (u)	Warrensburg	MO
Webb City High School	Singers (v)	Webb City	MO
Bay High School	Momentum (v) 2004	Bay St. Louis	MS
Biloxi High School	Cabaret (v)	Biloxi	MS
Forrest County Agricultural High School	Aggie Accents (v)	Brooklyn	MS
Pearl River Central High School	Central Attraction (v)	Carriere	MS
Clinton High School	Attache (v)	Clinton	MS
Columbia Academy	Premiere (v)	Columbia	MS
Columbia High School	Limited Edition (v)	Columbia	MS
Columbus High School	Front Line (v) 2004	Columbus	MS
Newton County High School	Vivace (v), Pizzazz (u)	Decatur	MS
South Jones High School	Company (v)	Ellisville	MS
Northwest Rankin High School	Renaissance (v)	Flowood	MS
Gautier High School	Sensations (v)	Gautier	MS
Grenada High School	Visions (v)	Grenada	MS
Hattiesburg High School	Expressions (v)	Hattiesburg	MS
North Forest High School	Illusions (v) 2006	Hattiesburg	MS
Oak Grove High School	Center Stage! (v)	Hattiesburg	MS
Horn Lake High School	Show Choir (v) 2004	Horn Lake	MS
Indianola Academy	Espirit (v)	Indianola	MS
Jackson Academy	Encore (v)	Jackson	MS
Jackson Preparatory School	Reveillon (v)	Jackson	MS
Northeast Jones Jr/Sr High School	Gold Horizons (v), Special Edition (u) 2006, Tiger Vibe (jv) 2005	Laurel	MS
West Jones High School	Imagination (v), Sassy (u)	Laurel	MS
Laurel High School	Showstoppers (v), 2006 Encore (u) 2006	Laurel	MS
Long Beach High School	Tropical Wave (v) 2005	Long Beach	MS
George County High School	Rebelution (v)	Lucedale	MS
Lumberton High School	A Touch of Class (v)	Lumberton	MS
Madison Central High School	Reveille (v)	Madison	MS
Pascagoula High School	Impact (v)	Pascagoula	MS
Petal High School	Soundsations (v), Innovations (u)	Petal	MS
Picayune Memorial High School	Tidal Rave (v), Girls! Girls! Girls! (u)	Picayune	MS
Purvis High School	Pizzazz (v)	Purvis	MS
Sumrall High School	Legacy (v)	Sumrall	MS
Taylorsville High School	Espirit de Corps (v)	Taylorsville	MS
Tupelo High School	Wave Connection (v), Soundwave (u)	Tupelo	MS
Wayne County High School	Orange Sensations (v)	Waynesboro	MS

West Point High School	Dynasty (v)	West Point	MS
Stone High School	Entourage (v)	Wiggins	MS
Montana Theaterworks	MTW Show Choir	Bozeman	MT
Fairfield High School	***Listed on SC.com but no record of an actual show choir***	Fairfield	MT
Charlotte Academy of Music	Charlotte Glee Club	Charlotte	NC
North Gaston High School	North Gaston Choral Society (v)	Dallas	NC
Riverside High School	Show Choir (v)	Durham	NC
Franklin High School	B-Naturals (m)	Franklin	NC
Holy Springs High School	Show Choir (v)	Holly Springs	NC
Alfred Luther Brown High School	Vocal Ensemble (v)	Kannapolis	NC
Broughton High School	Carolina Spirit (v) 2004, Capital Touch (u) 2005, Carolina Company 2005	Raleigh	NC
Cardinal Gibbons High School	Show Choir (v)	Raleigh	NC
Red Springs High School	NA	Red Springs	NC
Spring Creek High School	***Listed on SC.com but no record of an actual show choir***	Seven Springs	NC
Green Central High School	The Ramblers, Varisty Singers	Snow Hill	NC
Fargo South High School	Pizzaz	Fargo	ND
Alliance High School	Harmonics (v), Velocity (u)	Alliance	NE
Auburn High School	Rhythm In Red (v)	Auburn	NE
Bayard High School	21st Centruy Singers (v), Magic Rhythm (jv)	Bayard	NE
Beatrice High School	Limited Edition (v)	Beatrice	NE
Bellevue East High School	Take II (v)	Bellevue	NE
Bellevue West High School	West Connection (v)	Bellevue	NE
Blair High School	Ovation (v), Encore (u)	Blair	NE
Chadron High School	Cardinal Singers (v)	Chadron	NE
Elkhorn High School	Excel (v), Expressions (u), Exclamation (jv)	Elkhorn	NE
Fairbury Jr/Sr High School	Crimson Elite (v), Show Choir (jv)	Fairbury	NE
Falls City High School	Applederas (v)	Falls City	NE
Norris High School	Norris Gold (v), 68th Street Singers (jv)	Firth	NE
Fort Calhoun Senior High School	Swing Choir (v)	Fort Calhoun	NE
Gering High School	Harmony (v), Dolce Bella (u)	Gering	NE
Grand Island Central Catholic High School	Crystal Blue (v), Show Choir (jv)	Grand Island	NE
Grand Island Northwest High School	14 Karat Gold (v), Bella Voce (jv)	Grand Island	NE
Grand Island Senior High School	Ultimate Image (v), Sweet Revelation (u), Future Image (jv)	Grand Island	NE
Gretna High School	Revolution (v), Evolution (u)	Gretna	NE
Chase County High School	Show Choir (v)	Imperial	NE
Kearney High School	Pops Choir (v), Sapphire & Gold Singers (u)	Kearney	NE
Lincoln East High School	Express (v), Elegance (u)	Lincoln	NE
Lincoln Lutheran Jr/Sr High School	***Listed on SC.com but no record of an actual show choir***	Lincoln	NE
Lincoln Northeast High School	Voices of Harmony (v)	Lincoln	NE
Lincoln Southeast High School	Countessess & Noblemen (v)	Lincoln	NE
Lincoln Southwest High School	Resonance (v), Ambiance (jv), Diva's Intuition (u) 2005	Lincoln	NE
Pius X High School	Spectrum Singers (v)	Lincoln	NE
Nebraska City High School	Expressions (v)	Nebraska City	NE
Elkhorn South High School	Varsity Show Choir (v), JV Show Choir (jv)	Omaha	NE
Millard North High School	Showstoppers (v), Illumination (u)	Omaha	NE
Millard South High School	Fresh Start (v)	Omaha	NE
Millard West High School	West in the Groove (v), Uptown Girls (u), Swing Cats (jv)	Omaha	NE
North High School	Explosion! (v)	Omaha	NE
Omaha Northwest High School	Pure Crimson & Gold (v), Scarlet Sensations (u)	Omaha	NE
Westside High School	Amazing Technicolor Show Choir (v), Simply Irresistible (u), Warrior Express (jv)	Omaha	NE
Ord Jr/Sr High School	18th Street Singers (v), Show Choir (jv)	Ord	NE
Southern Valley High School	Show Choir (v)	Oxford	NE
Papillion La Vista High School	Free Spirit (v), In Motion (jv), Heart & Soul (u)	Papillion	NE
Papillion La Vista South High School	Titanium (v), Illumination (u), Titan Prep (jv)	Papillion	NE
Pawnee City High School	Showstoppers (v)	Pawnee City	NE
Plattsmouth High School	Sapphire and Ice (v)	Plattsmouth	NE
Ralston High School	RUSH (v), Runway (u)	Ralston	NE
Scottsbluff High School	Choraliers (v) 2002, 27th Street Singers (jv)	Scottsbluff	NE
Seward High School	Singers (v)	Seward	NE

South Sioux City High School	Sound Sensations (v), Royalettes (u)	South Sioux City	NE
Platteview High School	Swing Choir (v)	Springfield	NE
Bishop Neumann High School	Scarlet Knights (v)	Wahoo	NE
Wahoo High School	Show Choir (v)	Wahoo	NE
Wilber-Clatonia High School	Emerald and Green (v)	Wilber	NE
Southern High School	Southern Harmony (v)	Wymore	NE
York High School	Dukes and Duchessess (v)	York	NE
Howell High School	Show Choir (v)	Farmingdale	NJ
Sayreville War Memorial High School	Vox Humana (v)	Parlin	NJ
Pennsauken High School	Double Dozen	Pennsauken	NJ
Point Pleasant Borough High School	***Listed on SC.com but no record of an actual show choir***	Point Pleasant	NJ
Sterling High School	Silvertones	Somerdale	NJ
Winslow Township High School	Soundwave	Winslow Township	NJ
Del Borte High School	Twilight Knights	Albuquerque	NM
Eldorado High School	Gold Rush (v), 24 Carat (u)	Albuquerque	NM
La Cueva High School	Main Street (v), 5th Avenue (u)	Albuquerque	NM
Manzano High School	Prestige (v)	Albuquerque	NM
Sandia High School	Continentals (v)	Albuquerque	NM
St. Puis X High School	Breath of Heaven (v)	Albuquerque	NM
Carlsbad High School	Show Choir (v) 2004, Encore (u) 2005	Carlsbad	NM
Las Cruces High School	Modernaires (v)	Las Cruces	NM
Onate High School	Legends (v)	Las Cruces	NM
Moriarity High School	Messengers (v)	Moriarity	NM
Portales High School	Red Hots (v)	Portales	NM
Capital High School	Show Choir (v)	Santa Fe	NM
Carson High School	Capital Stars (v)	Carson City	NV
Palo Verde High School	Vocal Infinity (v) 2005	Las Vegas	NV
The Meadows School	***Listed on SC.com but no record of an actual show choir***	Las Vegas	NV
Brockport High School	***Listed on SC.com but no record of an actual show choir***	Brockport	NY
Mount Mercy Academy	Pure Magic (v)	Buffalo	NY
Central Islip High School	Show Choir (v)	Central Islip	NY
Liverpool High School	***Listed on SC.com but no record of an actual show choir***	Liverpool	NY
Lockport High School	***Listed on SC.com but no record of an actual show choir***	Lockport	NY
Sanford H. Calhoun High School	Crescendo (v)	Merrick	NY
Middletown High School	Pipers (v)	Middletown	NY
Greece Athena High School	Show Choir (v)	Rochester	NY
Our Lady of Mercy High School	Show Choir (u)	Rochester	NY
Ada High School	Varsity Singers (v)	Ada	OH
Alliance High School	Jet Singers (v)	Alliance	OH
Marlington High School	Duke Street, Jazz Choir	Alliance	OH
Ashland High School	Arrow Dynamics (v)	Ashland	OH
Teays Valley High School	Prominent Rendition (v)	Ashville	OH
Aurora High School	Emerald Ensemble (v)	Aurora	OH
Beavercreek High School	Friends (v)	Beavercreek	OH
West Branch High School	Young & Alive (v)	Beloit	OH
Brunswick High School	Young Folk (v) 2002	Brunswick	OH
Bluffton High School	Center Stage (v)	Buffton	OH
River Valley High School	Music Company (v), New Addition (u)	Caledonia	OH
Miami East High School	Explosion (v)	Casstown	OH
Chardon High School	Free Harmony (v) 2002	Chardon	OH
Chesapeake High School	Show Stoppers (v)	Chesapeake	OH
Unioto High School	Rhapsody (v)	Chillicothe	OH
Colerain High School	Show Cards (v), Cardinal Company (u)	Cincinnati	OH
North College Hill High School	Mirage Show Choir (v)	Cincinnati	OH
West Clermont High School (Glen Este Campus)	Counterpoint (v) 2006	Cincinnati	OH
Cleveland Heights High School	Heights Singers (v) 2005	Cleveland Heights	OH
Capital High School	VIP's (v)	Columbus	OH
Crestview High School	Knight Vision (v)	Convoy	OH
Cuyahoga Falls High School	Melodymen & Melodettes (v)	Cuyahoga Falls	OH
Walsh Jesuit High School	Harmony Gold (v)	Cuyahoga Falls	OH
Buckeye Valley High School	Visions (v)	Delaware	OH

Dover High School	Crimson Chorale (v) 2006	Dover	OH
Euclid High School	Varsity Chorale (v)	Euclid	OH
Fairfield Senior High School	Choraliers (v), Pure Elegance (u)	Fairfield	OH
Findlay High School	First Edition (v), Voices In Perfection (jv)	Findlay	OH
Fort Recovery High School	Purple Pride (v), Elegance (u)	Fort Recovery	OH
Gahanna Lincoln High School	Chorale (v)	Gahanna	OH
Galion High School	Showtunes (v)	Galion	OH
Garfield Heights High School	Music Express (v)	Garfield Heights	OH
Goshen High School	Center Stage (u) 2004	Goshen	OH
Greenville Senior High School	Wavaires (v) 2009	Greenville	OH
Central Crossing High School	Excelsior (v)	Grove City	OH
Grove City High School	Touch of Class (v), Class Act (u)	Grove City	OH
Hamilton High School	Rhapsody in Blue (v), Fascinating Rhythm (u)	Hamilton	OH
Wayne High School	***Listed on SC.com but no record of an actual show choir***	Huber Heights	OH
Kenton High School	Top 20 (v)	Kenton	OH
Kettering Fairmont High School	Illusion (v), Mirage (u) 2007	Kettering	OH
Lebanon High School	Singers (v)	Lebanon	OH
Olentangy High School	Keynotes (v)	Lewis Center	OH
Olentangy Orange High School	Revolution (v)	Lewis Center	OH
Indian Lake High School	Meistersingers (v)	Lewistown	OH
Loveland High School	By Request (v)	Loveland	OH
Brush High School	Soundsation (v), Vocal Motion (jv) 2003	Lyndhurst	OH
Nordonia High School	Music Machine (v)	Macedonia	OH
Malvern Middle/High School	Accents (v)	Malvern	OH
Marietta High School	Premiere (v)	Marietta	OH
Elgin High School	Energizers (v)	Marion	OH
Marion Harding High School	Harding Singers (v)	Marion	OH
Marysville High School	Swingers Unlimited (v)	Marysville	OH
Mason High School	Parallel Motion (v)	Mason	OH
Mayfield High School	Limited Edition (v)	Mayfield Village	OH
Medina High School	Encore Entertainment Company (v)	Medina	OH
Lake Catholic High School	***Listed on SC.com but no record of an actual show choir***	Mentor	OH
Mentor High School	Top 25 (v)	Mentor	OH
Midpark High School	Magic (v)	Middleburg Heights	OH
Middletown High School	Purple Pizzazz (v)	Middletown	OH
Millersport Junior/Senior High School	Illumination (v), Select (jv)	Millersport	OH
Lemon Monroe High School	Monroe In Blue (v)	Monroe	OH
Ridgedale Junior/Senior High School	Rocket Ovation (v)	Morral	OH
Riverdale High School	Soundsation (v)	Mount Blanchard	OH
Licking Valley High School	Vocal Impact (v)	Newark	OH
North Ridgeville High School	Spectrum of Sound (v)	North Ridgeville	OH
Colonel Crawford	Vision (v)	North Robinson	OH
Norwalk High School	Trucker Tones	Norwalk	OH
Clay High School	Showstoppers (v) 2005	Oregon	OH
Ottawa-Glandorf High School	Out of the Blue (v)	Ottawa	OH
Perry High School	Buccaneers (v)	Perry	OH
Perrysburg High School	Jazz Singers (v), Women's Select (u)	Perrysburg	OH
Philo High School	Philo Show Choir (v)	Philo	OH
Piqua High School	The Company (v)	Piqua	OH
Jonathan Alder High School	High Society (v)	Plain City	OH
Portsmouth High School	Expressions (v)	Portsmouth	OH
Cory-Rawson High School	Impressions (v)	Rawson	OH
North Union High School	Noteable (v)	Richwood	OH
River Valley High School	New Addition (v)	River Valley	OH
Rocky River High School	River's Edge (v)	Rocky River	OH
Ross High School	Rhythm and Motion (v)	Hamilton	OH
East High School	Madrigals (v)	Sciotoville	OH
Lehman Catholic High School	Limelighters (v) 2009	Sidney	OH
Solon High School	Music in Motion (v)	Solon	OH
South Webster Junior/Senior High School	Show Choir (v)	South Webster	OH
Greenon High School	Opening Knights (v)	Springfield	OH

St. Clairsville High School	Singers (v)	St. Clairsville	OH
Stow Munroe Falls High School	Sensations (v)	Stow	OH
Strongsville High School	Mustang Express (v)	Strongsville	OH
Southview High School	Show Choir (v)	Sylvania	OH
Sheridan High School	Northern Stars (v)	Thornville	OH
Waite High School	Show Choir (v)	Toledo	OH
Edgewood High School	Choraliers (v)	Trenton	OH
Trotwood-Madison High School	***Listed on SC.com but no record of an actual show choir***	Trotwood	OH
Twinsburg High School	Great Expectations (v)	Twinsburg	OH
Lake High School	Reflections (v)	Uniuntown	OH
Upper Sandusky High School	The Upper Class (v)	Upper Sandusky	OH
Van Buren High School	The Association (v)	Van Buren	OH
Vermillion High School	Soundsation (v)	Vermillion	OH
Wapakoneta High School	Singsation (v), Starlettes (u)	Wapakoneta	OH
West Jefferson High School	Gold Ensemble (v)	West Jefferson	OH
Westerville North High School	Noteables (v)	Westerville	OH
Westlake High School	Company D (v)	Westlake	OH
Whitehall Yearling High School	***Listed on SC.com but no record of an actual show choir***	Whitehall	OH
Chaney High School	Choral Company (v)	Youngstown	OH
Alva High School	Electric Gold (v)	Alva	OK
Durant High School	"Mane" Attraction (v)	Durant	OK
Hugo High School	Neon (v)	Hugo	OK
Jenks High School	Trojanaires (v), Trojan Expression (jv), Trojan Connection (jv), Treble Tones (u)	Jenks	OK
Eisenhower High School	We B Vocal (v)	Lawton	OK
Lexington High School	Southern Accents (v)	Lexington	OK
Carl Albert High School	Soundsations (v)	Midwest City	OK
Putnam City North High School	Show Choir (v)	Oklahoma City	OK
Western Heights High School	Encore and Co. (v)	Oklahoma City	OK
Picher-Cardin High School	***Listed on SC.com but no record of an actual show choir***	Picher	OK
Stilwell High School	Reflections (v)	Stilwell	OK
Yukon High School	Yukon Show Choir (v)	Yukon	OK
North Valley High School	Free Design (v) 2004	Grant Pass	OR
Parkrose High School	Debonaires (u)	Portland	OR
Bangor Area High School	Show Choir (v) 2004	Bangor	PA
Boyertown Senior High School	Show Choir (v)	Boyertown	PA
South Western Senior High School	Singchronicity (v)	Hanover	PA
Penndale High School	Show Choir (v)	Lansdale	PA
Lehighton Area High School	Music Express (v)	Lehighton	PA
Laurel Jr/Sr High School	Show Choir (v)	New Castle	PA
Shippensburg Area Senior High School	Audio Audacity (v)	Shippensburg	PA
Clover High School	***Listed on SC.com but no record of an actual show choir***	Clover	SC
South Florence High School	Choraliers (v) 2006	Florence	SC
West Florence High School	The Knight Edition (v)	Florence	SC
J.L. Mann High School	Southern Sensations (v)	Greenville	SC
Lexington High School	Golden Blues of Lexington (v)	Lexington	SC
Carolina Forest High School	Showcase (v) 2005	Myrtle Beach	SC
Wren High School	Show Chorus (v) 2005	Piedmont	SC
Sumter High School	Show Choir (v)	Sumter	SC
Aberdeen Central High School	Central Singers, Inc. (v), Special Request (u)	Aberdeen	SD
Avon High School	Gold (v)	Avon	SD
Chamberlain High School	River City Groove (v)	Chamberlain	SD
Clark High School	ICC Show Choir (v)	Clark	SD
De Smet High School	Vive Voce (v)	De Smet	SD
Elk Point High School	SshhaaBAM (v)	Elk Point	SD
Groton High School	Prosmatic Sensations (v)	Groton	SD
Hot Springs High School	Les Chanteurs (v)	Hot Springs	SD
Lake Preston High School	Gold Xperience (v)	Lake Preston	SD
Leola High School	Show Choir (v)	Leola	SD
Madison High School	Madtown (v)	Madison	SD
Menno High School	Menno Swing (v)	Menno	SD

Mitchell High School	Friend de Coup (v)	Mitchell	SD
Scotland High School	Show Choir (v)	Scotland	SD
Washington High School	Classic Connection (v), Stagelights (u)	Sioux Falls	SD
O'Gorman High School	Ovation! (v), KnightLights (u)	Sioux Falls	SD
Roosevelt High School	Executive Suite (v)	Sioux Falls	SD
Vermillion High School	Rhythm In Red (v)	Vermillion	SD
Bradley Central High School	Vocal Motion (v)	Cleveland	TN
Cleveland High School	Renaissance (v)	Cleveland	TN
Culleoka High School	Singers (v)	Culleoka	TN
Houston High School	Natural Rendition (v)	Germantown	TN
Greeneville High School	Show Choir (v)	Greeneville	TN
Beech High School	Melodic Impact (v), Divine Divas (u)	Hendersonville	TN
Dobyns-Bennett High School	Impact (v), Pizzazy Ladies (u)	Kingsport	TN
Bearden High School	Treblemakers (u)	Knoxville	TN
Lexington High School	Golden Blues (v)	Lexington	TN
Donelson Christian Academy	Legacy (v)	Nashville	TN
Hume-Fogg High School	The Blue Notes (v)	Nashville	TN
McGavock High School	Capital Sounds (v), Ladies (u)	Nashville	TN
Ripley High School	Show Choir (v)	Ripley	TN
Tullahoma High School	Aristocats (v)	Tullahoma	TN
Lamar High School	***Listed on SC.com but no record of an actual show choir***	Arlington	TX
Coppell High School	Vivace (v)	Coppell	TX
Harlingen High School	Broadway Bound (v)	Harlingen	TX
Keller Central High School	Voices of Central (v)	Keller	TX
Legacy High School	Legacy Magic (v)	Mansfield	TX
Canyon High School	Platinum (v)	New Braunfels	TX
Plano East Senior High School	Show Stoppers, Sound Intervention	Plano	TX
The Colony High School	***Listed on SC.com but no record of an actual show choir***	The Colony	TX
Waco High School	Mane Attraction	Waco	TX
Judge Memorial Catholic High School	Judge Show Choir (v)	Salt Lake City	UT
American Leadership Acedemy	Evolution (v), Premier (u)	Spanish Fork	UT
Spanish Fork High School	Ambassadors (v)	Spanish Fork	UT
Tooele High School	Cabaret (v)	Tooele	UT
Hunter High School	***Listed on SC.com but no record of an actual show choir***	West Valley City	UT
Amherst County High School	Amherechos (v), Belles of Amherst (u)	Amherst	VA
Patrick Henry High School	Soundsations (v), Essence (u)	Ashland	VA
Chantilly High School	Touch of Class (v), Magic Touch (u)	Chantilly	VA
Albemarle High School	Vocal Ascension (v)	Charlottesville	VA
Western Branch High School	Varsity Singers (v)	Chesapeake	VA
Thomas Dale High School	Knightscence (v), Knightingales (u-w), U-Knighted (u-m)	Chester	VA
Lloyd C. Bird High School	Sudden Image (v), Reflections (u)	Chesterfield	VA
Matoaca High School	High Impact (v), Up Front (u)	Chesterfield	VA
Deep Run High School	Sound Steps (u)	Glen Allen	VA
Kecoughtan High School	Harbor Lights (v), Touch of Jade (u)	Hampton	VA
Douglas S. Freeman High School	Harmony In Motion (u)	Henrico	VA
Herndon High School	Sound Wave, Heat Wave	Herndon	VA
Hopewell High School	Female Intuition (u)	Hopewell	VA
Atlee High School	Illusion (v), Elegance	Mechanicsville	VA
Hanover High School	Sound FX (v), Highlights (u)	Mechanicsville	VA
Lee-Davis High School	Madrijazz (v), New Horizons (u), A Few Good Men	Mechanicsville	VA
Clover Hill High School	New Dimensions (v), Iridescence (u)	Midlothian	VA
Cosby High School	Spotlight (v), Rhapsody (u)	Midlothian	VA
James River High School	Current Edition (v), Anything Goes (u), Priority Male	Midlothian	VA
Manchester High School	Captial Swing (v), Touch of Swing (u-w), Just Swingin' (u-m)	Midlothian	VA
Midlothian High School	Just For Show (v), City Lights (u)	Midlothian	VA
Denbigh High School	***Listed on SC.com but no record of an actual show choir***	Newport News	VA
Menchville High School	(m)pulse (v), Monarch Magic (jv)	Newport News	VA
Appomattox Regional Governor's School	InAChordDance (v)	Petersburg	VA
Poquoson High School	Soundsation (v), Garnet & Gold (u)	Poquoson	VA
Powhatan High School	Revv'd Up (u)	Powhatan	VA
Douglas Freeman High School	Harmony In Motion	Richmond	VA

Meadowbrook High School	Showin' Off (v), Visions (u)	Richmond	VA
Mills E. Godwin High School	Debut (v), Modern Appeal (u)	Richmond	VA
Monacan High School	Center Stage (v), Innovation (u)	Richmond	VA
Varina High School	Struttin'-R-Stuff (v), Sassy-N-Sapphire (u)	Richmond	VA
Colonial Forge High School	Select (v), Treble Makers (u)	Stafford	VA
Gar-Field Senior High School	Dominants (v)	Woodbridge	VA
Auburn High School	Guys and Dolls (v)	Auburn	WA
Bellingham High School	Showstoppers (v)	Bellingham	WA
Pasco High School	10th Avenue Singers (v)	Pasco	WA
Wilson High School	Scintillation! (v)	Tacoma	WA
Altoona High School	Locomotion (v), Enginuity (u)	Altoona	WI
Ashwaubenon High School	Encore (v)	Ashwaubenon	WI
Beaver Dam High School	BD Swaz (v)	Beaver Dam	WI
Brodhead High School	Guys and Dolls (v)	Brodhead	WI
Burlington High School	B*JAZZled (v)	Burlington	WI
Chippewa Falls High School	Chi-Hi Harmonics (v)	Chippewa Falls	WI
Colby High School	Coalition (v), Hornettes (u)	Colby	WI
De Pere High School	Jam Session (v), Charisma	De Pere	WI
Durand High School	The Singsations (v)	Durand	WI
Memorial High School	Old Abe Show Choir (v), Eagle Show Choir (jv), Eaglettes (u)	Eau Claire	WI
North High School	Nothernaires (v)	Eau Claire	WI
Elk Mound High School	Sound Sensation (v)	Elk Mound	WI
Fall Creek High School	Cricket Choralation (v)	Fall Creek	WI
Winnebago Lutheran Academy	Academy Kids (v)	Fond du Lac	WI
Fort Atkinson High School	South High Street Singers (v), Lexington Singers (u)	Fort Atkinson	WI
East High School	Rhapsody In Red (v)	Green Bay	WI
Green Bay Preble High School	Center Stage (v), Rendezvous (u)	Green Bay	WI
Southwest High School	***Listed on SC.com but no record of an actual show choir***	Green Bay	WI
West High School	West High Wildcats	Green Bay	WI
Arrowhead High School	Broadway Bound (v)	Hartland	WI
Holmen High School	Midwest Express (v), Midwest Magic (u), Midwest Momentum (jv)	Holmen	WI
Craig High School	Spotlighters (v)	Janesville	WI
Kiel High School	Waves Of Rhythm (v)	Kiel	WI
Logan High School	Class Act (v), Classy Ladies (u)	La Crosse	WI
La Crosse Central High School	Grand Central Station (v), Central Connection (u)	La Crosse	WI
Union High School	***Listed on SC.com but no record of an actual show choir***	La Porte	WI
Lodi High School	Special Effect (v)	Lodi	WI
Madison East High School	Encore (v), Mad City Swing (u)	Madison	WI
Mayville High School	Cardinal Singers (v)	Mayville	WI
Menasha High School	Blue Persuasion (v)	Menasha	WI
Middleton High School	Choralaries (v)	Middleton	WI
Milton High School	Choralation (v), Rising Stars (jv)	Milton	WI
Thomas More High School	Show Choir (v)	Milwaukee	WI
Monona Grove High School	Silver Connection (v), Silver Dimension (u)	Monona	WI
Mukwango High School	Guys and Dolls (v), Starstruck (u)	Mukwonago	WI
Neenah High School	Vintage (v), Act II (jv)	Neenah	WI
Nekoosa High School	Sound Advantage (v)	Nekoosa	WI
New London High School	Vision (v)	New London	WI
Onalaska High School	Hilltoppers (v), Express (jv)	Onalaska	WI
Parkview High School	Pizazz (v)	Orfordville	WI
Sauk Prairie High School	Executive Session (v), YTBN (u)	Prairie Du Sac	WI
Reedsburg Area High School	Choraliers (v)	Reedsburg	WI
Rice Lake High School	Gold (v)	Rice Lake	WI
Westosha Central High School	Cenral Swing, Inc.	Salem	WI
Sheboygan North High School	Northern Lights (v)	Sheboygan	WI
Slinger High School	Nightwatch (v)	Slinger	WI
Tomah High School	Limited Edition (v), One Note Above	Tomah	WI
Flambeau High School	Sound Dimension (v)	Tony	WI
Washburn High School	Fire and Ice (v), Superior Ladies (u)	Washburn	WI
Watertown High School	WHS Show Choir (v)	Watertown	WI

School	Choir	City	State
West Salem High School	Singsations (u)	West Salem	WI
Wisconsin Dells High School	The Coporation (v)	Wisconsin Dells	WI
Riverside High School	Melodic Fusion (v)	Belle	WV
Berkeley Springs High School	Show Choir (v)	Berkeley Springs	WV
Bridgeport High School	Show Choir (v)	Bridgeport	WV
Buckhannon-Upshur High School	Buccanaires	Buckhannon	WV
Buffalo High School	Show Time (v)	Buffalo	WV
Capital High School	Voices In Perfection (v)	Charleston	WV
Sissonville High School	Touch of Class (v)	Charleston	WV
Liberty High School	Women's Show Choir (u)	Clarksburg	WV
Robert C. Byrd High School	Radiant Rhythm (v)	Clarksburg	WV
Herbert Hoover High School	High Impact (v)	Clendenin	WV
Nitro High School	Expressions (v)	Cross Lanes	WV
North Marion High School	Noteables (v)	Farmington	WV
Grafton High School	Entertainers (v)	Grafton	WV
Hedgesville High School	Wings (v)	Hedgesville	WV
Huntington High School	Illusions (v)	Huntington	WV
Hurricane High School	Red Hot (v)	Hurricane	WV
Musselman High School	Kaleidoscope (v), Vivid Image, Elite Dimensions	Inwood	WV
Greenbrier East High School	East Side Swing	Lewisburg	WV
South Harrison High School	Hawks In Harmony (v)	Lost Creek	WV
Martinsburg High School	Good Times (v), Encore (u)	Martinsburg	WV
Morgantown High School	Images (v)	Morgantown	WV
Nitro High School	Showcats (v)	Nitro	WV
Cabell Midland High School	Rhythm In Red (v)	Ona	WV
Poca High School	Visual Volume (v), Music in Motion (u)	Poca	WV
Point Pleasant Junior/Senior High School	Sound Wave (v)	Point Pleasant	WV
Princeton High School	Centerstange (v)	Princeton	WV
Ravenswood High School	Rave Revue (v)	Ravenswood	WV
Ripley High School	Blue Persuasion (v)	Ripley	WV
Saint Albans High School	Classix (v), Class Act (u)	Saint Albans	WV
Jefferson High School	Pop Singers (v)	Shenandoah Junction	WV
Nicholas County High School	***Listed on SC.com but no record of an actual show choir***	Summersville	WV
Winfield High School	General Admission (v)	Winfield	WV
Niobrara High School	Choralaries (v)	Lusk	WY
Sundance High School	Adrenaline (v)	Sundance	WY

CANADIAN SHOW CHOIRS

Name of High School	City	Prov
Adrenaline!	Marc Garneau	Toronto	ON
Splash	Etobicoke School of the Arts	Etobicoke	ON
Vocal Thunder	J. Clarke Richardson Collegiate	Ajax	ON
Vocal Fusion	Richmond Hill High School	Richmond Hill	ON
The Gleediators	John Fraser Secondary School	Mississauga	ON
Earl Haig Show Choir	Earl Haig SS	Toronto	ON
Cheat Notes	York Mills CI	Toronto	ON
	Unionville CI	Unionville	ON
SPSC	St Peter Catholic HS	Ottawa	ON
Wexford Glee	Wexford Collegiate School for the Arts	Toronto	ON
Youth Singers of Calgary		Calgary	AB
Niagara Star Singers		Niagara	ON
KW Glee		Waterloo	ON
	Glendale SS	Hamilton	ON
Northern Lights	Don Mills CI	Toronto	ON

UK SHOW CHOIRS

Bridgwater College Show Choir	Bridgwater, Somerset, UK
West End Kids	Rochester, Kent, UK

BIBLIOGRAPHY

Alexander, Chad. Choreographer and competition director for FAME Events. Personal interview, January 21, 2011.

American Choral Directors Association. "About the ACDA" webpage, February 5, 2001

Anderson, Doug. Author, *The Show Choir Handbook*. Personal interview, January 23, 2000.

Anderson, Milton C. Founder and director of the Young Americans. Personal interview, November 30, 2010.

Berry, Jim. Choral director. Personal interview, July 3, 2011.

Biggs, Joel. President and CEO of FAME Events. Personal interview, February 7, 2011.

Bolles, Ron. Former choral director Bonita Vista. Chula Vista, CA. Personal interview, December 30, 2010.

Booster, The La Crosse Central High School yearbook, Lacrosse, WI: 1948–1950.

Boye, Larry. Associate director for the Young American. Personal interview, September 28, 2000.

Brackette, Kye. Singer, actor, choreographer. Personal interview, 30 November 30, 2010.

Brown, Charles T. *The Art of Rock and Roll*. Englewood Cliffs, NJ: Prentice-Hall, 1983.

Butler, Kevin. Music educator. Personal interview, January 4, 2001 and December 30, 2010.

By Way of Introduction. Bishop Luers First Annual Swing Choir Contest Program. February 22, 1975.

Castleman, Harry, and Walter J. Podrazik. *Harry and Wally's Favorite TV Shows*. New York: Prentice-Hall, 1989.

Clark, Jeff. Choral director. Personal interview, January 4, 2011.

Clark, John. Former conductor with the Kids from Wisconsin Singers. Personal interview, December 29, 2000.

Crocker, Emily. Head choral editor, Hal Leonard Publications. Personal interview, December 29, 2000.

Cusack, Jim. Former director Chula Vista School for the Creative Performing Arts. Personal interview, January 2, 2011.

Eklund, Peter A. Director of choral activities, University of Nebraska. Personal interview, February 8, 2011.

Fehr, David. Arranger and choral director. Clinton, MS. Personal interview, November 29, 2011

Force, Marta. Director of the North Carolina Summer Institute for Choral Arts. Personal interview. July 5, 2011.

Gilpin, Greg., Writer/arranger. Personal interview, December 12, 2010.

Griffith, Sandy. Former singer for Lawrence Welk. Personal interview, December 30, 2000.

Green, Stanley. *Hollywood Musicals Year by Year*. Milwaukee: Hal Leonard, 1990.

Grove, Greg. Choral director. Personal interview. July 3, 2011.

Gulsvig, Paul. Music educator. Personal interview, February 1, 2000.

Haak, Elizabeth. Director of Marketing for Wenger Corporation. Personal interview, January 23, 2000.

Haines, Andy. Choreographer. Personal interview, February 5, 2011.

Haley, Chuck. Choreographer. Personal interview, December 30, 2000.

Hellems, Ronald. Personal interview, September 28, 2000, and February 11, 2011.

Heins, Bill. September 26, 2000.

Hills, Robert. Former director of Eastern Illinois University Collegians. Personal interview, September 26, 2000.

Hill-Swander, Betty. Business owner. Personal interview, December 30, 2010.

Holman, Sona, and Lillian Friedman. *How to Lie About Your Age*. New York: Collier-Macmillan, 1979.

Hoopingarner, Pam. Former singer/dancer. Personal interview, December 1, 2010

Hoover's Guide to Media Companies. Austin: Hoover's, 1996.

Howard, Michael. Department chair, head of musical theater program. Personal interview, November 29, 2010

Huff, Mac. Song writer/arranger. Personal interview, February 1, 2001.

Invitational Story, The. Bishop Luers Swing Choir Invitational program. February 27, 1999. Fort Wayne, IN, 1999.

Isaacs, Mary. Booster president in La Crosse, WI. Personal interview, January 16, 2011.

Jaeger, Richard. Former music educator. Personal interview, December 29, 2000.

James, April. Choreographer. Personal interview, February 2, 2011.

Jennings, Brendan. Choral director. Burbank, CA. November 30, 2010.

Johnson, Jason. Choreographer. Personal interview, January 11, 2011.

Jordan, Dwight. Director/choreographer. Personal interview, January 2, 2001, and February 10, 2011.

Keifer, Peter. Coordinator for Fred Waring's America Library at Penn State. Personal interview, February 2, 2001.

Kessler, Tom. Retired choral director, West Covina, CA. Personal interview, January 27, 2011.

Kimmel, James. Associate Professor of Music at Belmont University. Personal interview, July 5, 2011.

Kinsey, Kim. Former director, Petal, MS. Personal interview, January 15, 2011.

Krouse, Karlene. Choral director at Bishop Luers High School. Personal interview January 27, 2011.

Legg, David. Writer/director. Personal interview, January 11, 2011.

Lippoldt-Mack, Valerie. Music educator. Personal interview, December 30, 2010.

Lojeski, Ed. Arranger. Personal interview, January 4, 2001.

Link, Father Fred. Promoter/producer. Personal interview, January 2001.

Malcolm, Hal. Music educator. Personal interview, February 2, 2001.

——————. *Genesis in Jazz Vocal Education*. Gresham, Oregon: Hal Malcolm, 1998.

Malone, Kim. Choral director. Personal interview, January 15, 2011.

Maxson, Rollie. Personal interview, November 29, 2010.

McBroom, Kraig. Choral director. Personal interview, January 24, 2011.

Moellenkamp, David. Choral director. Personal interview, February 2, 2010.

Mountford, Fritz. Conductor and former Fred Waring's Pennsylvanians. Personal interviews, September 26, 2000, and January 4, 2001.

Mountford, Fritz. *The Art of Entertainment*. Milwaukee: Hal Leonard, 1991.

MTV and *TV Guide Present the 100 Greatest Videos Ever Made*. Viacom Press Release, November 29, 1999. Internet: Viacom, 1999.

Mulligan, Connie. Choral director. Personal interview, January 30, 2011.

Neary, Kevin, and Dave Smith. *The Ultimate Disney Trivia Book*. New York: Hyperion, 1992.

Neuen, Donald. Choral conductor/founder of the Ball State Singers. Personal interview, September 26, 2000.

Oliver, Pat Phillips. Fred Waring, "Glory, Glory, Hallelujah!" *Palm Springs Life*, March 1965.

Pennsylvania Center for the Book: Fred Waring (Web site).

Pfeiler, Cathy. Choral director. Personal interview, January 4, 2011.

Ridgell, Lamont. Founding member and choreographer for Western Michigan University's Gold Company. Personal interview. July 5, 2011.

Sage, Randy. Choreographer. Personal interview, January 11, 2011.

Saul, Wanda. Former choral director. Personal interview, November 11, 2010.

Slinkard, Verda, Choral director. Personal interview, November 29, 2010.

Snyder, Linda. Choral director. Personal interview, February 1, 2011.

Spradling, Diana. Former ACDA National Chair for Jazz and Show Choir. Personal interview, December 27, 2000.

—————. Selected papers from the 2000 ACDA repertoire and standards committee on jazz and show choirs meeting. August 5–6, 2000. Kalamazoo: Spradling, 2000.

Stoll, Robert. Former director of choral activities at Indiana State University. Personal interview, September 28, 2000.

Schwartzhoff, Gary. Director, Kids of Wisconsin. Personal interview, February 5, 2001.

Sundry, Häakon. Founder of Show Choir Community/Showchoir.com. Personal interview, February 1, 2011.

Terrien, Tom. Choreographer. Personal interview, September 26, 2000.

Thorn, Jeff. Director, Kids of Wisconsin Singers. Personal interview, September 26, 2000.

Tober, Tara. Choreographer. Personal interview, February 6, 2001.

Tuleja, Tad. *Popular Americana*. New York: Stonesong, 1994.

Van Cleave, Eric. Writer/Arranger. Personal interview, December 27, 2010.

Walton, Jim. Actor. Personal interview, January 2, 2011.

Waldschmidt, Peg. Director. Personal interview, December 30, 2010.

Willert, Dave. Choral director. Personal interviews, January 16, 2011, and February 21, 2011.

Wetterau, Bruce. *The New York Public Library Book of Chronologies*. New York: Stonesong, 1990.

Zaninelli, Luigi. Arranger for Fred Waring and the Pennsylvanians. Personal interview, September 27, 2000.

INDEX OF SHOW CHOIRS

Photo and Lyric Credits

PHOTO CREDITS

3mi Photography: 87
Adam Miller: 133
Adam Sorenson: 136, 137
Alex Keatinge: 132
America Sings:87
American Choral Directors Association/Tim Sharp: 32
Andrew Drinkall: 128
Anita Easton: 118
Ball State Singers: 34, 123
Barry Thompson: 78, 118
Betty Hill Swander: 4
Big Red Singers: 128
Bill Bradshaw: 148
Bill Miller: 124
Bishop Luers High School: 42, 43, 44, 45, 46, 47
Bishop Luers HS Yearbook: Accolade/Abigail "Abby" Ehinger: 97
Brendan Jennings: 58, 80, 115
Brian McConkey: 153
Bruce Sharp: 71
Bud Ford: Ford Studios/Stephen Lloyd: 101
Bunny Oldman: 131
C. Mauzy: 118
Carolyn Rains: 96, 113
Catherine Gatewood: 127
Charles Cheeseman: 117
Cindy Quisenberry and Sal Frenda: 114
Colette's Cakes: 79
Colleen Hart: ix, x, 166
Corbis: 138, 139
David Sackschewsky: 128
Debbie Swander: 4
Doug Uhler: 93
Dwight Jordan: 73

Elizabeth Tape: 129
Everett Collection: 138, 153, 155
Fame Events: 68, 77, 90, 92–93, 98, 99
Fread Waring's America at Penn State University: xii–xiii, 11, 12, 13, 14, 15, 16, 17, 18, 79
Getty Imaages: 2, 3, 6, 7, 25, 140, 153
Google: 142
Gordon Blackburn: 82
Häakon Sundry: 48, 58, 74,75, 95, 142
Hal Leonard: 53
Helen Rotnem Vivian: 155
Indiana University Singing Hoosiers: 34, 119
Indy Action Photos: 72, 112, 118, 119, 120, 121, 122, 123, 124,
Istock: 82, 83, 84, 85, 86, 104
Jamie Lynn Marble: 119
Jeanine Meyers: 153
Jeff Haught: 132
Jeffrey Thorne: 43, 44, 53, 90, 97
Jerry Levy: 101, 116
Jim Walton: 152
Joe Prosser: 70
Joel Biggs: 72
John Ganun: 154
John Hendrix: 154
Johnny Brewer: 169
Jordan Matter: 153
Julia Andrews: 131
June Talley: 128
Kaitlin Dale: 153
Kathrine Kouns: 114
Kathryn Stevens: 148
Katie Bishop: 155

Katie Lee: 154
Kenneth Schemffler/KMKS Photo: 126
Kevin Flogel: 133
Kevin O'Leary: 130
Kevin Sesko: 119
Kids From Wisconsin: 28, 29, 135
LaCrosse Central HS: 17
Laura Rose: 152
Len Struttman: 124
Lisa Brannen: 114
Lisa Harrington: 101
Lost Cinema Archives/Mark Heggen: 5
Marcia Wooley: 130
Mary Rago: 47, 48
Matthew Ragas: 153
Maurizio Babaldi: 153
Michael T Sater: 91
Michael Weaver: 13, 16, 45, 47, 74, 76, 78, 79, 84, 107, 149
Mt Hood College: 40
On3Fotos: 88, 89, 94, 115, 131, 153
Onalaska Hilltopper archives: 135
PARADE Magazine: 143
Patricia Fadsen: 158
Photofest: 5, 7, 8, 9, 16, 20, 22–23, 24, 25, 26, 27, 30, 31, 32, 33, 50, 51, 52, 53, 56, 57, 59, 60, 61, 63, 64, 65, 66, 67, 79, 90, 97, 142, 152, 153, 154
Playbill®: 57
ProCat: 101, 128
Rada Cutlery: 84
Randy Luher: 109, 135, 160, 161
Randy Ruttger: 126
Rob Sapp: 154

Ron Bolles: 41, 48, 61
Ron Hellems: 54, 90
Ronald Hellems: xi, 101
RS Owen Company: 79
Sam A. Milosevich
Sanford Sardo: 130
Scott Ahlersmeyer: 85
Scott Smith PhotoGliff: 128
Steve McCoy: 15
Steve Neal: 130
Susan Kuzia: 118
Susan Uhler Bowman: 70
Tamera Garner: 114
Ted Arnold: 14
Terry Bateman: 121, 122
The West End Kids: 147
The Young Americans: 34, 35, 49
Tiffany Blanchard: 154
Tim Randall: 131
Tri Tran Photography
TV Guide: 15
University of Iowa: 3
University of Wisconsin Singers: 36, 37, 134–135
Up with People: 35, 117
Valerie Lippoldt Mack: 125
Victoria McGuire: Victoria V's Gallery: 127
Wenger Corporation: 77, 78
West End Kids: 73

LYRIC CREDITS

What Would I Do Without My Music
Words and Music by Bruce Belland and Harry Middlebrooks
© 1978 EMI BLACKWOOD MUSIC INC., FULLNESS MUSIC, CENTERSTREAM MUSIC, EMI APRIL MUSIC INC., LAZY LIBRA MUSIC and MARVELHOUSE MUSIC
All Rights for FULLNESS MUSIC and CENTERSTREAM MUSIC Controlled and Administered by EMI BLACKWOOD MUSIC INC.
All Rights for LAZY LIBRA MUSIC and MARVELHOUSE MUSIC Controlled and Administered by EMI APRIL MUSIC INC.
All Rights Reserved. International Copyright Secured. Used by Permission.
Reprinted with Permission of Hal Leonard Corporation

Every reasonable effort has been made to contact copyright holders and secure permissions. Omissions can be remedied in future editions.